ANTI-INDIVIDUALISM

In this book Sanford Goldberg argues that a proper account of the communication of knowledge through speech has anti-individualistic implications for both epistemology and the philosophy of mind and language. In Part 1 he offers a novel argument for anti-individualism about mind and language, the view that the contents of one's thoughts and the meanings of one's words depend for their individuation on one's social and natural environment. In Part 2 he discusses the epistemic dimension of knowledge communication, arguing that the epistemic characteristics of communication-based beliefs depend on features of the cognitive and linguistic acts of the subject's social peers. In acknowledging an ineliminable social dimension to mind, language, and the epistemic categories of knowledge, justification, and rationality, his book develops fundamental links between externalism in the philosophy of mind and language, on the one hand, and externalism in epistemology, on the other.

SANFORD GOLDBERG is Professor of Philosophy at Northwestern University.

CAMBRIDGE STUDIES IN PHILOSOPHY

General editors

JONATHAN LOWE *University of Durham*
WALTER SINNOTT-ARMSTRONG *Dartmouth College*

Advisory editors

JONATHAN DANCY *University of Texas, Austin*
JOHN HALDANE *University of St Andrews*
GILBERT HARMAN *Princeton University*
FRANK JACKSON *Australian National University*
WILLIAM G. LYCAN *University of North Carolina at Chapel Hill*
SYDNEY SHOEMAKER *Cornell University*
JUDITH J. THOMSON *Massachusetts Institute of Technology*

Recent titles

RAYMOND MARTIN *Self-Concern*
ANNETTE BARNES *Seeing Through Self-Deception*
MICHAEL BRATMAN *Faces of Intention*
AMIE THOMASSON *Fiction and Metaphysics*
DAVID LEWIS *Papers on Ethics and Social Philosophy*
FRED DRETSKE *Perception, Knowledge, and Belief*
LYNNE RUDDER BAKER *Persons and Bodies*
ROSANNA KEEFE *Theories of Vagueness*
JOHN GRECO *Putting Skeptics in Their Place*
RUTH GARRETT MILLIKAN *On Clear and Confused Ideas*
DERK PEREBOOM *Living Without Free Will*
BRIAN ELLIS *Scientific Essentialism*
ALAN H. GOLDMAN *Practical Rules: When We Need Them and When We Don't*
CHRISTOPHER HILL *Thought and World*
ANDREW NEWMAN *The Correspondence Theory of Truth*
ISHTIYAQUE HAJI *Deontic Morality and Control*
WAYNE A. DAVIS *Meaning, Expression and Thought*
PETER RAILTON *Facts, Values, and Norms*
JANE HEAL *Mind, Reason and Imagination*
JONATHAN KVANVIG *The Value of Knowledge and the Pursuit of Understanding*
ANDREW MELNYK *A Physicalist Manifesto*
WILLIAM S. ROBINSON *Understanding Phenomenal Consciousness*
D. M. ARMSTRONG *Truth and Truthmakers*
KEITH FRANKISH *Mind and Supermind*
MICHAEL SMITH *Ethics and the A Priori*
NOAH LEMOS *Common Sense*

Anti-Individualism

Mind and Language, Knowledge and Justification

SANFORD C. GOLDBERG
Northwestern University

CAMBRIDGE
UNIVERSITY PRESS

B
824
. G65
2007

CAMBRIDGE UNIVERSITY PRESS
Cambridge, New York, Melbourne, Madrid, Cape Town, Singapore, São Paulo, Delhi

Cambridge University Press
The Edinburgh Building, Cambridge CB2 8RU, UK

Published in the United States of America by Cambridge University Press, New York

www.cambridge.org
Information on this title: www.cambridge.org/9780521880480

H

First published 2007

Printed in the United Kingdom at the University Press, Cambridge

A catalogue record for this publication is available from the British Library

ISBN 978-0-521-88048-0 hardback

To Gideon, Ethan, Nadia, and Judy –
no better family could there be

Contents

Preface

The topic of this book is linguistic communication. More specifically, the topic is the nature of the sort of knowledge one acquires through accepting another speaker's say-so. My attraction to this topic derives from the prospect it holds for enabling one to bring together the three philosophical subfields I work in: philosophy of language, philosophy of mind, and epistemology. My core thesis is that a proper account of the nature of 'testimonial' knowledge (as it is called) will have us endorse anti-individualistic theses about language and mind, knowledge and justification.

My approach to the topic of testimonial knowledge can be described as 'inter(sub)disciplinary.' An overarching aim of the book is to illustrate the benefits of taking such an approach. But there are risks associated as well. Above all, there is the risk of superficiality in each of the relevant (sub)-disciplines. I expose myself to this risk in the hope of bringing a unity that I have felt missing in other discussions of testimonial knowledge and linguistic communication. It goes without saying that in pursuing such a wide-ranging discussion I have been particularly dependent on the help and feedback of many others. I count myself unusually fortunate in the indulgence shown to me by teachers, colleagues, and friends, as I talked about – OK, obsessed over – the nature of the testimonial exchange. This book has been shaped by many conversations, over many years, with more people than I can remember. They include Fred Adams, Ken Aizawa, Michael Antony, Dorit Bar-On, Katie Barret, Bob Barnard, Kelly Becker, Itzak Ben Baji, Yemima Ben Menachem, John Bickle, Akeel Bilgrami, John Bolander, Larry Bonjour, David Bradshaw, Tad Brennan, Berit Brogaard, Andy Brook, Jessica Brown, Tony Brueckner, Tyler Burge, Charles Chastain, Zhihua Cheng, Earl Conee, Kristie Dotson, Eli Dresner, Jay Drydyk, Gary Ebbs, Catherine Elgin, David Enoch, Paul Faulkner, Arthur Fine, Dan Frank, Lizzie Fricker, Richard Fumerton, Jon Garthoff, Chris Gauker, Mikkel Gerken, Amihud Gilead, Alvin Goldman, Peter Graham, John Greco, David Henderson, Gail Heyman, Dien Ho,

Harmon Holcomb, Terry Horgan, Claire Horisk, Scott James, Deepthi Kamawar, Charlotte Katzoff, Tim Kenyon, Max Kölbel, Richard Kraut, Jon Kvanvig, Igal Kvart, Jennifer Lackey, Skip Larkin, Jo-Anne LeFevre, Ernie Lepore, Brandon Look, Peter Ludlow, Heidi Maibom, Neil Manson, Dave Mattheson, Kay Mathieson, Ariel Meirav, Andrew Melnyk, Brad Monton, Sidney Morgenbesser, Ohad Nachtomy, Ram Neta, George Pappas, Nicolaj Jang Pedersen, Phillip Pettit, Avital Pilpel, Tom Polger, Ted Poston, Duncan Pritchard, Jim Pryor, Wayne Riggs, Michael Rosenthal, Joe Salerno, Sarah Sawyer, Ted Schatzki, Ira Schnall, Oron Shagrir, Ivy Sichel, Keith Simmons, Liza Skidelski, Miriam Solomon, Rob Stainton, Kent Staley, Mirit Stav, Mark Steiner, Anita Superson, William Talbott, Paul Thagard, Deb Tollefson, Chris Viger, Jonathan Weinberg, David Widercker, Alison Wylie, Guiming Yang, Nick Zangwill, Tad Zawidzki, and Chris Zurn. I am very grateful to all of these individuals. I would also like to thank the many graduate students who, over the years, let me try out half-baked ideas and first-draft arguments, and who kept me honest throughout: Alex Doherty, Carl Ehrett, Michael Horton, Kamper Floyd, Matthew Mullins, Erin Murphy, Gil Sagi, Assaf Sharon, Levi Spectre, Jennifer Woodward, and Jonathan Yaari.

More individuals – many, many more – would have to be thanked if this list were to be exhaustive. Instead I will have to be satisfied with thanking those in the audiences of the various venues at which I have given portions of this book as talks. These venues include Bar-Ilan University (Ramat Gan, Israel); Bowling Green State University; Carleton University (Ottawa, Canada); Hebei University (Hebei, China); the Cognitive Science and Philosophy Departments at Hebrew University (Jerusalem, Israel); the Graduate School of the Chinese Academy of Sciences (Beijing, China); the Foreign Language School and the Institute of Philosophy and Research at Shanxi University (Taiyuan City, China); Northwestern University; the University of Haifa (Haifa, Israel); the University of Memphis; the University of Mississippi; the University of Missouri; the University of Washington; the 2005 meeting of the Central States Philosophical Association (Presidential Address); and a symposium at the 2006 Pacific Division Meeting of the APA.

I have also been fortunate in the support I have received from various institutions and fellowships. Special thanks here belong to the College of Arts and Sciences at the University of Kentucky, for sabbatical and research support during the interval during which I completed this book; the Lady Davis Fellowship Trust, for support during the period of the writing of this book; the Philosophy Department at Hebrew University, for hosting me during some of the period of the writing of this book; Mr. Baoming Yang and Mr. Guiming Yang, for inviting me to China to give a series of lectures on topics pertaining to linguistic communication; and the Spindel family, for support for the 2005 Spindel Conference on Social Epistemology at the University of Memphis (my talk there was incorporated into the book).

Thanks belong as well to the journals *Philosophy and Phenomenological Research* and *The Southern Journal of Philosophy*, which granted me permission to reprint portions of papers that first appeared in them. Chapter 6 borrows from "Monitoring and the Epistemology of Testimony," *Philosophy and Phenomenological Research* 72:3, 576–93 (co-authored with David Henderson); chapter 7 is a substantially revised version of a paper that first appeared as "The Social Diffusion of Warrant and Rationality," *The Southern Journal of Philosophy* 44: 118–38 (Spindel supplement); and chapter 8 is an expanded version of "Testimonial knowledge in early childhood, revisited," *Philosophy and Phenomenological Research* (forthcoming).

In addition, I am grateful to Walter Sinnott-Armstrong, for his very helpful recommendations on an earlier draft of this manuscript; two referees from Cambridge University Press, for their detailed and insightful comments on that draft; and Hilary Gaskin, for the help she provided in her role as editor.

My biggest debt of gratitude is owed to my wife, Judy, and my three children, Gideon, Ethan, and Nadia. For years they have been humoring me by putting up with my philosophizing – or, as it is commonly known in our house, with my *michigas* (a Yiddish word whose rough equivalent in English is 'craziness'). It is to them, with my deepest love and gratitude, that I dedicate this book.

Introduction

Linguistic communication is a pervasive feature of human life. Some of this communication involves the transmission of a piece of knowledge from speaker to hearer. In this book I argue that a proper account of the sort of communication that aims at the transmission of knowledge will have substantial implications for both the philosophy of mind and language, and for epistemology.

The burden of Part I (chapters 1–4) is to provide a novel argument for anti-individualism about mind and language. According to such views, the psychological properties instantiated by a subject, as well as the semantic (meaning) properties of her words, depend for their individuation on features of her social and natural environment. These views are quite popular, owing in large part to the seminal work of Tyler Burge and Hilary Putnam. Here I offer a novel argument for such views. Standardly, anti-individualistic views in the philosophy of mind and language are taken to be supported by considerations such as the semantics of speech- and attitude-reports, subjects' incomplete grasp of their own concepts, speakers' semantic deference to (some subset of) speakers in their linguistic community, the possibility of non-standard theorizing, or the objectivity of perceptual representations. My argument, by contrast, depends on none of these considerations. Rather, it reorients the discussion, focusing instead on the conditions on knowledge communication: I argue that a proper account of the semantic dimension of linguistic communication (pertaining to the hearer's comprehension of the source speech act), together with humdrum facts about the sorts of circumstance under which hearers acquire a communicated piece of knowledge, yield anti-individualistic results regarding linguistic meaning, speech content, and the propositional attitudes.

In Part II of the book (chapters 5–8) I move from the semantic to the epistemic dimension of knowledge communication. My claim here is that,

1

when it comes to the sort of belief one acquires through accepting another's testimony, the belief's epistemic characteristics – including whether it amounts to knowledge, and (more controversially) whether it is justified and/or rationally sustained – depend on facts regarding the members of the linguistic community within which one has acquired and sustained the testimonial belief. Such a view falls within a category I designate as *epistemic* anti-individualism: the view is a version of epistemic externalism, in that it entails that not all of the materials that make for epistemic justification can be discerned through the subject's searching reflection; but it is a novel, *anti-individualistic* sort of epistemic externalism, in that it regards the epistemic characteristics of a subject's (testimony based) beliefs as depending on features of the cognitive and linguistic acts *of the subject's social peers.*

The book's overarching ambition, then, is to show that the conditions on knowledge communication motivate a broadly anti-individualistic account of both *what* we know (i.e., the conceptual, propositional contents of our knowledge), and the fact *that* we know (or justifiedly believe).

0.2 THE SEMANTIC DIMENSION OF COMMUNICATION

Chapter 1 sets the stage by describing the nature of the sort of knowledge whose conditions I subsequently go on to explore in the rest of the book. Schematically, testimonial knowledge is testimonially grounded belief whose testimonial grounds satisfy the conditions on knowledge. The notion of testimonially grounded belief is spelled out in terms of the notion of the hearer's *epistemic reliance* on a piece of testimony. Borrowing from the literature on the norm of assertion, I argue that a hearer relies epistemically on testimony when she acquires a belief grounded in her (implicit) assumption that the testimony in question satisfies the epistemic norm(s) appropriate to testimony. (One's view of the precise epistemic strength of this ground will depend on one's view of the norm of assertion; my argument is neutral on this matter.) I go on to argue that a testimonially grounded belief amounts to testimonial knowledge when, in virtue of features of its testimonial ground, it satisfies the remaining conditions on knowledge. These conditions I spell out by using the notion of reliability to stand in for the non-accidentality condition on knowledge. The result, I argue, is that testimonially grounded belief amounts to testimonial knowledge only if (a) the *source testimony* itself was reliable, in the sense that the testimony would have been proferred only if true; (b) the hearer's recovery of the attested proposition was based on a *reliable comprehension* process; and (c) the hearer's acceptance of the testimony was the upshot of a reliable capacity to *distinguish reliable attestations from unreliable ones*. The structure of the book is then organized around these three necessary conditions on testimonial knowledge. The remainder of Part I (chapters 2–4) concerns the semantic dimension of a hearer's reaction to proffered testimony, and so focuses mainly on (b); Part II (chapters 5–8) concerns those aspects of communication that are more traditionally regarded as constituting the epistemic dimension of communication, focusing on (a) and (c).

In chapter 2 I present the first of two arguments in support of the postulation of public linguistic norms. Here the argument is from successful communication, cases in which a hearer comes to know that *p*, through recognizing that she has been told that *p*. Since successful communication involves cases in which the hearer acquires the very piece of knowledge expressed in the assertion, such cases presuppose the satisfaction of condition (b), the reliable comprehension condition. But successful communication has several other characteristics which make it hard to see how (b) could be satisfied in all of the cases in which knowledge is testimonially transmitted. In particular, successful communication is *prevalent*; it amounts to an *efficient* way to spread knowledge; and it is *linguistically undemanding*, in the sense that it remains an efficient and pervasive way to spread knowledge even under conditions in which the speaker and hearer know nothing about each other's speech and interpretative dispositions, save what is manifest in their brief communicative exchange itself. My thesis is that without appeal to public linguistic norms, we have no explanation for how successful communication *could* have these characteristics, since we would then have no explanation for the prevalence of cases satisfying the reliable comprehension condition.

In chapter 3 I present the second of my two arguments in support of the postulation of public linguistic norms. While the argument here still highlights condition (b), the reliable comprehension condition, the crucial premise concerns cases in which this condition *fails* to be satisfied. In particular, I argue that a proper account of *mis*understanding (in cases of would-be knowledge communication) also requires the postulation of such norms. Cases of misunderstanding are cases of a breakdown in the activity whereby a speaker aims to share knowledge. I argue that responsibility for the breakdown cannot be determined in a principled way without recourse to the norms of the shared language. This is because the ascription of responsibility must determine whether the case is one in which the speaker mis-spoke, or one in which the hearer misinterpreted the speaker's remark. Such a matter cannot be answered in a principled way, I argue, unless there is a 'standard' interpretation of *S*'s remark, since it is the standard interpretation that enables us to distinguish cases of misspeaking from cases of misinterpretation. I go on to argue that there is nothing that might provide the 'standard' interpretation save the linguistic norms of a shared, public language.

In chapter 4 I appeal to the existence of public linguistic norms as part of an extended argument for various anti-individualistic results – regarding speech content, linguistic meaning, and ultimately the attitudes. Here I develop the idea that, if public linguistic norms are to play the roles assigned to them in the arguments of chapters 2 and 3, these norms must specify the conditions on correct application for the various expressions in one's idiolect. Various anti-individualistic doctrines can then be reached by a familiar sort of thought experiment in which we vary the public linguistic norms at play in a speech exchange, without varying any of the individualistic facts regarding the hearer. When we do so, we see that there could be two hearers, type-identical in their intrinsic (non-relational) properties, who differ in what they believe owing to differences in the public linguistic norms in play. (This difference of belief follows from the prior difference in knowledge: the respective testimonies communicate different pieces of knowledge to the two hearers, so, on the assumption that knowledge implies belief, the hearers believe different things.)

As an argument for anti-individualism about language and thought, this sort of argument can appear quite similar to arguments Tyler Burge has given. However, two features of my argument are noteworthy. First, as an argument for Attitude Anti-Individualism (AAI), the premises I use do not rely on any of the premises used in traditional arguments for AAI. Rather, the argument seeks to establish AAI directly by appeal to the conditions on knowledge communication, together with humdrum facts regarding the actual prevalence and efficiency of such communication. Relatedly, and second, my argument reveals that the phenomena often taken to be at the core of the case for AAI – in particular, incomplete grasp and semantic deference – can themselves be traced to the conditions on knowledge communication, and in particular to our *epistemic reliance* on the other members of our linguistic community.

The conclusion of Part I is that, to the extent that we depend for our knowledge of the world on the say-so of others, *what* we know are contents constituted by the concepts and categories we inherit from the public language – concepts and categories that a hearer consumes (or sustains) in the very act of consuming others' say-so itself.

0.3 THE EPISTEMIC DIMENSION OF COMMUNICATION

In Part II I move from the linguistic dimension of knowledge communication – the process by which communicated messages are *understood* – to those features of knowledge communication that are more commonly taken up in discussions of the epistemological dimension of communication – conditions (a) and (c) of the three necessary conditions above. My main thesis in Part II is that, in cases of testimonially grounded belief, one's instantiation of *many* epistemic properties – knowledge, warrant, justification, and rationality – depends on facts about one's social environment. As a result, taking a proper account of the epistemic dimension of this process will involve endorsing various *epistemically anti-individualist* doctrines.

In chapter 5, I present an initial case, to be supplemented in subsequent chapters, for several epistemically anti-individualistic results. I begin by arguing for two theses that may be uncontroversial in any case: whether a hearer counts as having acquired knowledge through another's testimony, and the amount of warrant enjoyed by her testimonial belief, both depend on facts pertaining to the satisfaction of (a), the condition on reliable testimony. These theses can be established by reflecting on pairs of cases, alike as to the hearers' excellent reasons for accepting the testimony and as to their properly functioning cognitive systems, but different as to the actual reliability of the testimony each has accepted. The result is that whether a hearer *knows* through testimony, and (more generally) the amount of warrant her testimonial belief enjoys, depend on more than her reasons for accepting the testimony and the proper functionality of her cognitive system. Since her status as knowing depends as well on epistemic properties of the testimony itself, anti-individualism about testimonial knowledge and warrant immediately follow. This conclusion is, perhaps, unremarkable, but it does have one interesting implication: knowledge-relevant exterrnal factors sometimes include those pertaining to the individual's *social* ('anti-individualistic') environment. I conclude chapter 5 by using this idea to make an initial case for a more controversial doctrine: whether a subject is *justified* in accepting a piece of testimony depends on features of her social ('anti-individualistic') environment. The controversial doctrine follows from *anti-reductionism*, an account of justified acceptance that (I argue) we have independent reasons to accept.

However, my positive case for anti-reductionism does not address some of the difficulties that anti-reductionist accounts are sometimes said to face. In chapter 6 I address the first of two such difficulties, based on Elizabeth Fricker's (1994) allegation that anti-reductionism is a recipe for gullibility. I argue that her contention is baseless. In the course of doing so, I identify another source of support for anti-reductionist approaches to the justified acceptance of testimony. I claim that such views are supported by a parallel with what makes for epistemic justification in other domains where reliable belief-fixation is achieved through largely subcognitive processing (memory and perception, for example).

In chapter 7 I address the second of the two difficulties that are thought to face more 'externalist' accounts of the conditions on justified acceptance (such as anti-reductionism). This difficulty, based on a point raised by Fricker in a more recent paper, is that more 'externalist' approaches sever the connection between justified acceptance of testimony and the rationality of testimonial belief. After developing this difficulty, I establish two points. First, anyone who accepts the anti-individualistic conclusion regarding testimonial warrant from chapter 5 – which is to say virtually everyone, *regardless* of their preferred account of justified acceptance of testimony – will be facing one or another difficulty on the present score. Second, once we compare the strengths and weaknesses of the various contending positions, none seems to provide anything as strong as a reason to reject the epistemically anti-individualistic results so far obtained. One implication of my argument here is that the very rationality of testimonial belief is itself socially diffuse: the rational standing of one's testimonial belief depends on facts regarding the (cognitive and epistemic) practices of one's co-linguals. I conclude the chapter by offering positive reasons for thinking that there is indeed an ineliminably social dimension to assessments of rationality generally (and of the rationality of testimonial belief in particular).

I conclude Part II (in chapter 8) by arguing that there are cases in which the satisfaction of condition (c) above, the reliable discrimination condition, implicates the agent's social surroundings. The argument here focuses on the consumption of testimony by cognitively immature children. Given their cognitive immaturity, very young children are not reliable in their discrimination of reliable from unreliable testimony. Even so, they acquire testimonial knowledge – so the reliable discrimination condition must somehow be satisfied. My claim is that a proper account of the process through which cognitively immature children consume testimony must include the credibility monitoring role performed *by the child's adult guardian(s)*. It is only in this way that the child's resulting testimonial beliefs can be seen as satisfying the reliable discrimination condition, despite their own cognitive immaturity, in all and only those cases in which, intuitively, we want to treat those beliefs as amounting to testimonial knowledge. Such a claim is an instance of what (following language of Andy Clark and David Chalmers) I will call an 'active' epistemic anti-individualism; and the position I develop bears some affinities to the hypothesis of extended (or distributed) cognition in the philosophy of mind. So the book closes on a note suggesting that the epistemic dimension of knowledge communication is even more social than traditional epistemic categories ('knowledge,' 'warrant,' 'justification,' 'rationality') would lead us to expect.

0.4 THE BIG PICTURE

I should note that the contemporary literature regarding the 'epistemology of testimony' has already devoted a good deal of attention to the nature of knowledge acquired through others' speech. Although I see the chapters of Part II as contributing to this discussion, there is an important sense in which my fundamental goal here is deeper than merely contributing to contemporary discussions on the epistemology of testimony. For although I will be developing a position that will be recognizable as an *anti-reductionistic* view in the epistemology of testimony, my more fundamental aim is to suggest that such a view is a response to one aspect of a phenomenon whose significance outstrips epistemology proper. The phenomenon, of course, is our epistemic reliance on other speakers. I believe that a proper appreciation of this reliance requires taking an anti-reductionistic (and so, I will argue, an anti-individualistic) position in the epistemology of testimony; but I also believe – and it is the burden of Part I to establish – that it requires taking an anti-individualistic position regarding linguistic meaning and mental content as well. To my mind, these various anti-individualist doctrines in semantics and epistemology are all parts of a single picture – a picture that emerges only when we consider communication in both its semantic and its epistemic dimensions. It is precisely this sort of picture that I aim to be developing in this book.

PART I

Semantic anti-individualism

1

The nature of knowledge communication

I.I INTRODUCTION

There can be little doubt that we acquire a good deal of our knowledge through the written or spoken word. Our knowledge of geography, science, and history; of current events; and even of our own names, parents, and birthdays – all of this (and more besides) involves knowledge we have acquired through accepting what others have told us. Without such knowledge we would be much less well-off, epistemically speaking, than we actually are.

While the existence of such knowledge is uncontroversial, its nature is not. There are debates regarding various related topics: whether another's say-so amounts to a kind of evidence (and if so, what kind); whether the justification or entitlement for accepting say-so derives from one's positive reasons for thinking that the say-so is credible; whether justification is even necessary for this sort of knowledge; whether the knowledge we acquire in this way is an epistemically basic sort of knowledge (and if so, in what sense); whether knowledge can be merely transmitted through testimony, or whether there can be cases in which a speaker *generates* knowledge for her hearer that she herself lacks; and how this sort of knowledge compares to other kinds of knowledge – in particular, perceptual or memorial knowledge.

I will have much to say on most of these topics, but for the most part I will reserve my own positive views on them for Part II of this book. Here, in Part I, I propose to remain as neutral as I can on these topics. I do so since my aim here is to establish certain conclusions regarding the *semantics* of communication. I believe that a proper account of knowledge communication through speech will have substantive implications on this score. My aim is to draw out these implications without taking on substantial commitments on the epistemic topics mentioned above.

This initial chapter serves that aim by presenting a characterization of the sort of knowledge that is at issue. In order to remain neutral on the epistemic issues mentioned above, my characterization here will of necessity be schematic: I will point out how those issues bear on my schematic account, without offering a definitive position on them. However, while it is schematic, my characterization will be far from empty: on the basis of it I will be arguing that the knowledge in question is epistemically distinctive (see esp. section 1.6 of this chapter), and that a proper account of this sort of distinctive knowledge calls for endorsing various anti-individualistic doctrines in semantics (chapters 2–4). (I go on, in Part II (chapters 5–8), to argue that a proper account of this sort of knowledge also calls for endorsing various anti-individualistic doctrines in epistemology as well: it is here that I will take sides on the issues above.)

To describe the sort of knowledge that will form the subject-matter of this book I will use 'knowledge through speech',[1] 'testimonial knowledge', and 'knowledge through testimony',[2] more or less interchangeably. In what follows I attempt to identify some non-trivial characteristics of this sort of knowledge. Where neutrality on the substantive epistemic issues identified above is not possible, I will offer arguments on behalf of the positions I do take up.

1.2 KNOWLEDGE THROUGH SPEECH: INTRODUCTION TO THE SUBJECT-MATTER

An initial question is this: how can a hearer acquire knowledge through observing another's speech? Assuming that knowledge involves belief that is non-accidentally true,[3] a first reformulation of our question might be: under what conditions does a hearer's observing another's speech result in the hearer's forming a belief that is non-accidentally true?

---

[1] I use 'knowledge through speech' as shorthand for a sort of knowledge one could acquire through written language as well. (Of course, knowledge through written language introduces a host of complications beyond those involved in knowledge through speech, mainly in connection with the issue of context. I will not have very much to say about these complications in this book; I hope to return to this at a later time.)

[2] 'Testimony' is the term used in the epistemology literature for speech acts apt for the transmission of this sort of knowledge.

[3] The idea that knowledge is incompatible with luck has been the basis of a new and very interesting development of an anti-luck epistemology: see Pritchard 2005. Of course, there are those who think knowledge is merely true belief: see for example Sartwell 1991 and 1992. See also Goldman 1999, where the suggestion is made that the notion of knowledge as merely true belief is useful for epistemology (even as he agrees that a more robust notion of knowledge is also useful).

An immediate question regards the non-accidentality condition on knowledge: there are various accounts of this condition, and the matter is controversial and complex. Although I do not want to make any controversial assumptions here, it will be convenient to work with a particular conception of non-accidentality – if only to suggest how the relevant issues can be formulated within a particular epistemic framework. For this purpose I will choose what I regard as a rather common (though still controversial) framework: that of the reliability theory of knowledge, according to which knowledge is true belief that is produced and sustained by reliable belief-producing and -sustaining methods.[4]

Call a belief *reliable* when it is true and it meets this reliability condition.[5] Now it is controversial to suppose that reliability is a necessary condition on *justified belief*: this thesis is the target of the so-called 'New Evil Demon' problem.[6] It is also controversial whether reliable belief *suffices* for knowledge. One's views on this matter will be shaped by one's views about the nature of epistemic justification and its relation to knowledge. But it is much less controversial to suppose that reliability is a *necessary* condition on *knowledge*. And this less controversial thesis is all that will be required for the semantic conclusions I seek to draw in Part I of this book. Further recourse is needed, of course, to address those philosophers who reject that reliability is a necessary condition on knowledge. Those who do should read this chapter by replacing my talk of 'reliability' with talk of 'non-accidentality', which they can understanding however they please. The main claims I wish to make in Part I will be unaffected by such a reading.

Assume, then, that reliable belief is a necessary condition on knowledge. Applied to the case of testimony, we get the result that the observation of another's speech gives rise to knowledge only when it gives rise to reliable belief, that is, only when such observation is part of a belief-producing (and-sustaining) process that is reliable. Though correct, this point does not demarcate the domain of knowledge that will be at issue

---

[4] I ignore issues pertaining to Gettierization.

[5] It is a controversial matter how to understand the relevant notion of reliability. Thus there is a common distinction between local and global reliability (McGinn (1984: 16) and Goldman (1986: 44–6)); there are proposals that tie reliability to the conditions of the actual world ('actual-world reliability'; see for example Sosa's distinction between aptness and adroitness, in Sosa (2002) and his contribution in Bonjour and Sosa (2003)); and there is a new proposal regarding transglobal reliability (Henderson and Horgan (forthcoming)).

[6] See Cohen 1984 and Sosa 1991.

here. The following case is instructive. Hearer *H* observes speaker *S* assertorically utter,

(1) Judy bought fourteen Gucci handbags at the mall today.

H is competent in the recognition of English sentences: she can reliably discriminate English sentences from non-English sentences. Consequently, on observing *S*'s utterance of (1) *H* learns (in the sense of *comes to know*) that *S* speaks English.[7] Here, *H*'s observation of *S*'s speech is part of a process that eventuates in *H*'s reliable belief that *S* speaks English; only this is not a case in which the knowledge comes *through* the speech, as it were. To be sure, since *H* is relying on her ability to recognize English sentences, she is attending to the linguistic features of *S*'s utterance. In this way her reliable belief here differs from the belief she forms, also from observing *S*'s utterance of (1), to the effect that *S* has a cold, where this belief is formed through *H*'s reliable ability to discriminate the stuffy-nose-sounds indicative of those with colds. Even so, the linguistic features to which *H* is attending, insofar as she acquires the belief that *S* speaks English, are not of the sort to underwrite testimonial knowledge.

As a kind of knowledge, then, testimonial knowledge is not to be distinguished merely by the fact that it involves belief formed through a reliable process whose initial input is the hearer's representation of observed speech. Can we fix this by saying that testimonial knowledge is knowledge involving reliable belief formed from (initially caused by?) one's having observed another's speech, where the content of the belief one forms is the content of the speech itself? An example modeled on a case described by Robert Audi (1997) shows that the proposed fix still fails. *H* observes *S* assert "I am a baritone." *S* is trying to deceive *H*, but incorrectly takes himself to be a tenor when in fact he is a baritone. Indeed, *S*'s testimony exemplifies the very baritone properties of his voice. And, on the basis of her reliable discernment of baritones (she can hear in *S*'s utterance those characteristic baritone sounds), *H* comes to believe that *S* is a baritone. Here *H*'s belief satisfies the conditions of the proposed fix, yet it is not a case in which the knowledge *H* acquires is testimonial knowledge.

---

[7] In what follows I will put '*S*' in oblique occurrence. This occurrence is not essential, as the knowledge in question can be rendered in a *de re* form: *H* can learn, regarding *S*, that she speaks English. Alternatively, the point I wish to illustrate can be made by choosing a case in which speaker and hearer are familiar to one another, in which case the content of the hearer's knowledge could be rendered in *de dicto* fashion.

Audi himself uses an example of this sort to illustrate the need for a distinction between knowledge that is merely *from* testimony, and knowledge that is *through* testimony. Where *H* acquired her belief that *S* is a baritone on the basis of her (*H*'s) ability to discriminate baritones from non-baritones *by the sound of the voice*, it would seem that testimonial knowledge properly so-called involves forming the belief in a way that is grounded on one's *acceptance of the testimony*. Here 'accept' and its derivatives are quasi-technical terms: to accept a piece of testimony in this sense is to accept (or form a belief in) what was attested, and to do so *on the basis of* its having been attested.

Consider then how the acceptance of testimony figures in an account of testimonial knowledge. Since accepting testimony is a matter of accepting the attested content on the basis of its having been attested, and since 'on the basis of' is an epistemic (grounding) relation, we get the following 'epistemic dependency thesis': beliefs formed through accepting testimony depend for their epistemic status – and in particular, for their status as *knowledge* – on the epistemic features of the testimony itself. The epistemic dependency thesis will enable us to rule out the case in which, having observed *S*'s testimony, *H* comes to believe that *S* speaks English, or has a cold. In these cases *H* could have acquired the knowledge she did even under conditions in which *S*'s testimony was not reliable with respect to what she attested. In addition, the epistemic dependency thesis will also enable us to rule out another case that should not count as testimonial knowledge. Consider in this light the case in which *H*, who knows that *S* makes comments about the weather only when nervous, comes to know that *S* is nervous through having observed *S* comment that the weather is lovely today. This case differs from the previous cases we have discussed, in that in this case *H* had to *understand* the speech she observed, and in particular had to understand that *S* was saying something about the weather, in order to arrive at the knowledge in question. Even so, *H*'s knowledge (to the effect that *S* is nervous) is not testimonial knowledge; and our the epistemic dependency thesis explains why not.

The present proposal, then, is this: testimonial knowledge is knowledge involving reliable belief formed through the process whereby a piece of testimony is accepted; that is, it is knowledge involving reliable belief in what was attested, formed on the basis of its having been attested.[8] In

---

[8] This characterization may now be too restrictive: must one believe precisely what one was told, in order to acquire knowledge through testimony? (For example, can't one form a

casting testimonial knowledge as involving belief formed *on the basis of* a content's having been attested, the proposed characterization highlights the element of the hearer's *epistemic reliance* on her source speaker. But what, precisely, is it to rely epistemically on one's source?

1.3 TESTIMONIAL KNOWLEDGE AND EPISTEMIC RELIANCE

Return to the case in which *H* comes to know that *S* is nervous, by observing *S* make a comment about the weather. In coming to know what she does, *H* is – or, so far as the knowledge *H* aims to acquire goes, can be – indifferent to *S*'s epistemic perspective regarding the speech contribution she (*S*) made. Although *H*'s acquisition of the knowledge that *S* is nervous depends on *H*'s having observed and understood *S*'s speech about the weather – he would not have acquired that particular piece of knowledge unless he observed *S*'s testimony (*S*'s nervousness being otherwise indiscernible), and unless he correctly understood that testimony to be a comment about the weather – it matters not a jot whether *S*'s speech itself was knowledgeable. Indeed, *none* of the epistemic properties of *S*'s speech are relevant to the epistemic status of *H*'s belief that *S* is nervous. The same goes for the other examples in which *H* acquires knowledge from, but not through, *S*'s speech. This suggests that what is distinctive of cases of knowledge through speech is precisely the element of epistemic reliance: in aiming to acquire knowledge through *S*'s testimony, *H* is relying on that testimony to have the epistemic features that, in virtue of its being a case of testimony, it ought to have.

Such a thesis calls for development.

I begin first with the claim that proffered testimony 'ought' to have certain epistemic features. Here I rely on the burgeoning literature regarding the epistemic norm of the speech act of *assertion*. Many authors have remarked that assertion is governed by an epistemic norm. To hold such a view is (roughly) to hold that assertion is that unique speech act instances of which are appropriately assessed by reference to the epistemic norm in question. To be sure, there is a lively dispute over what the norm is:

belief in an obvious implicature generated by the speaker's having testified as she did, yet still count as having thereby acquired knowledge through the testimony?) I will have something to say about this matter in chapter 3. Until that time I simply stipulate that I am interested in knowledge transmission in cases whether the propositional content of the knowledge acquired is precisely that of the testimonial speech act.

some hold that it is knowledge (Unger 1975; Brandom 1983 and 1994; DeRose 1991; Adler 1996; and Williamson (2000)), while others suggest that it is some epistemic status short of knowledge (Kvanvig (2003 and forthcoming), Lackey (unpublished manuscript)). But everyone – or at least everyone who thinks that assertion is governed by epistemic norms of some sort or another[9] – agrees on one important point. All agree that in asserting *p* a speaker presents herself as being in one or another epistemic-ally privileged position *vis-à-vis* the truth-value of *p*, such that if she does not occupy such a position, she is susceptible to criticism *qua* assertor. This reflects an 'ought' relevant to assertion: one ought to assert *p*, only if *q*, where '*q*' is replaced by a sentence expressing the condition whose obtaining would render the assertion normatively acceptable.

In a context in which we are interested in the features which testimony as such 'ought' to have, the relevance of the epistemic norm of assertion is straightforward. On many accounts of testimony, to testify just is to assert.[10] But whether or not this identification holds, on any plausible conception of testimony, assertion is the sort of speech act that is a candidate for constitut-ing testimony. This much appears to be common to all those who theorize about testimony – the difference between them being what *other* conditions, if any, need to be satisfied if an assertion is to count as a case of testimony.[11] What is more, no matter one's views regarding the relation between testimony and assertion, both have a core feature in common: both are speech acts whose paradigmatic upshot is to make a content available in such a way that a hearer who, having formed a belief through her acceptance of the speech contribution, has formed a belief whose status as knowledge (or not) turns on the epistemic features of the speech act itself. In light of this, what is true of assertion is true of testimony: there are epistemic standards for speech acts of this sort, violation of which renders

---

[9] Not all proposals for the norm of assertion are epistemic norms. Williamson (2000) considers the norm of truth, as given by the rule: assert *p*, only if *p* is true. (As a defender of the knowledge rule, Williamson rejects the truth norm as the norm of assertion.) Now my linkage of the norm of testimony with the norm of assertion will be undermined if assertion's norm is, as the truth-rule is, non-epistemic. Happily, the proposal that assertion is governed by the truth rule would appear to face insurmountable difficulties: see Williamson (2000: 244–9). Consequently, I will assume that assertion is governed by an epistemic norm – though in keeping with my neutrality on contested epistemic matters I will remain neutral on which of the epistemic candidates provides the norm in question.

[10] For example, see Fricker 1987 and Sosa 1994.

[11] Thus Coady 1992 argues that the speech act of testifying is a speech act that must be performed as the answer to some question presently at issue. But see Graham 1997 for an argument against imposing this restriction.

the speaker susceptible to criticism *qua* assertor or testifier. Just as with asserting, so too with testifying: the speaker presents herself as in a privileged position *vis-à-vis* the truth of the content attested to, and the testimony ought to have those properties in virtue of which the speaker would occupy that happy epistemic position.

So far I have been suggesting that testimony is governed by an epistemic norm *because assertion is.* But the claim that testimony is governed by an epistemic norm is actually plausible independent of the corresponding claims regarding assertion.[12] Whatever else one takes testimony to be, it is the sort of speech act that (minimally) aims to be reliable in what it (linguistically) represents to be the case. What is more, this aim is distinctive of testimony. We can get a sense of this by contrasting testimony with other speech acts that (in some broad sense) aim at truth. For example, whereas speculation and guessing might also aim at truth – one who speculates or guesses with no interest in truth would be said to be deficient *qua* speculator or guesser – nevertheless one's aim at truth when one speculates that *p* does not impose any demand for reliability – one whose speculation is not reliable is not *ipso facto* deficient *qua* speculator. Precisely not, since the very point of speculating or guessing is to advance a content as true under conditions in which a question has arisen, but where no candidate answer is taken to satisfy any substantive epistemic standards. This explains why it is that, at least in cases in which the hearer is encountering the speaker for the first time, the hearer cannot acquire the knowledge that *p* through accepting what is merely the speaker's *speculation* that *p*.[13] The epistemic norms governing speculation are such that, even if *p* is true, a speaker's speculation that *p* is not (or at least not typically) suitably related to the fact that *p*, to serve as the sort of speech act that can ground another's acquisition of knowledge through her acceptance of that speech act. This singles out what is unique about testimony *qua* speech act aiming at truth: testimony is a speech act aiming not just at truth but at *reliable* truth. (As we will see below, it is for this reason that testimony can ground the unique sort of knowledge I am calling

---

[12] I thank Eli Dresner for discussion of this point.

[13] It's controversial whether a hearer can acquire the knowledge that *p* through accepting a speaker's *assertion* that *p*. This will depend in part on the correct view regarding the conditions on being entitled to accept an assertion. But it should be uncontroversial that a hearer cannot acquire the knowledge that *p* through accepting a speaker's *speculation* that *p*. This is enough to suggest that, as speech acts, speculation and assertion have what we might call a different *pragmatic–epistemic potential*. See what follows in the text.

'testimonial knowledge.') At a minimum, then, we can say that testimony-constituting speech acts are appropriately assessed in such terms: testimony that fails to be reliable is *ipso facto* deficient *qua* testimony. In short, testimony is governed by the epistemic norm appropriate to the aim of reliable (linguistic) representation: at a minimum, a piece of testimony ought to have those features, whatever they are, that render the speech act a case of reliable (linguistic) representation.

If I am right about this, then one might use this point about testimony, together with the idea that *by its very nature* assertion is the sort of speech act that can constitute testimony, to argue that assertion, too, is governed by an epistemic norm. To argue in this way would be to reverse the order of explanation above: here we hold that assertion is governed by an epistemic norm *because testimony is*. However, I won't attempt such an argument here.[14] For present purposes, all that is needed is that testimony is governed by an epistemic norm – whether or not that norm is the norm of assertion, and indeed whether or not assertion is governed by an epistemic norm in the first place.

The foregoing considerations suggest the following picture. In accepting another's testimony (or assertion; in what follows I won't bother distinguishing these), a hearer is relying on the speaker to have lived up to the epistemic norm governing testimony. This point enables us to formulate the sort of grounds that are characteristic of testimonial knowledge: such knowledge involves a belief acquired through the hearer's (*de facto*) reliance on the speaker's having satisfied the relevant norm governing testimony. Insofar as we are assuming (for the purposes of illustration) a reliabilist epistemology, we can regard this norm as one requiring that the testimony itself be reliable, in something like the following sense: it would have been made only if it were true.

So far I have been arguing that testimonial knowledge is knowledge grounded in a hearer's epistemic reliance on the speaker, where the latter is characterized as the hearer's (*de facto*) reliance on the speaker's having satisfied testimony's norm in her testimony-constituting speech act. But while epistemic reliance *in some sense or other* is required for testimonial knowledge, it is controversial to suppose that this is the form that it takes. For, arguably, a hearer can rely epistemically on a speaker, in the sense relevant to acquiring testimonial knowledge (or at least testimonial belief)

---

[14] See Goldberg (forthcoming d) where I present and critically discuss a variant on this argument, whose conclusion is that knowledge is the proper norm of assertion.

through her acceptance of the speaker's testimony, even when the hearer regards the speaker's testimony as failing to be normatively acceptable *qua* assertion (or *qua* testimony). If so, then we will need to modify our conception of epistemic reliance itself. Since the examples that illustrate the need to so do also bear against the transmission view of testimonial knowledge, and since this view is of some independent interest in its own right, it is worth spending some time on the matter. I do so in the next section.

1.4 THE NATURE OF EPISTEMIC RELIANCE AND THE TRANSMISSION MODEL OF TESTIMONIAL KNOWLEDGE

The proposal above, regarding the sort of grounds characteristic of testimonial knowledge, involves a certain conception of what is involved in a hearer's epistemically relying on a speaker. My claim has been that the reliance in question involves a hearer's reliance on the speaker as having conformed to the norm governing testimony. (Given my reliabilist orientation, I have been regarding this norm as requiring, at a minimum, reliable linguistic representation.) The challenge that I am about to present to this proposal depends on cases in which the speaker fails to live up to this norm. Assuming (as I am) that knowledge requires reliable belief, and assuming (what is plausible) that a speaker who offers unreliable testimony has given expression to an unreliable belief, we get the result that, in these cases, the speaker fails to have the knowledge (or reliable belief) that she aims to be transmitting to the hearer. In this way we see that the challenge I am presenting against the proposed characterization of epistemic reliance is also, and at the same time, a challenge to the transmission model of testimonial knowledge. According to such a model, one can acquire knowledge through testimony only if the speaker herself had the knowledge in question.[15] In presenting a challenge to that view,[16] I am aiming to complicate my account of the sort of epistemic reliance that grounds testimonial knowledge; I do so in order to ensure the adequacy of that account *even if* it should turn out that the transmission view is not correct.

---

[15] Variants on the transmission view have been explicitly defended by Audi (1997: 410); Ross (1975: 53); Welbourne (1994: 302); Burge (1993: 486); (Dummett 1994: 264); and Fricker (2006: 239–41). It is also assumed, although without argument, in Schmitt (2006).

[16] Other challenges to that model can be found in Lackey 1999; Graham 1999; and Goldberg 2005b and (forthcoming c).

(Of course, those who are unconvinced by my examples will not see the need to modify the foregoing account of epistemic reliance.)

Why might one think that the foregoing account of epistemic reliance – and with it, the transmission model of testimonial knowledge – are not acceptable? Consider a case in which a hearer *H* observes an assertion under conditions in which she recognizes that there is a relevant alternative that the speaker *S* cannot rule out, but where (*H* is aware that) *H* herself can rule that alternative out. In that case *H* might still accept the testimony (assuming that *H* has no testimony-independent access to the truth of the attested content); but insofar as *H* did accept the testimony, she would not be relying on *S*'s having lived up to the norm of testimony on this occasion. After all, if *H* regards the testimony as based on evidence that doesn't rule out a relevant alternative, then *H* will regard that testimony itself as unreliable, and hence – assuming that reliability cashes out the epistemic norm of testimony – as failing to live up to that norm. Insofar as she is inclined to accept the testimony anyway, *H* would be relying on *S* to have lived up to that norm *but for the relevant alternative she (S) can't rule out*. Assuming that cases of this sort would still count as cases of testimonial knowledge, we reach two conclusions. First: the sort of epistemic reliance presupposed by the acquisition of testimonial knowledge does not require that the hearer regard the speaker as having lived up to the norm of testimony (taken to require reliable linguistic representation). Second: testimony can generate knowledge for a hearer that the source herself lacks.

This schematic presentation may not convince. Those who wish to retain the transmission model of testimonial knowledge might think to do so by questioning whether the cases schematized above can be correctly described as cases in which the hearer's knowledge was *testimonial* knowledge. They might grant that the hearers know, but deny that the knowledge is testimonial knowledge.

However, there are reasons to think that such a move is unacceptable.

A first point to make here is a defensive one: what is arguably the main reason that could be offered, in defense of the claim that cases of this sort are not to be treated as testimonial knowledge, is not a good reason. The purported reason is this: *H*'s knowledge should not be counted as *testimonial* knowledge because it is based on background information she brings to bear in the process of forming the belief in question. But such a reason is too strong: it would show that most of the knowledge we count as testimonial knowledge does not so count. For, as I go on to show in greater detail in chapter 6, it is plausible to think that hearers *always* bring background information to bear in the process through which a piece of testimony is accepted or rejected. (Admittedly, the process by which a hearer's background beliefs are brought to bear in evaluating the *prima facie* plausibility of testimony is typically subcognitive; but it is one in which the background information does figure nevertheless.) I learn through taking your word that it is 95 degrees today. But even in this paradigmatic case of knowledge through testimony, my move to accept your word is informed in part by my background belief that what you said is well within the range of what one would expect regarding temperatures around here for this time of year. Nor should one make too much of the fact that, for her part, *H* is *consciously* using background information as part of the process through which she is acquiring her belief. This is not sufficient to rule out the case as one of testimonial knowledge. Compare: if, observing your testimony that *p*, I consciously ask myself whether to trust you and, reviewing the factors that justify my doing so, accept your testimony, surely this still counts as a case of testimonial belief (and knowledge).

At this point, a critic of my claim that *H*'s knowledge is testimonial knowledge might complain that, in addition to *H*'s own background information playing a substantive epistemic role *vis-à-vis* the belief *H* acquires, *H*'s epistemic reliance on *S* is too meager for this to count as a case of testimonial knowledge. But I think that this charge can be met, and in so doing I present a positive case for thinking that this is to be treated as a case of testimonial knowledge. It is true that *H* is not depending on *S*'s testimony to satisfy the norm of testimony, construed as enjoining reliable testimony. After all, *H* knows of a relevant defeater *S* can't rule out, and so *H* knows that *S* would have offered the testimony even if it had been false (in the way anticipated by the defeater). Even so, *H* is depending on *S*'s testimony to be such that, *on the assumption that we can regard the defeater in question as irrelevant*, the testimony is normatively acceptable. It should be clear from the story above that *H* is so regarding *S*'s testimony. The knowledge that enables *H* to defeat the defeater renders that defeater irrelevant to *H*'s own epistemic perspective. What is more, *H* would not have acquired the knowledge he did were it not for the fact that, bracketing the defeater in question, the testimony is otherwise normatively acceptable. Thus it would appear that *H* is relying on *S*'s testimony in this way. And this is precisely the sort of reliance that, I noted above, grounds testimonial knowledge.

A less schematic case might make the present point clear. Let *S*'s assertion be one regarding a particular wall that is perceptually accessible to *S* but not to *H*, to the effect that it is red. Let the relevant alternative (the defeater) be the hypothesis that the wall is white but is presently being illuminated by a uniform red light – it being known to *H* but not to *S* that this part of town is the 'red light district'. And let *H* be aware, as *S* is not, that *S* happens to be on one of the few streets in that district with no red lights. *H*'s move to accept *S*'s testimony is informed by his reliance on the uptake of *S*'s perceptual system (reported in *S*'s testimony); only *H* does not regard this uptake as (locally) reliable full-stop, but rather as (locally) reliable *given that the red light hypothesis can be disregarded*. Here, the fact that this hypothesis can be disregarded by *H* *but not by S* is irrelevant to the (qualified) reliance *H* exhibits towards *S*'s testimony. This reliance, it would seem, is of the sort that underwrites the claim that *H* has acquired testimonial knowledge through his acceptance of *S*'s testimony.[17]

If I am correct about this, then we need to complicate our account of the sort of epistemic reliance that is at the heart of the acceptance of testimony. Happily, a fix is near-to-hand. We can say that, in accepting testimony, a hearer is relying on the testimony to be such that, either it is normatively acceptable (satisfying the norm of testimony), or else (if it is not normatively acceptable) whatever defects prevent it from being normatively acceptable can be 'repaired' by information the hearer herself has. The relevant notion of 'repair' can be spelled out in reliabilist terms, as follows: given a hearer *H* who accepts *S*'s testimony on *O*, *H*'s background information 'repairs' *S*'s testimony when (i) *S*'s testimony on *O* was not normatively acceptable, (ii) *H* accepts the attested content, (iii) among the grounds of *H*'s resulting belief, an ineliminable role is played by both (a) *S*'s grounds for the testimony and (b) the background information *H* brings to bear on her assessment of the acceptability of the testimony, and (iv) the process through which *H* accepts *S*'s testimony on *O* results in a reliable belief. (*H*'s reliance on the testimony is seen in the ineliminability of (a) in an account of the epistemic status of *H*'s belief.) I submit that it is reliance *in this sense* that lies at the heart of accepting testimony.[18]

The proposed fix, and with it the proposal regarding the sort of epistemic reliance that grounds testimonial knowledge, can be motivated by the non-accidentality condition on knowledge. We are after cases in which the reliability condition on knowledge is satisfied by reliable belief

---

[17] See Goldberg 2005b for a defense of this sort of claim, in an analogous case.

[18] I thank Assaf Sharon, David Enoch, and Igal Kvart for help in thinking about this issue.

produced by the hearer's epistemic reliance on a speaker's say-so. The cases above are all cases in which the speaker's say-so is not itself reliable, owing to the relevance of an alternative that the speaker herself cannot rule out, yet where, because the hearer *can* rule out that alternative (and all other relevant ones), the hearer's acceptance of this unreliable say-so would produce reliable belief. These cases indicate that it is not *the testimony itself*, so much as the testimony-as-having-been-scrutinized-and-consumed-by-the-hearer, that must be reliable.[19] This suggests that the hearer is relying on the speaker to have testified in such a way that, whatever it is that supports the testimony, together with the background information that the hearer brings to bear in accepting the testimony, make for the acquisition of a reliable testimonial belief. In standard cases, of course, the hearer will be relying on the speaker to have the knowledge in question: these will be cases in which the hearer's epistemic reliance on the speaker will take the form of relying on her to have lived up to the norm of assertion (or testimony). But we can allow cases of the above sort, too, where the hearer relies on her own background information to "repair" the defects in the testimony in such a way as to acquire a belief that is non-accidentally true. The idea is that, in such cases, the testimony's epistemic features provide something in the way of positive epistemic support for the hearer's belief – support without which the hearer would not be in a position to acquire the knowledge in question in the first place – where this support falls short of that needed for knowledge, but where the background information the hearer brings to bear on the testimony can fill in the gap, resulting in a belief that is epistemically supported in a way sufficient for knowledge.

An analogous point can be made in connection with the transmission model of testimonial knowledge. Given that testimonial knowledge is knowledge, and that knowledge presupposes reliable belief, we might say that the transmission model is based on a further assumption: the only way to acquire a reliable belief through the acceptance of testimony, where the resulting testimonial belief would satisfy the conditions on testimonial knowledge, is for the testifier to have the knowledge (hence reliable belief) she is purporting to express in her testimony. However, we have seen that this is simply false. One can acquire a reliable belief through one's acceptance of testimony, where the resulting belief satisfies the

---

[19] I discuss what form such scrutiny takes, and how it relates to the reliability of the testimonial belief that is produced, in chapters 6 and 8.

remaining conditions on knowledge, even when the testimony itself (and hence the belief expressed in the testimony) is itself unreliable. That such a case of knowledge is correctly described as *testimonial* knowledge simply reflects the fact that it depends for its status as knowledge on one's (qualified) epistemic reliance on the testimony itself.

Now much more could be said in defense of my claims regarding the transmission model and the sort of epistemic reliance that grounds testimonial knowledge. However, I do not propose to defend either of these claims further.[20] Instead, I propose to use this amended account of epistemic reliance, in order to discern some of the necessary conditions on testimonial knowledge. To simplify my exposition, I will put the account as follows: in accepting a piece of testimony, a hearer is epistemically relying on the speaker to have testified in a normatively* acceptable way (relative to the hearer), where one has testified in a normatively* acceptable way (relative to a hearer) when *either* the testimony is normatively acceptable (satisfying the norm of testimony) *or else* the hearer has background information which enables her to 'repair' the deficiencies of the testimony in the manner indicated (resulting in a reliable testimonial belief).

1.5 TESTIMONIAL RELIABILITY

I have been arguing that testimonial knowledge must be grounded in a hearer's epistemic reliance on a speaker; and I have proposed how such epistemic reliance is to be understood. We might say that satisfying the epistemic reliance condition ensures that one's belief is grounded in the manner appropriate to a *testimony-based* belief, and hence is a candidate for testimonial knowledge. Whether a testimony-based belief amounts to testimonial knowledge will then depend on whether, in virtue of the features of this grounding, it satisfies the remaining conditions on knowledge. In this section I begin the process of identifying these further conditions. In discussing this it will be best to begin, not with the disjunctive conception of epistemic reliance just noted (in which the hearer takes the testimony to be normatively* acceptable), but rather with the simpler conception of epistemic reliance, on which the hearer relies on the speaker to have lived up to the norm of testimony (assertion). The simpler

---

[20] But see Goldberg 2005b, (forthcoming c), and (forthcoming d).

conception will better enable us to disentangle the conditions on the speaker from those on the hearer. Once we are clear about these, we can accommodate the points within an account utilizing the more sophisticated, disjunctive conception of epistemic reliance.

Our question is this: given that a hearer forms a belief through epistemic reliance on a speaker (taking her testimony to be normatively acceptable), what further conditions must be met in order for *H*'s belief to amount to testimonial knowledge? One condition is clear: given a case in which the hearer is depending on the testimony to be normatively acceptable (as opposed to normatively* acceptable), the testimony must actually be (as the hearer takes it to be) normatively acceptable. This point should not be controversial. Suppose that Gideon forms a belief that *p* through epistemic reliance on Sara's testimony that *p*. Gideon has excellent reasons for regarding Sara as reliable, his cognitive system is working properly, and indeed Sara's testimony is knowledgeable. In that case, Gideon's belief is knowledge. But now imagine a variant, like the above except that Sara's assertion is not only not knowledgeable, she's just making it up. (This is very out of character for her, she is normally hyper-reliable, but she very much wants Gideon to believe *p*, and so asserts *p* with all the trappings of confidence she normally has when she makes an assertion.) Unbeknown to Sara, *p* happens to be true. Even so, Gideon's true belief, based on her testimony, fails to amount to knowledge. The obvious diagnosis is that Gideon fails to know because Sara's testimony was not normatively acceptable – at the very least, Sara's testimony was not suitably related to the fact in question.

The foregoing diagnosis is supported by the non-accidentality condition on knowledge: Gideon's belief is only accidentally true, where the source of the accidentality in question is the source testimony. The point can be put in terms of the notion of reliability, as follows. Sara's testimony was not reliable: it is not the case that she would have testified that *p* only if *p* were true. But in most or all nearby worlds in which she falsely testifies to *p*, Gideon (having there the same accessible reasons to regard her as credible as he has in the actual world) still accepts the testimony. This shows that his testimonial belief is unreliable: he would have believed *p*, in the same (testimonial) way he did, even if *p* had been false. What is more, this belief is unreliable precisely *because* the testimony he accepted is unreliable. What we have, then, is one necessary condition on testimonial knowledge: given a belief formed through epistemic reliance on a speaker, the hearer's belief amounts to testimonial knowledge only if the testimony was in fact reliable. More generally still: given a belief formed through (unqualified) epistemic reliance on a speaker, the hearer's belief amounts to testimonial knowledge only if the testimony was normatively acceptable (satisfying the norm of assertion).

1.6 UNDERSTANDING TESTIMONY

So far we have the following picture: when a hearer aims to acquire testimonial knowledge through her unqualified epistemic reliance on a speaker's say-so, her acquisition of such knowledge requires that the say-so is reliable (or, if it is preferred, satisfies testimony's norm). Suppose then that we have a case meeting these conditions. Does this suffice for reliable testimonial belief, and hence satisfy the non-accidentality requirement on knowledge? It still does not.

Here I focus on the possibility of a linguistic source of unreliability – one in which the hearer fails to recover the propositional content of the testimony itself. The case I envisage is as follows. Hearer H observes S's testimony, and represents the testimony as having had p as its propositional content. So, on the basis of her implicitly regarding S as in an epistemically privileged position regarding the truth of p (that is, as having given normatively acceptable testimony), H forms the belief that p. However, even though S's testimony was normatively acceptable (and so was reliable), H's belief is unreliable. It turns out that the content of S's testimony was (not p, but) q, logically independent of p.

The foregoing type of situation, whose possibility is patent, goes some distance towards explaining one persistent feature of the literature on the epistemology of testimony. It is common for those writing on the topic to restrict their attention to *content-preserving* cases of communication, where H comes to believe the very proposition attested to (on the basis of its having been attested to).[21] Most writers restrict their attention in this way with little or no comment about this restrictive focus. Indeed, my characterization above of what is involved in 'accepting testimony' was similarly restrictive, as it involved accepting *the very content attested to* on the basis of its having been attested. We now see one justification for restricting our theoretical focus to content-preserving cases. If the content of the belief H acquires from S's testimony is identical to the content of that

---

[21] I borrow the term 'content-preserving,' as used in the context of communication, from Burge 1993.

testimony, then the reliability of that testimony is reliability regarding the truth of *the very content that the hearer believes*. It does not follow, of course, that in such a case the hearer's testimonial belief is thereby reliable: perhaps the hearer has a defeater that the speaker lacked. But if the content believed is the content attested to, the hearer's belief would then be reliable *given that certain further epistemic conditions (to be identified below) were satisfied*. The same cannot be said for the case in which the hearer forms a belief based on a misunderstanding of the testimony.[22] For in that case, the reliability of the testimony would be reliability regarding the truth of a content that, if it bears an interesting logical or semantic relation to the content that the hearer came to believe, does so only fortuitously. The fortuitousness here reflects the fact that the case was one of misunderstanding: even if it turned out that the hearer's belief (based on her misunderstanding the speaker) was true, this would be an accident, and in any case it would not reflect the reliability of the testimony she aimed to accept. This would not be a case of knowledge, period – let alone knowledge through testimony – as it would fail to satisfy the non-accidentality condition on knowledge.

The foregoing makes clear that reliable testimonial belief involves more than merely being acquired through epistemic reliance on what in fact is normatively acceptable (reliable) testimony, as discussed in 1.5. If we want an account of how the reliability condition on knowledge is satisfied in cases of testimonial knowledge, we need to include a condition requiring the hearer's *reliable recovery of the proposition attested to*. The point here is that it is not enough for the hearer H to rely on the normative acceptability of the testimony, if all that this comes to is a matter of H's forming a belief on the basis of her (perhaps implicit) assumption that the testimony was normatively acceptable. For such acceptance is compatible with misunderstanding the testimony, and we have just seen that misunderstanding testimony is a way of introducing a knowledge-undermining element of luck into the process of belief-formation. Restricting ourselves to cases conforming to the schema *coming to know that p through recognizing that one has been told that p* – in chapter 2 I will examine what to say about other cases – the hearer's apprehension of the content of the testimony must be

---

[22] I ignore for the moment the case in which the hearer recovers a content that bears some interesting *pragmatic* relation to the content asserted – as when she recovers a content that the speaker conversationally implicated. These cases are discussed in chapter 3.

reliable, in something like the following sense: H would apprehend testimony as having the propositional content, p, only under those conditions in which the testimony did have p as its propositional content. What is required here is not just the recovery of the proposition attested to, but the *reliable* recovery of that proposition: a correct guess as to what another said in her testimony would be incompatible with acquiring knowledge through the testimony. What makes guessing an epistemically poor way to form beliefs in general, holds in the particular case of forming a belief through accepting what one guesses was what another person attested to: namely, one might have formed the belief one did, in the way that one did, even under circumstances in which the belief was false.

I.7 RELIABLY DISCRIMINATING EPISTEMIC RELIANCE

Suppose that H observes and understands a piece of testimony, that the testimony is reliable, and that H accepts the testimony because she regards it as reliable (which is to say H exhibits the sort of epistemic reliance characteristic of testimonial knowledge). Does this suffice for reliable testimonial belief, and hence for the satisfaction of the non-accidentality condition on knowledge? No: in addition to the possibility (mentioned above) that the hearer has a defeater that the speaker lacked, there is also the possibility that the hearer was overly credulous in her acceptance (she would have accepted the testimony even if it had been proffered by a notorious liar who was aiming to deceive her). The latter possibility suggests that, insofar as we want an account of the satisfaction of the reliability condition on testimonial knowledge (in cases involving unqualified epistemic reliance), we need yet another necessary condition: in addition to exhibiting such reliance on what in fact is reliable testimony, under conditions in which one's recovery of the content attested to is itself reliable, one's acceptance of that testimony must be based on a reliable capacity for distinguishing reliable from unreliable testimony.[23] (One must be discriminating in one's epistemic reliance on others; credulity is not an epistemic virtue.) We might put the point by saying that one's disposition

---

[23] If undefeated defeaters make for unreliability, then this third condition handles the former sort of case as well (involving the hearer's having a relevant defeater). But if not, we would still need to add a 'no defeater' condition, as a fourth necessary condition on reliable testimonial belief. I will disregard this complication here, as not central to my present concerns.

to rely epistemically on others must itself be reliable, in that one is disposed to rely epistemically only (or at least mainly) on reliable testimony.

It is clear how a failure on this score could result in unreliable testimonial belief. Consider the case of gullible Jim. Jim is linguistically competent: whenever he confronts the speech of others, he always recovers the propositional content of the speech. What is more, he competently identifies the type of speech act performed in each case: he can reliably discriminate assertion from guess, request from command, and so forth. And he typically forms beliefs in what was said only when he discerns the case as one of assertion; but in such cases he *always* accepts the testimony (at least whenever he doesn't already have the belief in question). Now suppose that Jim occupies a room full of liars. But suppose that, luckily, he happens upon the only truth-teller in the room. Observing her assertion, he immediately accepts what she says on the basis of her having said so. Here he is epistemically relying on what in fact is a reliable piece of testimony whose content he has reliably recovered; and yet his testimonial belief is not reliable for all that. After all, he would have come to believe what he did, in the way that he did (namely, through testimony), even under conditions in which what he believed was false. Had a liar falsely told him so, he would have believed it anyway. As a result, his actual testimonial belief, though true and formed through his epistemic reliance on a reliable source he understood, was nevertheless unreliably formed. It would appear, then, that we need to add a *reliably discriminating epistemic reliance* condition to our previous two necessary conditions on reliable testimonial belief.

We have come to identify three necessary conditions on reliable testimonial belief. In cases in which the hearer's testimonial belief is grounded on her *unqualified* epistemic reliance on a piece of say-so, her belief is a reliable testimonial belief (and so satisfies the reliability condition on knowledge) just in case the following conditions are satisfied:

(i) the testimony consumed was normatively acceptable;
(ii) the hearer non-accidentally recovered the proposition attested to through a process of comprehension; and
(iii) the hearer's acceptance of the testimony was the upshot of a capacity for distinguishing normatively acceptable from normatively unacceptable testimony.

If we then assume that reliability is the key epistemic property in terms of which to understand the normative propriety of assertion and the non-accidentality condition on knowledge, we then get the following construals of (i)–(iii), as three necessary conditions on testimonial knowledge:

(a) the testimony consumed was reliable (i.e., was such that it would be proferred only if true);
(b) the hearer recovered the proposition attested to through a reliable process of comprehension; and
(c) the hearer's acceptance of the testimony was the upshot of a reliable capacity for distinguishing reliable from unreliable testimony.

How can this be modified to cover the case in which the hearer's testimonial belief is grounded on her *qualified* epistemic reliance on a piece of say-so? In such cases (i) and (iii) are not quite right; and for this reason the corresponding (a) and (c) are not quite right either (even assuming that reliability is the right way to gloss the normative propriety of assertion and the non-accidentality condition on knoweldge). In the case of (i) and (iii), the fix is simply to replace 'normatively acceptable' with 'normatively★ acceptable.' In the case of (a) and (c), the fix will be a bit more involved. Briefly, the idea would be to replace both (a) and (c) with the following single condition:

(c★) the hearer's acceptance of the testimony was the upshot of a reliable capacity for acquiring reliable belief through epistemic reliance.

However, rather than go into the details here,[24] it will suffice simply to note that conditions (a)–(c) will provide three necessary conditions on testimonial knowledge in all standard cases, where a case is standard whenever the hearer exhibits an unqualified epistemic reliance on the speaker's say-so. (In such cases, all of the background information that the hearer brings to bear on (whether to accept) the testimony bears on the normative acceptability of the testimony – and not on "repairing" any flaws that prevent the testimony from being normatively acceptable.) Since most of the arguments I wish to make throughout this book will be focusing on these sorts of standard cases (and I will note where this is not so), I will simply ignore these complications and accept (a)–(c) as three necessary conditions on testimonial knowledge. (I ask the reader to bear in mind, however, that this is a simplification.)

---

[24] I have done so elsewhere; see Goldberg 2005b and (forthcoming c).

1.8 THE CHARACTERISTIC UPSHOT OF SUCCESSFUL EPISTEMIC RELIANCE

I have just identified three necessary conditions on reliable testimonial belief, and hence – assuming reliable testimonial belief is a necessary condition on testimonial knowledge – on testimonial knowledge. I now want to put these conditions to use. I do so here by introducing two superficially similar cases of knowledge acquisition, only one of which involves epistemic reliance. My claims will be, first, that the case involving epistemic reliance is epistemically distinctive, and second, that this epistemic distinctiveness can be traced to the nature of epistemic reliance itself. If this analysis is correct, then there is what I will call a characteristic epistemic upshot of acquiring knowledge through epistemic reliance – one that speaks to the very nature of the sort of knowledge I am calling 'testimonial knowledge.'

Here are the two cases. In the first case, a doctor, Henrietta, comes to know that it is a sunny day today, through observing a patient of hers, Slobodan, report that he is in a good mood. Since Henrietta has been indoors on call for the past day, she has not observed the weather for herself; rather, her knowledge that it is sunny today is based on the empirical generalization, which she has confirmed through careful observation of Slobodan, that he reports being in a good mood only on sunny days. She has confirmed this generalization with numerous positive instances in a variety of otherwise very different circumstances, and has encountered no negative instances. Here it will be granted that, even supposing that Henrietta does know that it is a sunny day today, Henrietta's knowledge is not correctly characterized as knowledge *through Slobodan's testimony*. The concept of epistemic reliance, introduced in section 1.3, easily explains this. This case thus contrasts with a second case in which Hallie, a doctor, observes the testimony of Steve, her patient, to the effect that it is sunny today. In that case, should Hallie accept the testimony, Hallie would then be relying epistemically on Steve, in the way characterized above. The result would be that her belief is then a candidate for testimonial knowledge. I take this as patent.

Consider now how these two cases differ from an epistemic point of view. In the former case, Henrietta is indifferent to Slobodan's epistemic perspective. Henrietta's knowledge that it is sunny (if she has attained such) depends merely on the epistemic status of two things: first, the empirical generalization linking Slobodan's good-mood-expressing reports and the sunny condition of the weather; and second, the description of Slobodan's current report, as a case that falls under the generalization in question. As a result, Henrietta is depending only on *her own* empirically well-supported generalization, and on her correct application of this generalization to the present case. The result is that the total knowledge-relevant support for her belief that it is sunny does not outstrip the support she has for the relevant generalization and for her characterization of Slobodan's act as falling under this generalization. Contrast this with the latter, communication-involving case. In that case Hallie is not indifferent to Steve's epistemic perspective. On the contrary, Hallie's knowledge that it is sunny (if she has attained such) depends on the epistemic features of Steve's testimony. This reflects the fact that Hallie is relying on Steve to have testified in a normatively acceptable way. But now suppose that Steve's testimony was normatively acceptable, and that Hallie was entitled to so regard it (which at a minimum involves Hallie's epistemic reliance here being reliably discriminating; see chapter 6 for further discussion). Given these conditions, the total knowledge-relevant epistemic support enjoyed by Hallie's belief that it is sunny *is not exhausted by* the support she has for any relevant inductive generalizations brought to bear in evaluating the credibility of this piece of testimony, together with the support she has for describing the testimony as falling under those generalizations. In particular, there remains the epistemic support Steve himself had for his testimony – support on whose adequacy Hallie was relying.

Let us describe a case in which a hearer H accepts a piece of testimony as 'happy' when the testimony itself was normatively acceptable, and H herself was entitled to so regard it. Then the present lesson is that happy cases (or at least those in which H attains a reliable comprehension of the testimony) have a characteristic epistemic upshot: in such cases, the total knowledge-relevant support enjoyed by the hearer H's testimonial belief outstrips the support provided by (one) the reasons hearer H had for trusting her source and (two) the proper functioning of H's cognitive system in the context in question. Return then to the contrast between the case of Henrietta and Slobodan, and Hallie and Steve. We now see that the epistemic difference between the cases can be traced to Hallie's epistemic reliance on Steve. For this reliance, together with the satisfaction of the other necessary conditions noted above, yields the characteristic epistemic upshot just noted: the total knowledge-relevant support enjoyed by Hallie's belief is not exhausted by the support she has for regarding

Steve's testimony as credible (or as satisfying the epistemic norm of assertion). This, then, is a distinctive characteristic of testimonial knowledge.

Although I will discuss it at greater length in chapter 5, the present point about the epistemic distinctiveness of testimonial knowledge bears emphasis. The point should be accepted even by those who are otherwise inclined to regard the epistemology of testimony in terms of the application, to particular occasions of testimony, of inductively confirmed generalizations regarding testimonial credibility.[25] Although I do not happen to think this is the right approach to the epistemology of testimony – for which see chapters 5 and 6 – here I want to suggest that even on such an approach, testimonial knowledge should be seen as epistemically distinctive in the manner indicated. Unlike ordinary inductive knowledge, testimonial knowledge rests on epistemic support that outstrips the subject's support for the relevant inductive generalization and for its application to the present case. What is more, this enhancement of epistemic support comes in virtue of the hearer's successful reliance on the speaker's having conformed in her assertoric (testimony-constituting) speech to the norms of such speech: given that the hearer recovered the proposition asserted, the support for her belief in that proposition is then enhanced by whatever supported the speaker's assertion. In this way we see that my proposed account of the distinctiveness of testimonial knowledge should be acceptable even to those who favor an 'inductivist' approach to the epistemology of testimony.

1.9 A UNIFIED ACCOUNT OF THE CONDITIONS ON TESTIMONIAL KNOWLEDGE

In this chapter I have focused on the nature of the sort of knowledge that is spread through verbal and written communication. The core of my account of such knowledge involves the notion of the hearer's *epistemic reliance* on her source. Only those beliefs acquired through epistemic reliance on a source's say-so are grounded in the way appropriate to knowledge through testimony. A belief grounded in this way amounts to testimonial knowledge when, in virtue of the features of its grounding in the subject's epistemic reliance on a piece of testimony, it satisfies the remaining conditions on knowledge. I spelled these conditions out in terms of the doctrine that knowledge involves belief that is non-accidentally

---

[25] I have in mind broadly 'reductionistic' approaches to the conditions on justified acceptance of testimony.

true. Applying this doctrine to the case of testimonial belief, we arrive at three further necessary conditions on testimonial knowledge. These I spelled out in terms of reliability: I argued that a belief formed through epistemic reliance on one's source is a case of testimonial knowledge only if (a) the testimony on which the hearer is relying is reliable,[26] (b) the hearer was reliable in her recovery of the proposition attested to, and (c) the hearer's acceptance of the testimony was based on her reliable capacity to distinguish reliable from unreliable testimony. These, I say, are necessary conditions on testimonial knowledge. If one endorses a reliabilist account of knowledge, then arguably they are jointly sufficient[27] – an idea I will be pursuing in Part II of this book. But for now I claim only that these conditions are necessary.

I turn now, in chapter 2, to a more detailed look at condition (b), the reliable comprehension condition – or, if it is preferred, the *non-accidental* comprehension condition – on testimonial knowledge. My thesis will be that, if the testimonial route to knowledge has the properties it is widely regarded as having – in particular, if it is as prevalent and as efficient a route to knowledge as we ordinarily think it is – then public linguist norms are ineliminably implicated in the processes through which testimony is produced and consumed. This should be an interesting result: what in the first instance is a condition on *reliable testimonial belief* nevertheless has interesting implications for the proper semantic treatment of language.

---

[26] At the very least, this condition will have to be met in standard cases (involving unqualified epistemic reliance).

[27] Again, *modulo* the possible need for a further 'no defeaters' condition: see footnote 23.

2

Public linguistic norms: the case from successful communication

In this chapter I argue for a key premise in the argument I will present (in chapter 4) for anti-individualism regarding the individuation of speech content, linguistic meaning, and (ultimately) the attitudes. The premise itself asserts the existence of *public linguistic norms*. As developed in the argument to follow, such norms are *normative* in that they provide standards for the correct usage and interpretation of lexical items (that is, they provide the semantic standards of these items); and such norms are *public*, first, in that they derive from the shared, public language that is common property to all members of a speech community, and second, in that participants in speech exchanges – speakers and hearers alike – are positively but defeasibly presumed to be answerable to these norms on each particular speech exchange.[1] In this chapter I will be pursuing the idea that the practice whereby knowledge is spread through a speaker's use of language itself *depends* on the existence of semantic standards provided by the shared public language. Or rather: such standards are required if this practice is to be, as we take it to be, a pervasive and efficient way to spread very specific pieces of knowledge, under conditions in which speaker and hearer may know nothing about one another's speech and interpretative dispositions beyond what is manifested in the brief speech exchange itself.

My main idea here, that the spreading of knowledge through testimony depends on a shared linguistic (and in particular semantic) inheritance, is not new. An early expression of such a view is found in Clifford's "The Ethics of Belief":

Our words, our phrases ... are common property, fashioned and perfected from age to age; an heirloom which every succeeding generation inherits as a precious deposit and a sacred trust to be handed on to the next one ... *Into this*, for good or

---

[1] Defeat of this presumption is discussed in chapter 3.

ill, *is woven every belief of every man who has the speech of his fellows.* (Clifford 1999: 73–4; italics mine)

Nor is Clifford alone in his recognition that the practice whereby beliefs are formed through "the speech of one's fellows" involves the inheritance or sustainment of the resources of a public language. More recently, others have emphasized the point that our encounters with the words of others provide us with the very concepts and categories that shape our cognitive life more generally. This theme is echoed, more or less explicitly, in the work of thinkers of diverse theoretical orientations, including Peter Strawson, Tyler Burge, Martin Kutsch, C. A. J. Coady, and Ruth Millikan:

Consider the overwhelming extent to which *what* we in fact perceive, the very nature or character of our perceptual experience itself, is determined by the instruction, the information, that we have already received from the word of others. (Strawson 1994; italics in original).

Comprehending standing, conceptual aspects of one's own thought and idiolect is itself, as a matter of psychological fact, normally dependent on having comprehended thoughts (one's own) that were shaped and expressed through the words of others. (Burge 1999: 243)

How can we hope to reduce testimony to perception if the way we perceive the world is to a considerable extent shaped by concepts and categories that we have learnt from others? (Kutsch 2002a: 341)

[There are] elements of dependence on others that are involved in the very use of an inherited and socially confirmed language. (Coady 2002: 358)

[There are] things you have heard about but would be unable to recognize in an ordinary way, such as Socrates and, if you like, molybdenum. How can you have concepts of these things on the theory of concepts I have suggested here [on which concept possession presupposes recognitional capacity]? ... Normally, language carries manifestations of distal affairs in the world in a way exactly analogous to the way light waves, sound waves, odors, tastes, gravitational fields and so forth do. Thus, in the Normal case (notice the capital 'N'),[2] believing what you are told is in relevant respects exactly like believing what you see ... One way of reidentifying an object or kind or property, then, is by knowing a word for it in the language spoken by the community you are in. (Millikan 2004: 237)

---

[2] For Millikan, 'Normal' is a technical term: roughly put, a situation is Normal with respect to the operation of a cognitive capacity R for organism O when and only when the situation is of a type whose instantiation throughout the history of O's species accounts for the members of this species not having been selected against in situations where members of the species not having R were or would have been selected against. See Millikan (2004: 229).

Each of these theorists accepts something to the effect that, in consuming the words of others, a hearer not only acquires knowledge (in the best case) but also, and perhaps more importantly, acquires or sustains the cognitive-cum-conceptual tools provided by the public language itself – tools the hearer will use throughout her cognitive life.

Of course it is one thing to say that, insofar as we rely epistemically on other people's say-so, we inherit (and/or sustain) their concepts. It is another to say that what was asserted to be the case in another's say-so is determined by norms governing *all members of the speech community*. The latter thesis, which is what the above theorists appear to accept, and which is what I will ultimately be trying to establish in this chapter, is significantly stronger. To see this, let it be granted that in any speech exchange in which a hearer accepts a speaker's say-so, the hearer inherits or sustains *that speaker's* concepts. This would enable us to account for knowledge transmission in particular cases, where this is understood to be a case of hearer *H*'s acquisition of the knowledge that *p* through her recognition that *S* told her that *p*. But this would stop short of establishing that, when conceptual contents are transmitted in speech, these contents themselves are (typically or usually) composed of concepts that *the public language* assigns to the (non-indexical) lexical items in the sentence used by the speaker.[3] In short, there is a gap separating the claim that content is transmitted in speech, and the claim that the contents transmitted in speech are those determined by the public language common to all members of the speech community. Among other things, the postulation of public linguistic norms is supposed to fill this gap.

In advance of offering an argument in defense of such a postulation, however, I want to note both the *naturalness* of the supposition that there are common, public linguistic standards governing speech exchanges, but also the *epistemic price* that we must pay for holding ourselves to these standards. In this vein the following remark by Jonathan Adler is especially apt:

Knowledge obtained purely by transmission or testimony is 'thin.' What the seeker knows via satisfying TK [a principle pertaining to testimonial knowledge] is simply the correctness of *p*. He does not, specifically, come thereby to understand at all why *p* is correct. The seeker need not even understand *p*. There are many who know from the testimony of others something to the effect that "Gödel's

---

[3] Here I am disregarding considerations of semantic context-sensitivity, where a distinction can be drawn between what the language assigns to the expression, and the semantic value of the expression as used on a given occasion.

Theory proves arithmetic incomplete" without grasping the rudiments of either the proof or the technical meaning of the crucial terms e.g. 'incomplete.' (Adler 1996: 107)[4]

I think that Adler is precisely right, both in his implicit semantic assumption – that in acquiring knowledge through testimony we simply inherit (or sustain) the concepts expressed in the say-so – and also in the epistemic implication he draws from this – that the result is that we acquire a distinctly 'thin' sort of knowledge. I discuss the epistemic implications of this in Part II of this book (especially in chapter 7); in this chapter I will be focusing on Adler's semantic point.[5] In this connection it is worth noting that Adler himself appears to be assuming the stronger thesis noted above. That is, he appears to be assuming that a proper account of knowledge communication presupposes not only that contents are transmitted in speech, but also that the contents that are transmitted are themselves determined by the standards of the public language itself. For, given that the hearer in his example does not grasp the technical meaning of the term 'incomplete', what else but the norms of the public language serve to fix the concept expressed by that term, and so serve to determine the content she knows through accepting her co-lingual's testimony?

Of course, it is one thing to cite a number of influential thinkers who appear to endorse the existence of public linguistic norms in connection with knowledge communication; it is another thing to *argue* for the existence of public linguistic norms in connection with knowledge communication. Since I do not want my argument to rest on the say-so of others, I will assume the burden of arguing directly for the postulation of public linguistic norms.

My motive for doing so, despite the fact that this postulation appears to be something that is commonly accepted, is two-fold.

---

[4] Adler's formulation of the knowledge in question is unfortunate. By speaking of those 'who know from the testimony of others something to the effect that "Gödel's Theory proves arithmetic incomplete," ' Adler's formulation is neutral as between whether the content of the knowledge is identical to the content of the sentence he quotes, or rather is some metalinguistic variant on this. However, as this is supposed to be an instance of knowledge that *p* where the hearer does not "even understand *p*," it is clear that Adler has in mind cases in which the person acquires knowledge whose content is the very content expressed in the testimony, rather than some metalinguistic variant on it. (I discuss the difficulties facing metalinguistic analyses of communication below, in sections 2.5 and 2.6.)

[5] See also chapter 4 section 4.11, where I will be arguing that the considerations underlying Adler's point about understanding can be used to explain the phenomena of incomplete grasp and semantic deference – phenomena often thought to be at the heart of the case for Attitude Anti-Individualism.

First, none of the aforementioned authors attempts to argue in detail for the claim that the testimonial spread of knowledge depends on the existence of public linguistic norms, and it would be nice to see whether this claim can be backed by something other than its intuitiveness. On this score I will be suggesting that the claim itself is motivated in the first instance by *epistemic* considerations, pertaining to the conditions on reliable (testimonial) belief. My argument will be that testimonial beliefs are reliably formed only if their formation satisfies the 'reliable comprehension' condition; and that, for at least a substantive subclass of these beliefs, the reliable comprehension condition will be satisfied only if the speaker and hearer alike rely on public linguistic norms in the production and comprehension of the speech act.

But I have a second motive for making out the argument from communication for public linguistic norms. In the course of my argument I will be identifying the basis for a novel route to anti-individualism regarding language and thought. There will be various points in my dialectic at which those hostile to anti-individualism might raise doubts. In addressing these doubts we can see how defensible the various forms of anti-individualism actually are, and how far critics of these doctrines must go in rebutting them.

2.2 OUTLINE OF THE ARGUMENT

My claim is that if the spread of knowledge through testimony is to have the features we ordinarily take it to have, then the satisfaction of the reliable comprehension condition will depend ineliminably on the existence of public linguistic norms. My argument is as follows.

Premise 1. If hearer *H* acquired the testimonial knowledge that *p* through speaker *S*'s testimony on utterance-occasion *O*, then *H* understood *S*'s testimony on *O* (in the manner appropriate to *H*'s acquisition of testimonial knowledge through *S*'s testimony on *O*).

Premise 2. *H* understood *S*'s testimony on *O* (in the manner appropriate to *H*'s acquisition of testimonial knowledge through *S*'s testimony on *O*) only if *H*'s understanding was the output of a process with the following property: confronted with an utterance of a sentence by one of the members of *H*'s speech community,[6] the process would represent the

---

[6] Let a speech community be understood roughly as the class of those whose linguistic interactions with one another are fluid and efficient. (No doubt, talk of such a 'class' is an idealization. In reality, linguistic communities have fuzzy boundaries.)

observed speech as having the propositional content p, in a situation like O, only when the target speech act had p as its propositional content.

Premise 3. There are cases in which a hearer H and speaker S have minimal background knowledge regarding each other's beliefs and (speech and interpretative) dispositions, yet where knowledge spreading nevertheless proceeds efficiently (H acquires the testimonial knowledge that p through S's testimony on O).

Premise 4. In cases of the sort described in premise 3, H's understanding is the output of a process with relevant property (as described in Premise 2) if and only if there are public linguistic norms – norms which (given the context of utterance) serve to determine the content S asserted, and by reliance on which H recovered what was asserted.

Conclusion. There are public linguistic norms which (given the context of utterance) serve to determine the content asserted, and in reliance on which H recovers what was asserted.

This argument, then, purports to establish the existence of public linguistic norms, by way of the conditions on the sort of understanding required by the acquisition of knowledge through speech. In what follows I will defend each of the premises in turn.

2.3 TESTIMONIAL KNOWLEDGE PRESUPPOSES UNDERSTANDING (PREMISE I)

I do not expect the first premise to be controversial, so I will restrict myself to expanding only a bit on what I have already said (in chapter 1) in its defense.

Let a speech exchange be called a case of 'Successful Communication' between S and H just in case it conforms to the following description: S asserts the proposition p, and on the basis of recognizing this and relying on S's say-so (under conditions in which she is entitled to do so), H thereby acquires the knowledge that p (where p is the propositional content of H's knowledge). This usage of 'Successful Communication' is meant to designate the sort of knowledge acquired in 'happy' cases of communication as described in chapter 1.

According to Premise 1, in any case of Successful Communication, H understood S's testimony. Why think that a hearer needs to understand proffered testimony in the first place? In chapter 1 I argued that the proper taxonomic kind for testimony will be a kind that includes its *semantic* (or, more accurately, its *representational*) features – that is, those features that are recovered in the process of (correct) understanding. My claim was this: it is only if testimony is so categorized, that it will be categorized in a way appropriate to belief that is grounded on the hearer's epistemic reliance on the speaker. Since testimonial knowledge involves the hearer's epistemic dependence on the speaker's testimony, the hearer must recover *how the speaker is representing the world* in that testimony. After all, the hearer is relying on the speaker's reliability with respect to the world's being as she (the speaker) has represented it to be in her testimony. So insofar as the hearer aims to acquire knowledge of how the world is *through* that testimony, he (the hearer) must recover how that testimony has represented the world to be. And this, of course, is another way of saying that the hearer must have understood the testimony.

This conclusion – that testimony as such must be typed in terms that are thoroughly semantic/representational – is further supported by a platitude about the testimonial spread of knowledge. The platitude is this: the content(s) that can be known through testimony, in the manner appropriate to the unique sort of knowledge characterized in chapter 1, appear to be invariant across the vast majority of non-semantic properties of the testimony-constituting speech act.[7] Thus, take a case in which a hearer learns through testimony something whose precise content is *that the Yankees acquired Johnny Damon on December 22, 2005*. The testimony-constituting utterance will have various non-semantic properties: it will have a certain temporal duration, it will have been made at a certain loudness level, by a subject of a certain hair color who (suppose) had a cold at the time of the testimony, and so on. Insofar as the piece of testimony was a source from which a hearer could acquire the knowledge that the Yankees acquired Johnny Damon on December 22, 2005, variations in any or all of these non-semantic features would not have affected the precise content hearers could come to know through the testimony. That is, such changes would not have affected matters on this score unless these changes either prevented the hearer from apprehending the

---

[7] 'Vast majority': there are some non-semantic properties that are relevant to the epistemology of beliefs based on testimony. Consider the following properties a piece of testimony might have: that of having been proferred by someone who is a known liar; that of having come from someone who is epistemically irresponsible; that of having been produced by someone who has only recently begun to learn the language she is presently struggling to use. Presumably, none of these are semantic features of testimony. Yet each of them is relevant to the epistemology of beliefs based on the testimony.

testimony in the first place, or else were such that the hearer had some reason to be suspicious of testimony with such features. This may happen in some unusual cases, but typically will not. So, given the *very specific* sorts of thing that can be learned through testimony, and given the variation in auditory and other non-semantic characteristics of instances of testimony, it would appear that the proper taxonomy of testimony is *semantic/representational through and through*.[8] We might even say that, from the perspective of the spreading of knowledge through communication, acoustically characterized utterances are to be grouped into (semantic/representational) equivalence classes that abstract away from their (non-semantic) acoustic properties. Of course, once we have established that testimony ought to be taxonomized by its semantic/representational properties, then the proper way to apprehend testimony is to *understand* it – in which case Premise 1 holds.

2.4 WHAT SORT OF UNDERSTANDING IS REQUIRED? (PREMISE 2)

But precisely what sort of understanding is required, if one is to count as having understood testimony in the way that underwrites the (possible) acquisition of testimonial knowledge through that testimony? Premise 2 states that this must be a reliable sort of understanding, where this means that the process of comprehension must be such that, confronted with a wide variety of observed speech acts, it represents the propositional content of a particular speech act as p, if and only if the observed speech act had p as its propositional content. The point here is that if one is to learn (in the sense of *come to know*) that p through recognizing that one has been told that p, then one's recognition that one has been told that p – and in particular one's apprehension of p as the content of the telling – cannot itself have been merely lucky. In the first instance this point is epistemic, not semantic. But given that the epistemic point pertains to the sort of *linguistic understanding* appropriate to testimonial knowledge, and that linguistic understanding involves a representation of the propositional content of another's utterance, the epistemic point has semantic implications.

---

[8] This is not to say that testimony is *exhaustively* taxonomized by its semantic characteristics. See footnote 7; and for further discussion, see chapter 6.

I briefly defended a claim in the vicinity of Premise 2 in chapter 1. To repeat what I said there: a process of testimonial belief-fixation that does not involve this sort of 'reliable comprehension' will not (typically) result in reliable testimonial belief, and hence will not result in testimonial knowledge. Suppose S tells H that p, but that for some reason or other the process by which H recovers the proposition attested to is not reliable. In that case, even if H correctly recovers the content of S's telling, this process of recovery will involve a knowledge-undermining element of luck. To see this, suppose that the content of S's actual telling was that p. There are nearby worlds in which what S told H was something else – that r, say. In that case, so long as p is a contingent proposition, in some of these worlds p will be false. Even so, in a good many of those worlds in which p is false, H will accept p, taking this (incorrectly) to be the upshot of what S said. Since p is false in such worlds, we will call such worlds *falsifier*-worlds (or '*f*-worlds' for short) relative to H's testimonial belief that p. The point I wish to make is that, if there is an element of luck in the process by which H recovered p as the content of S's (actual) telling, then H's testimonial belief that p (acquired through accepting what H took S to have told him) *is unreliable*, since in that case there are relevant *f*-worlds nearby. The nearness of relevant *f*-worlds establishes that H would have formed a belief in p, in the very manner that she actually did (i.e., through accepting what she takes to be testimony to that effect), yet it is false that p. H's belief is unreliable, owing to her failure to have understood the testimony.

The foregoing offers a positive reason for thinking that testimonial knowledge depends on reliable comprehension of the testimony. But vindication of this point requires addressing two potential objections. Both of these objections purport to show that testimonial belief can be reliable without being formed through a process involving reliable comprehension in the sense defined. The first objection denies that reliable testimonial belief requires comprehension involving a *correct* representation of the propositional content of the testimony; the second grants the need for correct comprehension, but denies that the process producing it needs to be *reliable*. I argue that both objections fail.

Consider first the allegation that a hearer H can acquire reliable testimonial belief even when H fails to recover the proposition attested to, that is, even when she fails to represent correctly the content of the attestation. This allegation might be backed by the contention that reliable testimonial belief need only be such that what is believed is likely to be true given the (reliability of the) testimony proffered. Granting that the paradigm case of this phenomenon is one in which what is believed just is what was attested, it might nevertheless be maintained that, so long as the hearer's belief is a belief in a content that is 'close enough' to what was actually said, then the belief in that 'close enough' content will likely be true, given the reliability of the source testimony, so long as the case is otherwise a 'happy' one (in the sense introduced in chapter 1). If so, the sort of understanding involved in testimonial knowledge does not require recovery of the very content attested to; close enough is good enough, epistemically speaking.[9]

There are several difficulties that the foregoing position must face.

First, it would appear that only a very strong form of the present objection will suffice to rebut the argument I want to make for public linguistic norms. To see this, suppose that there are a good deal of cases of Successful Communication. Then my argument can be run on the cases in question – *whether or not* there are other cases conforming to the 'close enough' model. The proponent of the 'close enough' model might try to accommodate cases of Successful Communication as falling well within the statistical norm, given a bunch of individuals speaking overlapping idiolects. However, the greater the number of cases of Successful Communication, the harder it will be to accommodate such cases in this way. And so it appears that rebutting the second premise by appeal to the 'close enough' model commits one to saying that cases of actual Successful Communication are not very common. This is a strong claim indeed, and appears to be gainsaid by the prevalence of ordinary examples to the contrary.

Second, the 'close enough comprehension' proposal has some unhappy epistemic implications. In particular, the sort of knowledge acquired in cases of 'close enough comprehension' fail to yield the sort of knowledge characterized in chapter 1 as 'testimonial knowledge.' Several points can be made in this regard.

An initial one is this. It appears that, on the 'close enough comprehension' model, the hearer's belief does not depend epistemically on the testimony in the first place. For consider. The 'close enough' model is motivated by the idea that, so long as the hearer's 'testimonial' belief was

---

[9] Here I do not have in mind cases in which a hearer comes to accept a content she takes the speaker to have implicated in her speech act. Arguably, a proper account of such cognition will represent the hearer as recovering the asserted content in the course of recovering the implicated content. I will discuss such cases in chapter 3. The sort of case I have in mind here is more radical than this: it is one in which the hearer never recovers the attested proposition, but only recovers the 'close enough' proposition.

acquired in a reliable way, it does not matter whether the hearer's understanding was correct – close enough is good enough. But whence the
insistence that the hearer's understanding be close enough in the first
place? Why not say that, so long as the hearer's belief was reliably acquired
from the testimony – so long as he (the hearer) would acquire the belief he
did, in the face of this sort of testimony, only if the belief was true – the
belief is a candidate for testimonial knowledge *whether or not* she has
attained any understanding of the testimony? The proponent of the
'close enough' model will want to resist this suggestion. But it is unclear
whether she can do so in a principled way. Here it is worth dwelling on
how the claim, that understanding is a necessary condition on testimonial
knowledge, was motivated above: it was motivated by appeal to the
hearer's need to recover how the speaker (in her testimony) is representing
the world to be. But the 'close enough' model *denies* that the hearer needs
to recover how the speaker is representing the world to be. Unless there is
some other way to motivate the claim that understanding is a necessary
condition on testimonial knowledge, the model's appeal to 'close enough
understanding' is unmotivated. Without this appeal, though, the proposal
is left with the claim that, so long as the hearer's belief was reliably acquired
from the testimony, it is a candidate for testimonial knowledge. And this
condition can be satisfied whether or not the testimony she consumed was
reliable. Under such conditions, the epistemic status of the hearer's belief
does not depend on the epistemic features of the testimony[10] – thereby
undermining the hypothesis that this is a case of testimonial knowledge (as
per chapter 1 section 1.2).

The present objection to the 'close enough' model of comprehension
can be deepened by developing a related point. It is unclear whether a
hearer *H* can be said to be 'epistemically relying' on a speaker *S*'s say-so
when *H* herself has not correctly represented (the content of) that say-so.
To rely epistemically on a speaker's say-so is a matter of relying on her to
have reliably gotten things right. But the notion of 'getting things right' is a
semantic/representational notion: it is a matter of representing things as
they are. Now in the proposed situation involving the hearer's recovery of
a content 'near enough' to what the speaker asserted, *H* is not forming her
belief through accepting *S*'s representation of how things stand – for such
an acceptance would presuppose that *H* grasps how *S* has represented

---

[10] Here, and in what follows, I am disregarding cases in which the hearer's epistemic reliance
on the say-so is 'qualified' in the manner described in chapter 1.

things as standing, and it is precisely this sort of understanding whose necessity the 'close enough' model denies. We might wonder, then: on the 'close enough' model, in what sense is H epistemically relying on S's say-so at all? To be sure, H is relying on a positive correlation between (i) S's having spoken as she has and (ii) the likelihood of the truth of what H came to believe. But we have already seen reasons to doubt that correlations of this sort suffice for epistemic reliance. As we saw in chapter 1 section 1.7, Henrietta was relying on a positive correlation between (i) Slobodan's having spoken as he did and (ii) the likelihood of the truth of what Henrietta came to believe (viz, that it is a sunny day); yet it is uncontroversial that this was not a case of epistemic reliance.

The proponent of the 'close enough' model might think to surmount this difficulty by revising our conception of epistemic reliance. In this vein, perhaps it will be argued that the hearer can be taken to be epistemically relying on the speaker's say-so as long as the hearer relies on the speaker to have made an assertion which prompts him, the hearer, to enter into a state of 'near enough comprehension', where the content he has recovered in this way is likely to be true given the truth and/or reliability of the testimony. We might designate the comprehension process involved in this process as 'near enough comprehension.' If the process of testimonial belief-fixation involves the process of 'near enough comprehension,' then (one might suppose) this process yields beliefs that are reliable enough to be candidates for testimonial knowledge. This is because in that case the process of 'near enough comprehension' will map observed speech onto contents that have an increased likelihood of truth, given the reliability of the speech act observed – even in cases in which the reliability of the speech act observed is a reliability regarding the truth of a *different content*, than what was yielded in the comprehension process.

But the 'near enough comprehension' ('NEC') proposal now faces three further difficulties. The first is actually a modified version of the objection posed by the case of Henrietta and Slobodan. Suppose that Pauline's cognitive system is normal in all respects save one: whenever she observes Slobodan make utterances about his good mood, she comprehends those utterances as amounting to statements about the weather. That is, where Henrietta observed Slobodan's utterances and *reasoned to the conclusion* that, since Slobodan reported being in a good mood, the day must be sunny, Pauline simply heard Slobodan's utterances as *stating* that the day is sunny. I submit that, even in that case, Pauline would not count as having acquired knowledge through Slobodan's testimony. Nor can the defender of the NEC proposal reply by explaining away this result in terms of the fact that Pauline misunderstood Slobodan: for the NEC proposal has already surrendered the idea that a correct understanding of testimony is required for testimonial knowledge. Thus, a modified version of the objection posed by the Henrietta–Slobodan case remains in place against the NEC proposal – the upshot being that the NEC proposal fails to accommodate the idea that testimonial knowledge involves a hearer's epistemic reliance on her source.

A second difficulty facing the NEC proposal is this. It is difficult to see how to explain the reliability of testimonial beliefs in contents recovered through the process of 'close enough comprehension', without at the same time smuggling in the sort of comprehension that the NEC proposal aims to avoid. For example, it would be simply question-begging to model the reliability of testimonial beliefs in 'near enough' contents on the reliability of the process whereby conversational implicatures are computed. This is question-begging since it is plausible to suppose that in the process whereby implicatures are computed, the hearer will first have recovered the content explicitly asserted: the fact that the speaker asserted the particular content she did is regarded as a key premise in the deduction whose conclusion is the claim that she has conversationally implicated another content.[11] Alternatively, a proposed explanation of the reliability of testimonial belief in 'close enough' contents would be smuggling in a reliance on public linguistic norms if it simply assumed that, as a matter of fact, regular exposure to language morphologically like one's own will induce in hearers a disposition to recover contents likely to be true given the reliability of the observed speech. For as I will go on to argue in sections 2.6 and 2.7 below, such a fact – if it is a fact – appears explicable only on the assumption of public linguistic norms. There may be other ways to try to explain the reliability of testimonial beliefs in 'near enough' contents; but the burden is on NEC's proponents to come up with them. Short of having one in hand, we can conclude that the most plausible explanations for the reliability of testimonial beliefs in 'near enough' contents either smuggle in public linguistic norms or else beg the question at issue.

---

[11] This is not to say that all accounts represent the hearer as explicitly reasoning in this way. Rather, the deduction itself is a rational reconstruction of the derivation of the implicature; how the deduction relates to psychological reality is a matter of some dispute. See Gauker 2001.

In addition, the NEC proposal faces a third difficulty. In chapter 1 I gave reasons for thinking that beliefs grounded in epistemic reliance have a feature whereby the hearer, in virtue of her comprehension of the content attested, is *ipso facto* entitled to regard the speaker as having a sufficiently high degree of knowledge-relevant warrant for her (the hearer's) belief. (How high a degree will depend on subsidiary views about testimony's norm – a matter on which I was neutral.) The difficulty is that it is hard to see how beliefs acquired through 'near enough comprehension' have this feature. Even if the content of one's testimonial belief is 'near enough', still it is not what the speaker asserted – so the norm of assertion will not require that the speaker have been in an epistemically privileged position *vis-à-vis* the truth of the 'near enough' content. To be sure, the hearer herself might have additional reasons for thinking that the 'near enough' content is likely to be true, given the reliability of the testimony. But in that case these reasons function as part of the epistemic support for the hearer's belief in the 'near enough' content, clearly going beyond the support provided by the testimony itself (as well as the support provided by the hearer's reasons for accepting that testimony). For this reason, it is unclear whether 'near-enough comprehension', even assuming that it gives rise to reliable belief, underwrites a kind of reliable belief involving the sort of warrant-expansion characteristic of testimonial belief (see chapter 1 section 1.6).[12]

I just gave several reasons for thinking that the appeal to 'near enough comprehension' will not mount a serious objection to Premise 2. We can conclude that, at the very least, testimonial knowledge presupposes correct comprehension, that is, presupposes the recovery of the very proposition attested to.

I now turn to a second objection to Premise 2 according to which, in order to acquire reliable testimonial belief, one's correct comprehension need not be *reliable*. In this vein we must confront a recent argument by Dean Pettit. In the course of arguing that linguistic understanding need not involve propositional knowledge, Pettit 2002 offers a case in which, by his lights, a hearer understands an utterance, yet where she acquires her understanding of one of the terms in an unreliable way. Pettit himself was

---

[12] This is not to say that beliefs formed through 'near enough comprehension' do not enjoy any warrant-expansion; only that, if they do, it would appear not to be of the sort characteristic of testimonial belief. I discuss this sort at greater length in Goldberg (2006).

not speaking of the sort of understanding presupposed by knowledge through testimony, and he did not use his example to address points about the reliability of the interpretations yielded by understanding. However, it is important for my purposes to consider his case in this context, since one might think to argue that if his description stands, then there are possible cases in which a subject understands an utterance yet lacks a reliable method for recovering the utterance's content – a counterexample to (the reliability aspect of) Premise 2.

Pettit's example is as follows (I have replaced the subject and adjusted the conjugation of the verbs accordingly):

Jones is traveling in Germany. She is a moderately competent speaker of German, but she comes across an unfamiliar word, say, the word 'Krankenschwester.' Jones sees a kindly looking, elderly German sitting on a bench nearby, and she asks him what 'Krankenschwester' means, hoping that he might know some English. With an air of authority, he smiles and politely replies in English 'It means *nurse*,' which is indeed what the word 'Krankenschwester' means. Satisfied with his answer, Jones thanks him and goes on her way. As a result of this exchange, Jones is now able to use this previously unfamiliar word correctly and correctly interpret it as it is used by other speakers of German. If a speaker of German assertively utters the sentence 'Die Krankenschwester ist nett,' for example, Jones will correctly take the speaker to be asserting that the nurse is nice . . . In short, in a familiar sort of way, Jones has come to understand the word 'Krankenschwester.' However, . . . unbeknownst to Jones, the elderly gentleman . . . is quite senile and doesn't know a word of English. His reply to her question (namely, 'it means *nurse*') is something he once overheard, but he has no idea what it means or what he is saying when he utters it. In his senility, he has taken to repeating this to tourists, regardless of what he is asked. By sheer coincidence, this was the right answer to the question Jones happened to ask him. But, had Jones asked him the location of the nearest post office, he would have said the very same thing. (Pettit 2002: 519–20)

Now Pettit himself is interested primarily in establishing that understanding – in this case, understanding the word 'Krankenschwester' – does not require having a piece of propositional knowledge (e.g. to the effect that 'Krankenschwester' means *nurse*). However his example, or at least his description of the example, might be thought to pose a challenge to Premise 2 as well. Pettit describes the subject as understanding 'Krankenschwester' despite having acquired this understanding in an unreliable way; and from here it might appear to be a short distance to the conclusion that, at least in periods prior to extensive exposure to 'Krankenschwester'-utterances, Jones understands the German word but is not in possession of a reliable method for interpreting (recovering the propositional content of) the 'Krankenschwester'-utterances she observes.

50

The claim that Pettit's example is a counterexample to Premise 2 can be met, either by denying that Jones understands (in the sense relevant to testimonial knowledge), or else by affirming that Jones does reliably comprehend the relevant report after all. Indeed, these options form the horns of a dilemma facing anyone who would appeal to Pettit's example as a counterexample to Premise 2.

To develop this dilemma, let us assume for the sake of argument that Pettit's example is best described as a case in which the hearer does *not* reliably comprehend 'Krankenschwester'-utterances. In that case his example is an analogue (in the case of testimonial knowledge) of the stopped clock case, in which a person glimpses at a clock whose face shows 12:00, where (unbeknownst to the viewer) the clock has been stopped for some time, but where her glimpse happened to have taken place at exactly 12:00. It is more or less uncontroversial to suppose that the accidentality of the belief's truth in this case is incompatible with its counting as a case of knowledge. In parallel fashion I submit that, if Pettit's Jones is correctly described as unreliable in her comprehension of 'Krankenschwester'-utterances, then, in a case in which she forms a belief through accepting what she takes a German speaker to have said when the German speaker made a 'Krankenschwester'-utterance, Jones does not thereby acquire knowledge, but at best acquires merely true belief. The argument for this is as above: Jones would have formed the belief that she did, in the manner that she did, under conditions in which the belief was false. But then Jones fails to understand the 'Krankenschwester'-utterance in the manner appropriate to testimonial knowledge. And this shows that, on assumption that Jones lacks reliable comprehension of 'Krankenschwester'-utterances, her grasp of 'Krankenschwester' is not such as to underwrite testimonial knowledge. In that case, even if Pettit's example succeeds in showing that (there is a sense of 'understanding' in which) Jones understands 'Krankenschwester'-utterances despite failing to knowing what 'Krankenschwester' means, even so the example is no counterexample to Premise 2, which explicitly restricts itself to the sort of understanding that underwrites testimonial knowledge.

Suppose then (the other horn of the dilemma) that those who would appeal to Pettit's example as a counterexample to Premise 2 insist that Jones does understand 'Krankenschwester'-utterances. In order to bear against Premise 2, the sort of understanding at issue must be the sort that underwrites testimonial knowledge. But we have already seen that this must be reliable comprehension (on pain of violating the reliability condition on knowledge, and so, by extension, on testimonial knowledge). The upshot is that if Jones has attained such an understanding, then this undermines the allegation that the case is a counterexample to Premise 2.

Either way, the would-be counterexample fails.

Still (the objector insists), *something* is unreliable about Jones' grasp of 'Krankenschwester', and if it is not her comprehension, then we want to know what it is. In response I submit that, on the assumption that Jones does reliably comprehend 'Krankenschwester'-utterances, we ought to distinguish the unreliability of the *way* Jones comes to acquire her (reliable) understanding of 'Krankenschwester', from the reliability this understanding provides (once she has it) with respect to her comprehension of subsequent 'Krankenschwester'-utterances.

To make the point, we can note that not all forms of luck are knowledge-undermining. Following Pritchard (2005), I distinguish *doxastic* luck, on which it is lucky that the agent believes what she does, from *veritic* luck, on which it is lucky that the agent's belief is true. As Pritchard himself argues, of these two types of luck only the latter is incompatible with knowledge. Indeed, a variant on Pettit's case of Jones can be used to make this very point. Suppose that a scientist has developed a certain pill whose ingestion will enable speakers who are ignorant of German to attain a reliable comprehension of German sentences.[13] If Smith happens to ingest the one 'real' pill out of the hundred pills that she is offered by the scientist (the other ninety-nine being placebos that have no linguistic effects), Smith was lucky to have done so; but, even so, on ingesting it Smith acquires the ability to reliably comprehend German sentences. We might say: Smith luckily (unreliably) acquired a reliable ability. In the analytic categories employed by Pritchard (2005), Smith's beliefs (regarding what the Germans are saying in their 'Krankenschwester'-utterances) are doxastically lucky, but they are not veritically lucky. The same thing can be said of Jones on our present assumption. Note, too, that the same *cannot* be said in the stopped clock case: since it is a one-off case, it cannot be analysed as the lucky acquisition *of a reliable ability*, that is, an ability that can be exploited in a variety of circumstances to yield reliable belief.

---

[13] The possibility of a language pill of this sort was first described (to my knowledge) in Danto (1969: 128); Chomsky (1980: 73) also uses it to score points about the epistemology of language cognition, similar to those I am urging here.

Indeed, Pettit himself appears to regard understanding as involving (something akin to) interpretative reliability. Here we can cite the evidence he himself offers in defense of the claim that Jones understands 'Krankenschwester.' He writes that she "is now able to use this previously unfamiliar word correctly *and correctly interpret it as it is used by other speakers of German.*" Pettit's use of the plural "German speakers" is presumably not accidental: what would it mean to say of some subject that she understands an expression but lacks a reliable method for recovering the content of utterances involving that expression?

At this point I should ward off any misguided attempt to read too much into what is involved in having such a reliable method. How the human mind/brain acquires such a method is a matter for empirical investigation, not philosophical reflection. What I am claiming is only that the ascription of understanding (of the sort relevant to acquiring knowledge through another's say-so) presupposes that the hearer have a reliable method for recovering the content of the utterance from the utterance itself. Here I am conceiving of the utterance as a sequence of sounds; and what I am describing as 'a reliable method for recovering the content of the utterance from the utterance itself' is simply a matter of the hearer's possessing some sort of competence whose characteristic manifestation involves her *de facto* assigning a semantic (propositional) interpretation to the various relevant sound sequences, in a manner conforming to the conditions on a reliable process.[14] So understood, I submit that Premise 2, too, is quite plausible: the demand that the understanding relevant to testimonial knowledge amount to what I have been calling *reliable comprehension* flows directly from the reliability condition on knowledge, together with the role understanding plays in the acquisition of testimonial knowledge.

2.5 CHARACTERISTICS OF SUCCESSFUL COMMUNICATION (PREMISE 3)

Successful Communication as I have defined it involves a speaker telling the hearer that *p*, thereby enabling the hearer to acquire the knowledge that *p* in a way that is epistemically dependent on the telling. Premise 3 pertains to some broadly sociological characteristics of this sort of

---

[14] The assignment of content to utterances need not be the result of a conscious procedure. In typical cases involving the apprehension of sentences of a familiar language, this process is not conscious: the contents of utterances simply 'strike one' immediately.

communication. In particular, it asserts that Successful Communication is prevalent, that it is an efficient way to spread knowledge, and that it enables very precise pieces of knowledge to be spread in a way that is linguistically undemanding.

I begin with the idea that Successful Communication enables very specific pieces of knowledge to be spread in a way that is linguistically undemanding. By this I mean that two individuals need not know anything substantive about each others' speech and interpretative dispositions, in order for one to Successfully Communicate a very specific piece of knowledge to the other. The claim that such cases are common would appear to be reflected in the typical examples given in the epistemological literature. These involve cases of getting information from a stranger (regarding directions, or some other matter of fact); consulting a textbook (in science, history, or geography); getting news from a newspaper or a talking head on TV (where the audience is unfamiliar with the reporter); and so on. The epistemological literature talks about these cases as if the transmission of knowledge obtains with great regularity, at least in those cases in which the source is in fact knowledgeable (and the hearer has no relevant defeaters). In fact, this assumption, that hearers regularly and unproblematically satisfy the reliable comprehension condition, appears to structure the main debates in the epistemology of testimony. So prevalent is the assumption that the comprehension dimension of communication is unproblematic – that hearers easily and reliably recover the proposition attested to – that there is virtually no discussion of the comprehension process whatsoever in the epistemological literature on testimony.[15] Instead, the literature focuses on the subsequent question, regarding when a hearer *who has understood a piece of testimony* counts as being in a position to acquire knowledge or justified belief through her understanding.

The following kinds of case, which are characteristic of the kinds of case discussed in the epistemology of testimony literature, illustrate my contention that those theorizing about testimony typically assume without further discussion that reliable comprehension is unproblematically achieved. (These cases could be multiplied, my aim being merely to show how common, and how pervasive, such cases are.)

---

[15] There are some exceptions. See McDowell 1981; Ross 1986; Jack 1994; Fricker 2003; and Goldberg 2004a.

- Confirming an upcoming flight on Korean Air to Beijing through Seoul, Grimshaw phones Korean Airlines and is told (in English) that he is confirmed in seat 42B on the flight to Seoul, and then in seat 15E on the flight to Beijing.
- Never having been to New York City before, Smith walks up to a stranger on the street and asks where the NY Public Library is, and is informed that the main (and most famous) branch is located on 42nd St. and 5th Ave.
- On the very first day of class of her very first college course, Jones is told by her physics instructor that light travels at a constant speed (it's the very first thing that the instructor says, once everyone is seated and quiet).
- Attending Yankee Stadium for the very first time, McSorley is informed by the stadium announcer that the Yankees' starting pitcher today will not be Randy Johnson, who has come down with the flu, but instead Mike Mussina, who will be pitching for only the fifth time in his career on three days' rest.
- Flipping through the channels on her TV, Wrigley learns (from a WGN talking head she has never before seen) that there is a street festival near the corner of Sheffield and Diversey on Chicago's north side.
- Purchasing a copy of a local newspaper he has never before read, Johnson learns that the building known as 'The Castle', located on Versailles Road and recently purchased by a lawyer from Miami, has been destroyed in a fire.

I highlight several features of these examples. First, they involve the transmission of very specific pieces of knowledge. Second, in such cases such transmission occurs despite the fact that the speaker and hearer have no prior knowledge of each others' beliefs and linguistic dispositions. Third, examples of this sort are commonplace. There can be little doubt that a good many actual cases actually possess these features.

Indeed, it would appear that the linguistically undemanding nature of Successful Communication is an important component in what makes Successful Communication as prevalent and efficient a means of knowledge sharing as it is. The intuitive point can be appreciated easily enough. Successful Communication involves a hearer's acquiring the knowledge that p through her recognizing a speaker to have told her that p. To the extent that one's theory raises the conditions on a hearer's counting as recognizing that she is being told that p, one's theory raises the conditions on her being party to Successful Communication. One's theory will make it even harder to satisfy the conditions on Successful Communication if the hearer's apprehension of the source speech act as a *telling-that-p* is taken by the theory to have the status of an *hypothesis* for which *evidence* is needed. And to the extent that one's theory also requires that the evidence in question be introspectively accessible to the hearer, one's theory will make it harder still to satisfy the conditions on Successful Communication. (See Goldberg 2004a for a discussion.)

In light of the foregoing, I submit that the testimonial spread of knowledge places an important constraint on theories of linguistic understanding: it should turn out that the linguistic understanding of the typical subject is such that she typically *does* attain a state of reliable comprehension of what she is told without further ado. An account of linguistic understanding denies this on pain of threatening to close off the human subject from what is arguably the most important source of knowledge she has, namely, the testimony of other speakers.

2.6 THE NEED FOR PUBLIC LINGUISTIC NORMS (PREMISE 4)

2.6.1

I come now to the crux of my argument. I contend that in a special subclass of cases of Successful Communication, the hearer has the relevant sort of understanding if and only if there are public linguistic norms – norms which (together with other features of the context of utterance) serve to determine the content asserted by the speaker, and by reliance on which the hearer recovers that content. The special subclass of cases are those in which Successful Communication proceeds smoothly and efficiently even though the hearer and speaker know nothing of each others' speech and interpretative dispositions beyond what is manifest in their brief speech exchange itself. Let us call these cases of Radical Communication (or 'RC-cases' for short).[16] My claim is that without appeal to (some doctrine

---

[16] My language here is borrowed from Jack 1994. However, I use the term differently than she does. Jack's usage of 'radical communication' is in the spirit of the Adler's phrase 'knowledge obtained purely by transmission or testimony' (see his 1996: 107). Their sense of the term is narrowly epistemic: communication is 'radical' in that sense owing to the hearer's negligible background knowledge regarding the truth of the proposition attested to. My use of the term, by contrast, is semantic: communication is 'radical' in my sense

entailing) the existence of public linguistic norms, Successful (knowledge-transmitting) Communication in RC-cases appears miraculous; whereas such cases are easily explicable on the assumption of such norms.

In outline form, the claim will be that, of all of the various postulated accounts on which hearers in RC-cases have a reliable method for recovering the content of a speech act from the utterance, the only plausible account – indeed, the only *remotely* plausible account – is one that postulates public linguistic norms. Although my argument here (like all arguments involving inference to the best explanation) will not be conclusive, I regard it as sufficiently strong to place the burden squarely on the shoulders of opponents of the hypothesis of public linguistic norms. Any account that such a theorist can offer for the linguistic sharing of knowledge in RC-cases will be significantly less plausible than the account to be had by positing public linguistic norms. I will go on to suggest that the implausibility of the former accounts can be traced to the limited materials with which one has to work, once one rejects the hypothesis of public linguistic norms – thereby suggesting that something is wrong *in principle* with such accounts.

To begin, suppose we have a situation involving Successful Communication in an RC-case. (To avoid this long phrase, I will speak of 'Successful RC.') That is, S tells H that p, and, on the basis of recognizing that she has been told that p (and satisfying the other conditions on testimonial knowledge), H thereby comes to know that p. Since H knows that p, her belief that p is reliable; and since her belief that p is a

---

owing to the hearer's and speaker's negligible knowledge of each other in their roles *as speaker and interpreter.*

I should note that, when it comes to examining the epistemology of testimony, it is hard to characterize precisely the category of knowledge intended by Jack 1994 under the label 'radical communication', and by Adler 1996 under the label "knowledge obtained purely by transmission or testimony." Presumably, knowledge obtained 'purely by testimony' still involves as part of its grounds the grounds the hearer has for regarding the testimony as credible; but acknowledging this makes one wonder about the work being done by 'purely' in "knowledge that is purely by testimony." Indeed, as will come out in chapters 5 and 6, I regard much of the controversy between so-called reductionists and anti-reductionists in the epistemology of testimony as having unclear contours, precisely because neither side has sufficiently clarified its conception of the bearing a hearer's background beliefs have on the conditions on justified acceptance of testimony. Reductionists (and even some anti-reductionists) tend to regard anti-reductionism, implausibly, as entailing strict limits in the role that a hearer's background beliefs can play in an account of the conditions on justified acceptance of testimony; whereas anti-reductionists (and even some reductionists) tend to regard reductionism, implausibly, as allowing for no interesting sense in which testimonial knowledge is epistemically unique. I discuss these matters in chapters 5 and 6; but see also Goldberg 2005b and 2006 for further discussion.

testimonial belief, its reliability implies *H*'s reliance on a process of reliable comprehension (as per section 2.4). Given that the case is one of Successful Communication, the process of reliable comprehension proceeded efficiently: *H* attained the state of reliable comprehension of *S*'s assertion very quickly, and with a minimum of conscious effort, despite the fact that *H* knew nothing of *S*'s speech dispositions beyond what was manifest in *S*'s testimony. Seen from a certain perspective, *H*'s accomplishment here is nothing short of astounding: she has somehow managed to reliably (and correctly) represent the propositional content of the sound sequence produced by *S*, without having any background knowledge of *S*'s speech behavior beyond what is manifest in the brief speech exchange. (I think many theorists are less impressed by this than we ought to be.)[17] How does *H* accomplish this?[18]

2.6.2

Before I proceed to various candidate answers to this question, it is worthwhile having a more detailed description of the situation, if only to better appreciate the nature of the problem one must confront in trying to answer this question. Here I want to note at the outset the chief problem that I will be identifying for those proposals that deny the existence of public linguistic norms. In the first instance, the problem will pertain to their ability to account for the *correctness* of a hearer's semantic representations of the speech acts of the various people with whom she interacts. So formulated, the problem does not explicitly raise the issue of the *reliability* (or the epistemic status more generally) of those representations. However, it is clear that if one's theory cannot account for so much as the *correctness* of hearers' semantic representations of other speakers' speech acts, then it is in trouble on the epistemic score as well. My claim will be that, without appeal to public linguistic norms, we have no satisfactory

---

[17] I should say that people who work in philosophy of language are usually appropriately impressed by this; but they typically do not consider the *epistemic* dimension (as opposed to the cognitive and/or linguistic dimensions) of this process.

[18] In what follows I will be moving back and forth, rather freely, between talk of the content of speech acts, on the one hand, and the meanings of lexical items, on the other. This is in advance of chapter 4, where I will discuss the conditions under which one can derive results regarding *linguistic meaning* from results regarding *the contents of speech*. Until that time I beg the reader's indulgence.

account of how hearers attain correct representations – and so, by extension, how they attain reliable comprehension – of the speech they observe.

The nature of the problem on this score is best appreciated by conceiving of the process of understanding as one that eventuates in the speaker's representation of the linguistic (syntactic, semantic, and pragmatic) features of the speaker's utterance.[19] Consider just that part of the process of understanding whereby (a hearer's mental representations of) the lexical items used by the speaker are mapped onto (the hearer's mental representations of) their meanings. This part of the process involves what we might call the hearer's mentally represented semantics for the speaker's language, which we can take to be a structure that determines a meaning assignment for each of the (hearer's mental representations of the) lexical items in the speaker's ideolect. Now suppose that the hearer's mentally represented semantics for the speaker's language is not a correct semantics. That is, it sometimes happens that the hearer's semantics maps a lexical item e (as used by the speaker) onto a meaning m, where m is not the meaning of e as e was used by the speaker in the observed utterance. On those occasions on which this does happen, the reliable comprehension condition on reliable testimonial belief will not be satisfied, since in that case the process of understanding will yield an incorrect verdict regarding the content of the speech act. The immediate lesson is this: if the reliable comprehension condition on reliable testimonial belief is to be satisfied on a given occasion, then the hearer's mentally represented semantics must make correct assignments for each of the lexical items in the sentence(s) uttered by the speaker on that occasion. Let us call this the *correct occasion-semantics* requirement: it requires that the hearer's semantics for the speaker's language yield a correct representation of the attested content on the occasion in question.

If Successful RC is to be (as we take it to be) commonplace, then the correct occasion-semantics requirement is clearly an instance of a more general requirement. Not only must the hearer's semantics map (the

---

[19] Here, and in what follows, I will occasionally employ the language of a hearer's 'mental representation' of (for example) the speaker's words and meanings. I find such talk of 'mental representation' to be helpful: it makes clear that, when a subject expresses a testimonial belief using a given sentence, her use of the sentence is informed by her having previously (if only implicitly) represented her source (the speaker through whose say-so she acquired the belief) as having asserted the proposition she is presently expressing. As it were: a testimony-based assertion of p is a linguistic representation whose content is that p, made on the basis of having recovered p as something represented by another speaker.

speaker's uses of) lexical items onto meanings in such a way as to correctly represent the meaning of the lexical items as these were used by this particular interlocutor on this particular occasion; the same point holds *over time*, for *each of the speakers* with whom the hearer interacts, and for *each occasion* of such interaction. That is, one's mentally represented semantics must be largely (if not entirely) correct *for each of one's (apparent) co-linguals*, and *throughout the period with which one interacts with them*. If this generalized condition is not satisfied, the hearer will not be in a position to acquire reliable testimonial belief, and hence testimonial knowledge, from a speaker on at least those occasions when the hearer's mapping would be incorrect. Let us call this requirement – the requirement whereby a hearer must attain a broadly correct semantics for the language(s) of each of the multitude of speakers with whom she interacts – the *generalized* correct occasion-semantics requirement, or generalized requirement for short.

Let us suppose that a semantics for a natural language must in the first instance treat of idiolects (languages of single individuals) rather than sociolects (languages of a community of speakers). The generalized requirement can then be put as follows: to the extent that a hearer H is to be in a position to acquire testimonial knowledge from arbitrary members of her speech community, she must be such, that for each of the speakers S with whom she interacts, H has a correct semantics for S's language. So stated, this requirement can be met by having a different semantics for each person in H's speech community. But it is clear that satisfying the generalized requirement in this way will not do. For one thing, it is dubious whether a single individual, *qua* hearer, could be able to keep track of a different semantics for each of the multitude of speakers with whom she interacts. For another, it is dubious whether a single individual, *qua* speaker, could in that case keep track of *her own* semantics – given that the semantics *of her own language* inherits at least some of its meaning-assignments from the speakers whose testimonies she has consumed.

The first point may be obvious; the latter deserves some attention. An example will make its purport clear. Suppose that hearer H observes speaker S assert, 'California has more inhabitants than Texas does.' On the basis of her epistemic reliance on S's say-so, H acquires a belief she expresses using the very same sentence (same sentence-type) as the one S used in that say-so. Given that this is a case of Successful Communication, the testimonial belief she expresses with this sentence-type is a belief in the very content S attested to. Since this is so, there is overlap in the semantic assignments of S's and H's respective idiolects with respect to the relevant items: 'California,' 'inhabitants,' and so forth. Of course, the lexical items in question (or at least morphologically type-identical lexical items) also figure in the expression of *other* beliefs *H* has – for example, she has beliefs she would express with sentences such as, 'California is on the West Coast,' 'New Jersey's inhabitants are particularly knowledgeable about their state,' and so forth. What is more, some of these other beliefs are beliefs that *H* acquired through the testimony of still other speakers. But then a similar line of reasoning argues for a relevant overlap between *H*'s idiolect and that of each of these other speakers, taken individually. Thus it would appear that the relevant kind of overlap will have to be more than just between two speakers and the words they happen to use in a given exchange; the relevant overlap will have to hold among *all* members of the speech community, and for most or all of the words in each's idiolect. For example, if *H* picks up distinct 'California'-beliefs through accepting various pieces of testimony (by different speakers), then, unless the various testifiers' respective uses of 'California' all make the same contribution to their respective assertions, the result will be that *H* (who acquired 'California'-beliefs from each of them) would have (almost) as many meanings associated with the 'California' entry *in her own lexicon* as there were occasions on which she acquired a 'California'-belief through another's testimony.[20] Clearly, this kind of consideration holds for most (if not all) of the expressions in her idiolect. The result is that when we speak of 'relevant overlap' among idiolects, this overlap must be great: it must cover *most or all of the words* in the idiolects of *most or all* of the members of a speech community. I will call this the *social calibration* requirement.

Of course, on the strength of the need to satisfy the social calibration requirement, we might well conclude by rejecting our assumption that it is idiolects, rather than sociolects, that are the initial object of semantic inquiry. But no matter our opinions on this methodological question, no semantic account is adequate to the facts of communication unless it explains how the various requirements – the correct occasion–semantics

---

[20] This is a bit of an idealization. No doubt, speakers' various uses of a given term will not always line up. To the extent that they do not, the acquisition of testimonial belief will bring in its tow new semantic entries for the lexical item in the idiolect in question. In such cases, the hearer herself will not typically appreciate these differences; and the result will be that her ability to use the term in question in sound reasoning – in reasoning that (among other things) avoids equivocations – will be affected. See Goldberg (forthcoming b) and (forthcoming f) for a discussion.

requirement, the generalized requirement, and the social calibration requirement – are met.

Before proceeding to see how these requirements might be met, it is worth noting that the requirements themselves exhibit something like a nested structure, at least in the following sense: the satisfaction of the social calibration requirement will suffice for the satisfaction of the generalized requirement (but not *vice versa*), and the satisfaction of the generalized requirement will suffice (at least in a good many cases – we must allow for idiosyncratic speakers) for the satisfaction of the correct occasion-semantics requirement (but not *vice versa*). More controversial is the question whether this nested structure reflects necessary conditions as well – whether, in order to satisfy the generalized requirement, it is necessary to satisfy the social calibration requirement and so forth. It is clearly *logically possible* for one to satisfy the generalized requirement without satisfying the social calibration requirement, and logically possible as well for one to satisfy the correct occasion-semantics requirement without satisfying the generalized requirement. The interesting question, rather, is whether *in point of fact* our satisfaction of each of these requirements is independent of our satisfaction of the others.

I will be arguing that, on the only natural account we have for how these requirements are satisfied, we get the result that hearers correctly comprehend individual speakers, and so satisfy the requirement of a correct occasion-semantics, in virtue of having socially calibrated idiolects (and so in virtue of satisfying the social calibration requirement). The idea here is that (one) there are public linguistic norms, shared by speakers and hearers alike; (two) these norms calibrate what the speaker's words mean and what the hearer takes them to mean; and (three) these norms play this role for each of the various speaker/hearer pairs in a given speech community, thereby enabling the satisfaction of the requirements just described. I will be suggesting an account of this sort as a natural account for the satisfaction of all three requirements, and I will be arguing that there are no other accounts that are even remotely plausible. I begin, however, with those other accounts.

2.6.3

Let us start with the most radically skeptical approach of all, which would be simply to deny these requirements are regularly satisfied. I will designate this view as 'radical skepticism'. It holds that hearers don't attain a correct, calibrated semantics for each of the multitude of speakers with whom they interact; that hearers don't often (ever?) attain a reliable comprehension of the speakers with whom they interact; and that it is not often (ever?) the case that hearers, knowing nothing of a speaker's speech dispositions save what is manifest in the brief speech exchange itself, nevertheless arrive at a reliable comprehension of the speech act. I regard this sort of skepticism as a non-starter. For one thing, most epistemologists recognize that a great deal of our mature knowledge, and perhaps most of it, depends either directly or indirectly on others' testimony. But I argued in chapter 1 and in section 2.4 above that the kind of knowledge I called 'testimonial knowledge' presupposes reliable comprehension. So unless the radically skeptical approach has some other way to vindicate our knowledge in these cases – some way that does not require treating such knowledge as 'testimonial knowledge' – the skeptical proposal will degenerate into a more global form of skepticism (an unacceptable result). For another thing, the skeptical proposal flies in the face of clear intuition. For it seems perfectly obvious that there are many cases like the following: you observe me assert, "The Yankees won 3–2 on August 8, 2005," and, on the basis of your epistemic reliance on me, you come to acquire the very piece of knowledge that I expressed in my testimony. To say that there are such cases seems so obvious as to be not worth mentioning; correspondingly, to deny that there are such cases (which the radical proposal appears to do) seems so absurd as not to be worth taking seriously.[21] In light of this, the best bet for those who wish to avoid the postulation of public linguistic norms would be to concede the existence of Successful RC cases, but to offer an account of (the reliable comprehension in) such cases which does not appeal to such norms.

2.6.4

In this vein, consider the suggestion that the three requirements above are satisfied, and so systematic reliable comprehension is made possible, by *de facto* uniformity in usage, and hence in ideolectical semantics, across speakers. Such uniformity ensures that, *modulo* considerations of context-sensitivity,

---

[21] Below I will consider a variant view according to which, while Successful Communication in the sense defined is prevalent, it does not presuppose content preservation, because '*S* knows that *p*' does not entail 'the content of *S*'s knowledge = that *p*.' My gripe with such a view will be not that it complicates the semantics of '*S* knows that *p*' (which it does), but that it fails to be adequate to the facts of Successful Communication.

the hearer is correct to interpret the speaker as expressing the propositional content that she (the hearer) would express with the same words. Let this suggestion be granted for the sake of argument, and let it be granted as well that, given such uniformity, the process of interpretation is both more efficient and more reliable than it would otherwise be. What I want to question is whether, without the postulation of public linguistic norms, we explain how such uniformity comes to pass. If we can't, then this proposal is a non-starter, as it would not enable us to avoid the postulation of such norms.

One possible way to explain uniformity in usage without appeal to public linguistic norms is in terms of social approbation. Here the suggestion might be that uniformity in usage is encouraged, and idiosyncracy discouraged, through the mechanisms of social approbation. Then, even on the assumption that there are no public linguistic norms, it might happen with some regularity that lexical items of the same morphological type can be assigned the same interpretation even across idiolects.[22] A minimalist account of the satisfaction of the calibration requirement (and, with this, of the two other requirements) would then be in place.

There are two related difficulties with this proposal. (I add that these difficulties attach to any other proposed explanation for uniformity in usage, insofar as the proposal stops short of postulating public linguistic norms.) The first is that cases of Successful Communication would not appear to be hostage to chance in the way the present proposal predicts. As a result, and second, the present proposal, which aims to avoid the difficulties facing the radically skeptical proposal of 2.6.3 above, risks degenerating into that more radical skeptical proposal.

In 2.4 I argued that the sort of understanding that underwrites Successful Communication is that which eventuates in reliable comprehension: the process eventuating in the hearer's state of comprehension must be such that she would reach that state of comprehension only if it accurately represented the propositional content of the speech acts she observed. Now, on the present view it is simply a contingent feature of one's linguistic environment whether or not the idiolect of a "co-lingual" interlocutor overlaps in relevant respects with one's own – something that depends on whether one's interlocutor has had the relevant portions of her idiolect shaped by the forces of social approbation. But in that case it would appear

---

[22] The sort of position I am describing is suggested in Bilgrami 1992, and perhaps in some of Davidson's writings.

that proponents of this social approbation explanation must confront the analogue, in the theory of comprehension, of Goldman's fake barn case (Goldman 1976). Take cases in which, as a matter of fact, one's present interlocutor utters a sentence of her idiolect in which all of the lexical items involved have an interpretation that overlaps with that of the morphologically type-identical lexical items in one's own idiolect (thereby rendering correct one's homophonic comprehension). Even so, in a good many of these cases there will be other speakers around whose idiolect contains morphologically type-identical items that do *not* overlap with one's own in this way. In such cases, the hearer will not count as having reliably comprehended her interlocutor, despite the fact that her comprehension correctly represents the content of the speech she observed – any more than one counts as reliably believing of a barn that it is a barn when one is in fake barn country. Indeed, here we are merely confronting the points noted in connection with the generalized and social calibration requirements above: to the extent that social pressures fail to ensure (or come close to ensuring) *comprehensive* and *systematic* overlaps in the semantics of idiolects among *all* of the people who engage in regular verbal interaction with one another, the theorist will face the analogue, in the domain of comprehension, of the fake barn case in the domain of perception. This result will threaten to undermine a good deal of what we should otherwise want to regard as testimonial knowledge. It would appear, then, that the distance of the present proposal from that of the radically skeptical one of 2.6.3 threatens to narrow.

2.6.5

But there is a way in which one might try to preserve the foregoing account of broad idiolectical semantic overlap, and in so doing to explain how the social calibration and other requirements are met, without having to endorse the hypothesis of public linguistic norms. It is to be recalled that the difficulty facing proposal of 2.6.4 is that the satisfaction of the calibration requirement requires more than the mechanisms of social approbation and disapproval: even as supplemented by other ways of attempting to enforce broad semantic overlap among idiolects, these mechanisms do not appear sufficient to ensure the systematic and comprehensive overlap needed for reliable comprehension in the battery of cases we pretheoretically take to be cases of Successful Communication. But perhaps these overlap-enforcing mechanisms would suffice for the task at hand on the assumption of a *strong concept innateness hypothesis*.

65

It is clear, at least in outline form, how such a proposal might be motivated. When confronted with a domain in which the evidence available to individual subjects is seriously impoverished relative to the complexity, specificity, and reliability of the mental representations the subjects generate in that domain, it is a common theoretical move among certain cognitive scientists and linguists to postulate a substantive innate contribution to the process that yields the representations in question. Familiar examples include the young child's recovery of syntax from the scattered observations she makes regarding sentences uttered in her presence, and the recovery of certain features of our three-dimensional world from the retinal projection of that world. Perhaps the task of comprehension poses another instance of this phenomenon. For example, it might be argued that the evidence each of us has, regarding the correctness of our semantics for the language of any particular co-lingual we encounter, is seriously impoverished relative to the complexity, specificity, and reliability of the representations we produce regarding the meanings of her words (and the contents of her speech). Perhaps then this domain too should be considered one in which there is a substantive innate contribution to the mental representations we generate regarding the semantic properties of our co-linguals' utterances. On this score, the nativist hypothesis might be, either that the process for forming concepts is itself innate, so that each of us is innately disposed to form the same concepts under similar sensory promptings; or else that our conceptual repertoire itself is (largely) innate to begin with, needing only sensory stimulation to be elicited.

On the assumption of a strong concept innateness hypothesis, the social calibration of the idiolects within a given speech community might be explained as follows. Concept innateness ensures that speakers everywhere will share a substantial portion (if not all) of their concepts with one another.[23] In that case idiolectical semantic overlap is achieved so long as speakers in a single speech community assign the same lexical item to the same concept, for most or all of the shared concepts in their repertoire. What is more, systematic reliable comprehension is achieved under these circumstances as well. For, while the comprehension task confronting the hearer would be still be the same – how to arrive at a correct mapping of lexical items in each of her interlocutors' idiolects onto the right

---

[23] If one's version of nativism holds that what is innate are our standards for concept-formation, then to get the desired result one will also have to assume widely shared environmental conditions.

concepts? – the difficulty of achieving the right mapping for each different speaker would be vastly reduced by the fact that we all share roughly the same stock of concepts. For then the only real question facing the hearer is whether a given speaker's idiolect has the same concept-word pairings as the hearer's idiolect has – and arguably that is something that can be discerned by a hearer even in limited interaction with a speaker.

No doubt the foregoing picture is crude in the extreme. But I will not bother complicating the picture, since my objection to it has nothing to do with its crudity. Rather, my objection is based on a familiar objection to concept-innateness hypotheses: there are a good deal of concepts expressed by words in our public language – or, if it is preferred, in one's own idiolect – regarding which it is patently implausible to think that those concepts are innate. For examples of such concepts, consider those expressed by such terms as 'top-hat,' 'toaster,' 'Tuesday', and 'Tory.' Since these terms are all terms that can be used in a knowledge-communicating way, they must express concepts that are innate if the present explanation of Successful RC is to account for reliable comprehension in such cases. Yet it is patently implausible to suppose that the concepts expressed by such terms are innate.

Admittedly the topic of innateness in cognitive science and in linguistics is notoriously slippery: it is difficult both to formulate the relevant claims, and then to determine how to test such claims empirically. With this in mind, I will restrict myself to making the following qualified comment. Given that a very strong concept-innateness hypothesis would have to be assumed in order to vindicate the present explanation of reliable comprehension in RC cases, and given the *prima facie* deep implausibility of such an hypothesis, it is to be hoped that we can explain the satisfaction of the social calibration requirement, and with it the satisfaction of the reliable comprehension condition in RC cases, without taking on such serious commitments. We have reason to prefer an alternative explanation.

2.6.6

I turn, then, to another proposed account of reliable comprehension in cases of Successful RC. Like the previous accounts, the account to be presented does not appeal to the hypothesis of public linguistic norms. Rather, it seeks to account for reliable comprehension in Successful RC cases in terms of two features that (it alleges) hold widely of communication cases. The first feature involves a phenomenon I will designate as *lexical recycling*, whereby a hearer who acquires a belief through accepting another's say-so will typically express her understanding of that say-so, and the subsequent testimonial belief she forms, by re-using ('recycling') the very sentence-type used by the speaker herself (*modulo* considerations of context-sensitivity). The second feature pertains to (what is alleged to be) the metalinguistic nature of the intention with which hearers recycle the sentence-types figuring in testimony they have accepted: the claim is that the hearer re-uses the sentence-type with the intention that her token sentence mean whatever it meant in the mouth of her interlocutor – in other words, that it inherit its meaning from her source's token.[24] I will call this proposed answer the *metalinguistic intention* proposal.

Obviously, the metalinguistic intention proposal must be complicated to handle context-sensitivity phenomena. But if such complications can be introduced in a motivated way, then we may have what we need. For it is arguable that this proposal can both endorse and explain how the social calibration requirement is satisfied: the sort of comprehensive and systematic ideolectical overlap that is needed in order to accommodate Successful RC is achieved in virtue of individual speakers' intentions to be using their words so as to preserve the meanings of their co-linguals' use of words of the very same morphological form.

However, reliable comprehension in Successful RC cases cannot be explained in the way that the metalinguistic intention proposal suggests – at least not if the explanation is to avoid the postulation of public linguistic norms. In particular, the proposed account is not sufficiently general, and in any case succeeds only on the assumption of public linguistic norms.

First, it is insufficiently general. It is dubious whether *every* case of Successful RC is a case in which the hearer forms the relevant metalinguistic intention. Consider that there can be cases of Successful RC involving young children. Presumably, such children can acquire knowledge through their interlocutor's say-so,[25] even when they lack the cognitive sophistication needed for meta-level intentions. It is a well-confirmed empirical result that children have no ability, or only a seriously

---

[24] This proposal should be distinguished from another metalinguistic proposal, according to which the very semantic content expressed by the hearer's re-use of the sentence-type in question incorporates a metalinguistic element – as if what I mean by 'chair' is expressed by "whatever other people in my community mean by 'chair.'" I will consider this proposal below. On the present view, it is the intention behind the use of the sentence that is metalinguistic, but the semantic content expressed by that use is not (unless the source speaker herself expressed a metalinguistic content in her use of that sentence-type).

[25] See chapter 8 section 8.2 for my defense of the ascription of testimonial knowledge to even cognitively immature children.

diminished ability, to employ metarepresentations[26] before the age of four.[27] Since the intention postulated by the present proposal is a meta-linguistic one, presumably it would take the form of a metarepresentation – in which case it would not be available to such children. But I submit that this lack of ability (or diminished ability) regarding metarepresentational deployment does not hinder children younger than four from learning through a trusting acceptance of what others tell them. Since they acquire knowledge through others' say-so, they count as a case that cannot be explained by the present proposal.

The insufficient generality of the metalinguistic intention proposal is seen in connection with adults as well. It is dubious whether it is always true that recipients of testimonial knowledge in Successful Communication have the requisite metalinguistic intention. Certainly it is not true that such recipients always have *consciously formed* the requisite intention. But if they have not consciously formed it, in what sense can they be held to have the intention at all? Perhaps the idea is that people can be held to have the intention implicitly – so long, that is, as they have no other relevant linguistic intention that is in conflict with the ascription of such an (implicit) intention to them. But this idea, though attractive in its own right, is of no help to those who wish to avoid the postulation of public linguistic norms.

We can bring out this last point by seeing that the present proposal gets things inverted. It is not that the idiolects of the members of a linguistic community largely overlap because these members (implicitly) intend to use their words as the other members in the community do. Rather, such an (implicit) intention on the part of the community's members would establish the overlap in question only on the assumption that *there is a prior commonality in others' usage*. This is because common usage is not the sort of thing over which one's intentions are authoritative: if your community is such that there is no common usage in connection with word-form *e*, then your intention to use *e* so as to be in accord with community usage is an

---

[26] Metarepresentations are representations of some lower-order representation, of the sort that corresponds to sentences of the form '*S* φs that *p*' for representational verbs φ – verbs such as 'say,' 'believe,' 'want,' and so forth.

[27] For the relevant empirical literature regarding children's capacity for metarepresentation, especially in connection with their capacity to learn through what others tell them, see Flavell 1979; Wimmer and Permer 1983; Gopnik and Graf 1988; O'Neill and Gopnik 1991; O'Neill *et al.* 1992; Mitchell *et al.* 1997; Sabbagh and Baldwin 2001; Wellman *et al.* 2001; and Lutz and Keil 2002.

intention that is bound to be frustrated. Of course, community usage might be united in that all members of the community take themselves to be, or are correctly taken to be, answerable to a common stock of linguistic norms. But it is precisely the appeal to such norms that the metalinguistic intention proposal seeks to avoid.

One final objection should be the nail in the coffin of the metalinguistic intention proposal, as it is fatal to the spirit, if not the letter, of the proposal. According to the proposal, idiolectical overlap is ensured in particular cases in virtue of the hearer's having the intention to be using her words in conformity with the usage of (some subset of) her co-linguals. But even if – contrary to what I have so far been arguing – this proposal succeeded in establishing how the social calibration requirement could be met in a way that did not involve public linguistic norms, even so the result *would be a victory for those who are anti-individualists about meaning and content.* For in effect the metalinguistic intention proposal would then be granting that what one person means with her words depends on what some other person(s) mean(s) with those words – in which case individualistic facts would not fix the meanings of her words or the contents of her speech. And since Successful Communication involves belief in the very content attested to, the result would be that what a hearer believes in these cases of Successful Communication would not be fixed by individualistic facts regarding the believer herself. I conclude, then, that the appeal to metalinguistic intentions is not the way to resist a communication-based argument for an anti-individualistic view of mind and language – whether or not it enables one to reject the hypothesis of public linguistic norms.

2.6.7

I have been considering various ways in which we might account for the satisfaction of the reliable comprehension condition in RC cases, without postulating the existence of public linguistic norms. One final proposal for doing so, also a metalinguistic one, ought to be considered. To contrast this view with the just-rejected metalinguistic intention proposal, I will call this the metalinguistic *interpretant* proposal. This proposal is like the previous (metalinguistic intention) proposal in that it, too, involves metalinguistic considerations; but it is unlike the previous proposal in the role that it ascribes to such considerations. Where the metalinguistic intention proposal took metalinguistic considerations to be part of the intentions which fixed the meanings of a speaker's words, and so the contents of her speech acts, without themselves being part of those meanings and contents, the metalinguistic interpretant proposal regards a speaker's metalinguistic intentions as part of the very meanings of her words and the contents of her speech acts.[28]

One implication of this view is worth noting straight off. According to the metalinguistic interpretant proposal, communication should be seen to be a matter, not of the preservation of *the content* of a speaker's assertion, but rather of *the truth-conditions* of that assertion, where a hearer *H* preserves the truth-conditions (though not the conceptual content) of her interlocutor *S*'s statement in virtue of *H*'s incorporating into her own ideolectical meanings and concepts her very reliance on (a specific subset of) her co-linguals.

A schematic illustration will help make the idea clear. Suppose that *H* observes *S*'s use of a word-form ω without fully grasping the concept *S* expresses with her use of ω, and that as a result the word-form ω enters into (or is reinforced in) *H*'s lexicon. In that case (the proposal goes) the interpretation-entry which *H*'s idiolectical semantics associates with ω is something akin to the concept WHAT OTHERS IN MY COMMUNITY REFER TO BY 'ω'. (Here, 'ω' is meant to be replaced by a name of the word in question.) The advantage of this proposal over the earlier metalinguistic intention proposal is clear. The metalinguistic intention proposal sought to secure idiolectical overlap by appeal to the intention to be using one's words in the way one's peers did; the result was that the very existence of a concept to be expressed depended on the prior existence of standard usage. In contrast, the present metalinguistic interpretant proposal seeks to secure idiolectical overlap in truth conditions (rather than conceptual contents) by rendering the concept expressed by the use

---

[28] It would appear that this is the view of Chomsky 1986. Commenting on his view of Putnam's (1975) Division of Linguistic Labor hypothesis, Chomsky writes: "suppose ... that someone knows that yawls and ketches are sailing vessels but is unsure of the exact reference of the words 'yawl' and 'ketch,' leaving it to specialists to fix this reference. In the lexicon of this person's language, the entries for 'yawl' and 'ketch' will be specified to the extent of his or her knowledge, with an indication that details are to be filled in by others ..." He goes on to note that this is a proposal "that can be made precise in various ways *but without going beyond the study of the system of knowledge of language of a particular individual.* Other social aspects of language can be regarded in a like manner ..." (p. 18; italics added).

However, it is unclear whether my attribution to Chomsky of the metalinguistic interpretant account is correct, as he notes that he is not to be read here as "deny[ing] the possibility or value of other kinds of study of language that incorporate social structure and interaction." (It is because I am uncertain of this attribution that I reserve this comment for a footnote.)

of a term as having a metalinguistic content – one that specifies, as part of its very content, an anaphoric link with community usage. The result is that even if there is no standard usage, this will not entail that there was no concept expressed; rather, it will entail that the concept expressed is, like that expressed by 'the largest natural number,' not correctly applicable to anything. It is also worth noting that the present proposal, unlike the metalinguistic intention proposal, does not entail anything problematic for an individualistic account of language and thought.

But the metalinguistic interpretant proposal has serious problems of its own. First, it should be clear that it is a non-starter when it comes to explaining Successful RC. Successful Communication (whether in an RC-case or not) involves the hearer's acquisition of knowledge whose *content* is identical to the content of the telling. Insofar as the metalinguistic interpretant proposal ascribes a metalinguistic content to the hearer, it gives up on this identification. This is because what the hearer comes to know – that is, the *content* that is known – in such cases is a metalinguistic variant on the content attested to. This means that the knowledge will not be of the unique sort characterized in chapter 1.

Proponents of this proposal may argue that we should simply accept this conclusion, rather than regard it as a *reductio* of the metalinguistic interpretant proposal itself. In defense of this, it might be said that, while a stark denial of the existence of Successful Communication would be implausible (as argued in connection with the radically skeptical proposal discussed above), such a denial is less implausible when combined with an account of communication on which hearers acquire beliefs whose *truth conditions* match those of the testimony they've consumed. Since this is something provided by the metalinguistic interpretant proposal, it is not objectionable in the way that the radically skeptical position above was.

But this effort to save the metalinguistic interpretant proposal is objectionable. The knowledge that is spread linguistically, paradigmatically in cases of Successful Communication, is knowledge of *the world*, not of one's own or the community's *language*. (This is so whenever the testimony itself expresses knowledge of the world, as opposed to knowledge of language.) On the present metalinguistic account of knowledge communication, however, it is a mistake to suppose that such knowledge is 'spread' (in the sense of 'transmitted') through language use. Rather, the present view is that, in any case in which the hearer *H* does not fully grasp the standard concept associated with a term used in the speaker's testimony, the knowledge *H* acquires through the testimony will be knowledge that is at least partially *metalinguistic in content*. To illustrate, if H does not fully grasp the standard concept expressed by 'electron', then, upon being confronted by S's assertoric utterance of 'Electrons have spin', and accepting this testimony (knowing full well that S is a physicist – or perhaps that S is what is commonly known in H's community as a 'physicist'), H will thereby come to know, not something whose content is *that electrons have spin*, but rather something whose content is (something like) *that the things commonly referred to as 'electrons' in this community have spin*. Of course, if H fails to fully grasp the standard 'spin'-concept as well, then the content H would thereby come to know would be (something like) *that the things commonly referred to as 'electrons' in this community have the property commonly known as 'spin' in this community*. So, too, with the concepts expressed by 'reference,' 'community,' 'property,' and so forth. Since full grasp is a rare phenomenon, our theorist will be forced to hold, in effect, that most cases of knowledge spreading are cases in which the knowledge acquired is metalinguistic knowledge of this sort. Given the pervasiveness of testimonial knowledge in our knowledge corpus, and given the grounding role that testimonial knowledge plays in our acquisition of yet other knowledge (testimonial or not), the result would be that on the present picture, most, if not all, of our knowledge (whether testimonially acquired or not) will be metalinguistic knowledge. If this is not a *reductio* of the metalinguistic interpretant proposal, I do not know what is.

2.6.8

So far, I have considered and rejected four distinct accounts that aim to explain the satisfaction of the reliable comprehension condition in cases of Successful RC, without appeal to public linguistic norms. None of these accounts succeeded, as none of them could offer a plausible explanation for the satisfaction of the social calibration requirement – the requirement that all of the various idiolects in a given speech community have broadly overlapping semantics. Before going on to suggest that the account we want is near-to-hand so long as we endorse the postulation of public linguistic norms, I want to strengthen my case for thinking that no such account is forthcoming once we deny the existence of public linguistic norms. Though what I have to say here is only suggestive, it is dialectically important nevertheless, since it suggests that the failure of the foregoing accounts is not a coincidence, but rather reflects an *in-principle difficulty* facing anyone who, aiming to account for (the satisfaction of the reliable comprehension condition in) Successful RC cases, nevertheless rejects the hypothesis of public linguistic norms.[29]

Let 'linguistic experience' designate any experience which is as of the linguistic properties of observed speech. And let the 'speaks the same language as' relation hold between two speakers H and S whenever a single semantic account is correct for at least the vast majority of the lexical items occurring in each of their respective idiolects. In this sense H's and S's idiolects can be seen to be imperfect 'copies' (as it were) of a single language. (This characterization is vague; but its vagueness would appear to reflect the actual vagueness of the English expression 'speak the same language'.) Then it would appear that anyone who would have us account for H's attaining a correct semantics for S's speech *without appealing to public linguistic norms* faces an inevitable dilemma, according to whether it is accepted or denied that H's attainment of a correct semantics for S's speech reflects the fact that H and S speak the same language.

Taking the first horn, suppose H's attainment of a correct semantics for S's language reflects the fact that H and S speak the same language. In that case we can ask: given just the resources that our imagined theorist has at her disposal, how does our theorist propose to explain how with respect to each other H and S manage to attain the state described as 'speaking the same language'? The difficulty on this score is even more dramatic than this, since really the issue is how *any* pair of members of a speech community manages to pull this off relative to one another: given any two arbitrary members of the same speech community, how does each manage to attain the state described as 'speaking the same language' as the other? Insofar as the assumption of a same language is meant to enable a theorist to avoid the postulation of public linguistic norms, it fails do so, since making such an assumption lands the theorist right back in the problems I identified in section 2.4.

Suppose then (second horn) that H's attainment of a correct semantics for S's speech does not reflect the fact that H and S speak the same language. Once again the question arises how H arrived at a correct semantics for the relevant portion of S's idiolect. The acuteness of this problem is seen in connection with communication involving concepts from the wide array of concepts not plausibly accounted for by appeal to the innateness hypothesis. In such cases, H must have attained a correct

---

[29] I thank Nick Zangwill for impressing upon me the desirability of this stronger kind of argument.

semantics for the relevant portion of S's language – that portion not accounted for by appeal to the innateness hypothesis alone – given only what is available innately, as supplemented by H's linguistic experience to date. But in RC cases, H's linguistic experience in connection with S is limited to H's experience of S's present speech act(s). Given that H and S are not being presumed to speak the same language, such an experiential basis would appear to be too meager to provide H with a correct semantics for the lexical items used by S in her speech act. This result holds even once it is granted, as in 2.6.7, that metalinguistic resources available to H would enable her to formulate a correct metalinguistic description of the truth conditions for S's speech. For we have already seen that this will not do as an account of H's *comprehension* of that speech – not, that is, if we hope to retain the hypothesis that the present case is a case of Successful RC.

At this point it might occur to one to deny that H's relevant linguistic experience – that which is relevant to the matter of H's comprehension of S's speech – is limited to H's experience of S's present speech act(s). It might be contended that, on the contrary, H has decidedly more relevant linguistic experience that he can bring to bear in comprehending S. For H's linguistic experience should be taken to include his experience of *all* of the speakers who appear to speak the same language as S – which is to say, his experience of all of the members of the speech community.[30] If so, H's reliable comprehension of S's meanings might be seen as a kind of induction from other speakers' usage. Having seen other speakers use each of the various word-forms in the sentence S uttered, H then draws the inductive inference that these word-forms mean the same in S's mouth as they did in the other speakers' mouths. The inductive inference takes H from the claim that S *appears* to speak like other people in H's environment, to the claim that S *does* speak like those others in H's environment. If it could be shown that this inductive inference is cogent, then it would have been shown that H's reliable comprehension of S's speech can be accounted for without appeal to public linguistic norms, simply by widening the linguistic evidence H brings to bear in the process of comprehending S's speech.

Such a view faces a direct challenge: it must be shown that the inference in question – from the claim that S appears to speak like most other speakers in H's community, to the claim that S does speak like them– is

---

[30] I thank Itzak Ben Baji for pressing the need to address this objection.

cogent. This challenge is great. To begin, we must keep in mind that the relevant sense of "speaks like" is the one pertaining to the satisfaction of the social calibration requirement: the relevant sense is that in which *S* "speaks like" the others in *H*'s speech community if and only if the there is one interpretation for the form of words *S* used which would be correct both for *S*'s use of those word-forms, and for the other speakers' use of those word-forms. (Again, I am helping myself to the simplifying assumption that we can bracket context-sensitivity considerations.) The defender of the cogency of the inductive inference must hold that the inference in question is cogent even if we read "speaks like" in this way. (In what follows I will understand the "speaks like" relation in this way, unless I explicitly state otherwise.)

Perhaps it will be thought that the cogency of the inference can be defended by reflecting on such things as (1) the unlikelihood that *S* would produce *just those sounds* if she were not speaking as others in *H*'s environment do, and (2) the fact that *S* did not produce any behaviors (such as accent, body language, tone of voice, etc.) that would signal some idiosyncracy in *S qua* speaker on this occasion.[31] However, it is dubious whether these sorts of considerations render the inference cogent.

Let it be granted that a hearer *H* who has limited exposure to a speaker *S* may nevertheless determine quite quickly, and with solid inductive support, that the word-forms in *S*'s idiolect largely overlap with the word-forms in the idiolects of others in *H*'s community. There is an exceedingly low probability that *S* would have produced a sound-sequence that engaged *H*'s word-recognition system in the way it was engaged, unless the word-forms of *S*'s idiolect largely overlap with those in *H*'s idiolect. But this point, which I take to be obvious, is a point about word-forms, not a point about the meanings or proper interpretation of those word-forms (in the mouth of the speaker). And the ease with which *S*'s utterance triggers *H*'s word-recognition system should not convince *H* that these word-forms *mean precisely the same thing* in *S*'s mouth as they do in the mouths of other community members.[32] Matters would be otherwise, of

---

[31] I thank an anonymous referee for suggesting that the present proposal might be defended in these ways.

[32] The possibility of raising this sort of question in connection with the issue of testimony is anticipated in Shogenji (2006: 336); he notes that identity in word-forms used does not, by itself, imply identity in meanings. (I should say that he notes this in the course of offering an argument that is sympathetic to the sort of induction-based reply I am presently criticizing. However, he gives no grounds for his confidence that the inductive reply will work.)

course, if we assume that everyone is speaking a public language. But we are pursuing a line of thought that tables this assumption, and that is trying to do without the appeal to public linguistic norms.

It would seem, then, that our inductive base is too meager to warrant the inference from *same word-forms* to *same meanings*. Consider how things stand from the perspective of those linguists and philosophers of language who maintain that the notion of a public language is a fiction, and that we each speak our own distinctive idiolect.[33] Surely they acknowledge that idiolects within a language community overlap (largely, if not entirely) at the level of word-forms in their lexicons. But the interest of their view lies precisely in *denying* that these lexicons made up of largely type-identical word-forms are type-identical as well in the meanings (or interpretations) to be assigned to the word-forms. It would seem, then, that to the extent that one really wants to do without public languages and public linguistic norms, sameness in the word-forms of the idiolects in a given speech community should not be taken without further ado to be a reliable indication of sameness at the level of the meanings associated with the word-forms.

In response, it might be said that various other factors render the inference (from same word-forms to same meanings) acceptable. These factors, it might be argued, suggest that those who use the same word-forms in communication exchanges can be expected to share meanings. For example, it might be argued that, under such circumstances, differences in meanings would be rather easy to confirm, at least if hearers had the tendency towards homophonic comprehension (comprehension that the hearer would manifest by using the very same word-forms in her own idiolect as those used by the speaker). Since in point of fact differences in meanings are not normally discerned in ordinary speech exchanges, this would suggest that those using the same word-forms are very likely to be meaning by their words what one oneself would mean with one's words.

But this response seriously underestimates the difficulty that must be faced. Successful RC requires not just *similarity* of meanings across idiolects (whatever that might mean), but *identical* meanings. The point is that such communicative exchanges result in the hearer's recovery of *precisely the content attested to*, not some 'close-enough' content (as per the discussion of

---

[33] The two most noteworthy proponents of such a view are Davidson (see especially his 1986) and Chomsky (in various places).

section 2.4). It is dubious whether a hearer's linguistic experience with the speakers of her community, by itself, suffices to discriminate the hypothesis of shared meanings, from that of similar-but-distinct meanings. Indeed, it is at precisely this point that we face a version of the problem I isolated in 2.6.4: that of explaining the *de facto* systematic and comprehensive overlap in the semantics of the idiolects of speakers in a given speech community, without appeal to the existence of public linguistic norms. On this score, the appeal to a hearer's extensive linguistic experience with other speakers is simply no help. For one thing, a hearer's extensive linguistic experience with other speakers will confirm the hypothesis of identical meanings only if meanings *are* identical (in at least a great many cases of conversational exchange), and we have yet to find a plausible explanation of how such an outcome (systematic and comprehensive shared meanings across idiolects in a given speech community) might come to pass. For another, as noted above, what a hearer's extensive linguistic experience with other speakers can be used to confirm is not what needs to be confirmed anyway. What that experience can be used to confirm is the hypothesis, regarding a given speaker observed only briefly, that her idiolect contains most or all of the same word-forms as those used by others in this community, or that her meanings are similar to those of others in the hearer's speech community. But what needs to be confirmed is the hypothesis, regarding a given speaker observed only briefly, that she means by her word-forms precisely what others in the community (including oneself) mean by their use of the same word-forms.

So far, I have been arguing that considerations of type (1) – those pertaining to the unlikelihood that S would produce *just those sounds* if she were not speaking as others in H's environment do – alone do not establish what the critic needs. Can we establish the needed claim by combining considerations of type (1) with those of type (2)? The latter, it will be recalled, pertain to the non-presence of any behaviors that would signal some idiosyncrasy in S *qua* speaker on this occasion. Unfortunately, this sort of evidence is of no help on the matter at hand. What factors such as tone of voice, accent, body language, and so forth enable us to confirm is that a speaker is *sincere*; we might even confirm that she is *competent* (or at least confident in her assertions). But none of this goes to the issue of *the precise content attested to* in this sincere and competent way.

In sum. The move to expand the relevant linguistic experience a hearer brings to comprehending a novel utterance, in an attempt to account for reliable comprehension without the appeal to public linguistic norms, appears to put the cart before the horse. It appears to assume that, rather than explaining how, everyone speaks the same language. It assumes this since, if it is not the case that everyone speaks the same language, then it is unclear why H's linguistic experience of *other speakers* is relevant to her efforts to attain a reliable comprehension of S's speech. It does not explain this since the explanation in question will require explaining how individuals attain the state of 'speaking the same language' – something that (we have seen) the present account cannot do.

Our conclusion, then, would appear to be general. In 2.6.4–2.6.8 I objected to various particular views that try to account for the pervasiveness and efficiency of (reliable comprehension in) Successful RC cases, without postulating public linguistic norms. It would now appear that these various attempts don't just *happen* to fail to account for the facts of comprehension in RC cases; rather, it appears that they were *bound* to fail, given the resources with which they had to work. In particular, once a theorist shelves the hypothesis of public linguistic norms, the resources available to the theory, in its attempt to explain how individual hearers systematically attain a reliable comprehension of the words of their (apparent) co-linguals, are too meager to account for the sort of comprehension that we suppose goes on all the time in our ordinary, everyday interactions with our linguistic peers.

2.6.9

Having argued that the satisfaction of the reliable comprehension condition on reliable testimonial belief (and hence on testimonial knowledge) cannot be accounted for once we surrender the hypothesis of public linguistic norms, I now want to argue that, once we endorse the postulation of public linguistic norms, we have a natural explanation of the phenomenon whereby reliable comprehension is effortlessly attained across a wide range of RC-cases. (This will complete my case for Premise 4, and with it the argument from Successful Communication for public linguistic norms.)

We can analyze the process of understanding in such cases as follows. On observing S's utterance, H – or rather: that part of H's cognitive system that interacts with linguistic inputs – maps (H's mental representations of) the sound-sequences in S's utterance onto word-forms. Insofar as these word-forms can be mapped onto lexical items in H's own lexicon, H does so, and assigns these lexical items the meanings that they have in H's idiolect. (Presumably this meaning assignment proceeds in some sort of compositional way.)[34] On the assumption that there are public linguistic norms that govern the entries of both the speaker's and the hearer's respective idiolects, *this sentence-to-sentence matching will be guaranteed to be content-preserving* (once again bracketing considerations of context-sensitivity). Such a method would then yield a very efficient and reliable comprehension process. What is more, by relying on this sort of comprehension process, *H* can efficiently and reliably comprehend *S*'s utterance even though, prior to their communicative exchange, *H* knew nothing of *S*'s speech or interpretative dispositions. Indeed, the process of understanding would then be (roughly) as reliable as is the process whereby the words used by another speaker are recovered from her utterance.[35] This is because, once the words have been recovered by the speaker, the public linguistic norms take over, ensuring agreement between speaker and hearer.

Seen from a certain vantage point, our result ought not to be very surprising. There is a sense in which communication involves a kind of coordination problem, where what needs to be coordinated is the speaker's and hearer's respective functions from lexical items to semantic values in their respective idiolects. Some *de facto* coordination of this sort is necessary if the speaker is to be able to rely on the hearer's reliability in recovering precisely the content attested to; and such coordination is also needed if the hearer is to be able to rely on the speaker's having produced a sentence that will reliably generate the recovery of the intended content in the process of comprehension. The question we are posing is how in general the semantics of various individuals' idiolects reach a state of more-or-less-mutual-coordination. The postulation of public linguistic norms would appear to be a natural suggestion here, since the public norms can be seen as solving the coordination problem by providing the standard against which the semantics of each of the speech community's individual idiolects are 'calibrated'. In the absence of such a postulation, though, it would appear that the theorist would be committed to a rather strong research agenda: that of showing how, given what is innate and what is acquired in our scattered and unsystematic verbal interactions with others, each of our

---

[34] No doubt complications will have to be introduced to handle such things as lexical ambiguity and polysemy, as well as any other pragmatic determinants of truth-conditional content. Here I disregard these phenomena, my intention being only to suggest the account in broad outline.

[35] Once again, we still have to allow for complications in connection with context-sensitivity.

idiolects (whose semantics are conceived individualistically) arrives at a state of more-or-less-coordination with the idiolects of all other members of our speech community – the sort of coordination required if we are to account for Successful RC.

One might charge that my appeal to public linguistic norms does not make reliable comprehension in Successful RC cases any less 'miraculous' unless these norms are somehow implicated in the causal processing that eventuates in the state of comprehension.[36] It is one thing to say that public linguistic norms serve to 'calibrate' the semantics of various idiolects, in the sense that we evaluate various idiolects against these norms, criticizing individual speakers and hearers for failing to conform to them. It is another thing entirely to claim that these norms themselves figure in the actual processing that eventuates in the hearer's attainment of a state of comprehension. This latter claim is a causal hypothesis regarding the processing that gives rise to language comprehension. The present charge is that, at best, my argument above establishes the first (calibration) claim, not the second (causal) one.

However, this worry can be met. Anyone who theorizes about linguistic comprehension will have to have some account of the processing that eventuates in the hearer's attainment of a state of comprehension. Such an account is called for *whatever* one's views on the existence of public linguistic norms. This account will have to specify the causal processes that yield the mental representations constituting the hearer's comprehension of speakers' utterances. Now it is true that there will be some disagreement as to how to individuate the contents to be assigned to these representations. Those who resist the postulation of public linguistic norms will think that contents can be assigned without appeal to such norms, whereas those who endorse this postulation will think that contents can be assigned only after we appeal to such norms. But the important point is that both sides can agree on the causal processes that drive comprehension. This is because the issue that separates the two sides is over the (individuation of the) *contents* to be ascribed to the relevant set of representations, not over the nature of the causal processing.

Another way to put this point is this. The benefit of postulating public linguistic norms is not that it illuminates the causal processing involved in linguistic comprehension: it doesn't, although it is not the worse for this, since as I have suggested it can co-opt whatever the correct story is in this

---

[36] This objection is owed to an anonymous referee.

regard. The benefit of postulating such norms is, rather, that it illuminates the individuation of the content of the representations in the domain of linguistic comprehension, thereby showing how Successful RC cases can be as prevalent as they are. And this shows that the appeal to public linguistic norms, as part of an account of the process of reliable comprehension in RC cases, is not susceptible to the charge that it leaves linguistic comprehension as mysterious as it was on those accounts I criticized.

I do not pretend that this sketch of an explanation is a complete account; no doubt many details need to be filled in. In particular, real-life communication is messier – indeed, much messier – than my public-linguistic-norm-account above suggests. (At the very least, it would have to be complicated to handle the phenomena of ambiguity, polysemy, indexicality, and any other forms of context-sensitivity – including, if such there be, widely pragmatic determinants of truth-conditional content.)[37] But I do maintain that the account on offer, rudimentary as it is, will be a core part of any more adequate account of knowledge communication, and that in any case it takes the mystery out of the phenomenon of Successful RC, in ways that none of the proposals above was able to do.

---

[37] I borrow the notion of 'widely' pragmatic determinants from Bach 1997b.

3

Public linguistic norms: the case from misunderstanding

In the previous chapter I defended the hypothesis of public linguistic norms by appeal to the nature of successful communication. The phenomenon to be accounted for was that whereby two participants in a speech exchange efficiently transmit very specific knowledge to one another through their speech, even under conditions in which they know nothing of each others' speech and interpretative dispositions save what is manifest in the brief speech exchange itself. The burden of chapter 2 was to argue that the reliable comprehension that is attained in such cases seems miraculous unless we suppose that there are such norms – norms which (given the concrete speech context) determine what the speaker literally said with her words, and which are at least implicitly exploited by the hearer in the process by which she arrives at a representation of the content of the speech she observed. Whereas that argument for public linguistic norms is thus an argument from Successful Communication, the present argument, in contrast, will be from a certain kind of unsuccessful communication – that arising from cases in which, though the speaker aims to be communicating knowledge, this aim is thwarted owing to *misunderstanding*. My central thesis will be that in these sorts of misunderstanding cases at least one of the parties is appropriately blamed for the breakdown in communication, and that (at least in RC-cases) warranted ascriptions of blame presuppose public linguistic norms. One interesting result will be that the legitimacy of the imposition of such norms on an arbitrary speech act is itself positive-presumptive (though defeasible).

So far as I can tell, the sort of argument I am about to provide for public linguistic norms has not been anticipated in the literature. This is not to say that no one has discerned any connection between the existence of public linguistic norms and the proper account of breakdowns in would-be knowledge-transmitting communication. However, discussions of these matters (see especially Ross 1986) typically focus on cases where the hearer's failure to acquire knowledge is owed to an *epistemic* breakdown in the process. Such cases can be distinguished from the sort of case I want to discuss here. In the cases traditionally considered, there is a successful transmission of content – the speaker said what she meant, and the hearer's uptake recovered the content in question – it's just that the speaker failed to have the knowledge she aimed to transmit. In the cases I will consider here, by contrast, the hearer's failure to acquire knowledge is owed to a failure along a distinctly semantic dimension: there is a disconnect between what the hearer *took* to be asserted in the testimony, and what the speaker herself 'meant.'

We might contrast the breakdown involved in these two types of case in terms of the three necessary conditions on testimonial knowledge, as set forth in chapter 1. The standard case in which a hearer's testimonial belief fails to amount to knowledge is one in which there is a failure along either the testimonial reliability dimension (as when the hearer has relied on unreliable testimony), or else along the reliable discernment dimension (as when the hearer has been overly credulous in her acceptance of testimony). In contrast, the case I will be describing here is one in which there is a failure along the reliable comprehension dimension. In this case, the unreliability of the hearer's testimonial belief reflects the disconnect between what the speaker meant in her attestation, and what the hearer came to believe on the basis of observing the attestation. In such a case, even if the speaker was reliable *vis-à-vis* what she meant to attest to, and even if the hearer was suitably discerning in her acceptance of (what she took to be) the testimony, the hearer's belief was not reliably formed. It is in this kind of case, I submit, where warranted ascriptions of blame require a appeal to the public linguistic norms in play: for the question here is whether it was the speaker's inept choice of words, or the hearer's inept comprehension[1] of them, that accounts for the misunderstanding. (The 'or' here is not exclusive.)

---

[1] It is important to be clear at the outset that, as it is being used in this chapter, 'comprehension' designates that state in which a hearer represents the content of a piece of observed speech. This usage is neutral on the correctness and reliability of that representation: 'inept comprehension' is not a contradiction in terms, and using 'reliable' to qualify 'comprehension' is not superfluous. (This usage holds throughout Part I; but it is not likely to cause confusion exception in this chapter, where I am explicitly taking up faulty comprehension.)

In drawing our attention to these kinds of cases, I am pointing out the various normative assessments that can be brought to bear in cases in which communication does not succeed in spreading knowledge. In particular, there are at least two ways in which a hearer might bear epistemic blame in a case in which she fails to acquire knowledge through another's speech aimed at that end: the hearer might fail to have attained a reliable comprehension of the testimony on which she relied, or else, having attained a reliable comprehension of the testimony, she might not be reliable in her discrimination of reliable from unreliable testimony.[2] In a roughly parallel fashion, there are at least two ways in which the speaker might bear epistemic blame in cases in which her testimony fails to 'let the hearer know': the speaker might fail to have the knowledge he means to be communicating to the hearer; or, alternatively, although he has the knowledge in question, he might fail to have expressed himself linguistically in such a way as to have enabled his audience to recover the known content he aimed to communicate. Whereas it is clear that in the former case we have a failure of the condition on testimonial reliability, how should we categorize the latter case? Given that there is a disconnect between the propositional content recovered by the hearer and the propositional content the speaker meant to transmit, this will be a case in which the hearer failed to attain a reliable comprehension of what the speaker meant. But this leaves open whether the fault is with the hearer (in the process of comprehension) or with the speaker (in the process of producing the testimony-constituting utterance).

I will be arguing that settling this kind of question as it arises in particular contexts is an important part of our knowledge-communicating practices, and that we can do so in a principled way only on the assumption of shared linguistic norms. For it is these norms that determine whether the speaker succeeded (in the utterance-context) in saying what he meant; and it is the speaker's status as having said what he meant (or not) that determines whether it is he, or his audience, who is to blame for the failed attempt at knowledge transmission.

---

[2] We should identify a third way in which a hearer might bear epistemic blame in a case in which she fails to acquire knowledge through another's speech: she might fail to have had the epistemic right to accept her interlocutor's word. Whether this failure goes beyond matters of her reliability in discriminating reliable from unreliable testimony will depend on one's account of the conditions on justified acceptance of testimony. I ignore this 'third way' here, as irrelevant to my semantic concerns; but I discuss it in chapters 5 and 6, where my focus turns to the epistemology of knowledge communication.

3.2 THE BLAME GAME: MOTIVATION

I begin with some programmatic remarks regarding why we bother playing the 'blame game' in cases in which the hearer fails to acquire knowledge through the speaker's attestation. I believe that this 'game' is a core
part of the background of the practice whereby knowledge is spread via
testimony.

Starting with the motive to blame, some general remarks are in order.
Suppose that your car has been giving you troubles recently. It still runs,
but various things have been going wrong (difficulties starting the car,
noises from the engine, etc.) You'd like to know what's at fault. Your
motive for wanting an insightful diagnosis – one that properly places the
'blame' – is both practical and economic. The ignoring of small problems
now might portend larger, more expensive problems later. Of course, you
could always adopt the policy of buying a new car whenever a car of yours
starts showing signs of trouble. However, in most cases it is better to
restrict yourself to the car troubles at hand. To do so you aim to identify
all and only those parts that are causing the trouble, in order to determine
what would most efficiently serve the aim of getting the car back into
acceptable shape.[3] You want to identify all of the problematic parts, since
you want to fix the problem; but you want to replace only the problematic
parts, since you don't want to fix what isn't broken – else your 'fix' will be
more expensive than it needs to be, and in any case might itself cause
difficulties you would have avoided if you had left well enough alone.

Let us say that we have a breakdown in purportedly knowledge-
transmitting communication whenever (i) a hearer acquires a belief through
her acceptance of what she took the speaker to have said, where (ii) the
speaker's aim to be transmitting knowledge to the hearer is nevertheless
frustrated (the hearer's belief does not amount to knowledge). It is in
everyone's interest to arrive at an insightful diagnosis. The motive here is
practical and – given one's practical aim – epistemic. All sides have a generic
interest in rendering as pervasive and efficient as possible the process
whereby knowledge is spread throughout a community. (I say this interest
is 'generic': I disregard private interests one might have in others' remaining
ignorant in certain domains, or in certain particular contexts.) Parties to a
breakdown could always adopt the policy never to extend trust, or to offer

---

[3] Acceptable shape itself will be determined as the balance you strike between maximizing
your future use of the car while minimizing the money and time you expend keeping it in
order.

information, to another person. But such a policy would be extremely inefficient with respect to one's generic interest in promoting and benefitting from the pervasive and efficient sharing of knowledge. Better yet, participants could aim to identify all and only those 'parts' of the 'transaction' that are causing the trouble, in order to determine what would best serve the aim of increasing the reliability and efficiency of the practice whereby knowledge is disseminated. One wants to identify all of the problematic parts, since one wants to fix the problem; but one wants to uncover only the problematic parts, since one doesn't want to fix what isn't broken – else one's 'fix' will be more epistemically expensive than it needs to be, and in any case might itself cause difficulties one would have avoided if one had left well enough alone.

Of course, it is easy to overstate the parallel between car troubles and communication breakdowns. One important difference is that in the latter case but not the former, the object being blamed is an *agent*. Since 'blame' connotes irresponsibility, car parts can be 'blamed' only in an attenuated sense. What is more, there would appear to be no clear analogue in the case of communication breakdown with the need to replace one's car from time to time. (Perhaps a loose analogue is this: occasionally there arises the need to discontinue talking with a party with which one has had nothing but systematic and deleterious miscommunication over some extended period of time.) Putting aside these differences for now, my point in making the limited parallel is to make clear that the 'blame game' is not something that is unique to communication, but rather is part of any complex system whose behavior can be evaluated in terms of how well it performs a certain function (reliable and efficient transportation; reliable and efficient spread of knowledge), where the system's performance depends on the coordinated activities of various of its interconnected components. Insofar as our system of linguistic communication can be thought of in such terms, the 'blame game' is an important part of that system.

3.3 GIVING ONE'S WORD: SEMANTICS AND PRAGMATICS

The blame game involves placing blame. In this case, the blame at issue pertains to cases in which knowledge fails to be transmitted through a speech act that purported to do just that. Here I want to connect the characterization I gave in chapter 1 regarding the sort of knowledge in question, with the issue of blame itself. The sort of blame at issue is vividly illustrated in those testimony cases in which a speaker *gives her word*, where that word turns out to be faulty. We will say that a speaker *S* 'gives her word' regarding *p* just in case *S* performs a speech act in which she both presents *p* as true and presents herself (at least implicitly) as knowing *p*. Depending on one's conception of testimony, cases of giving one's word are either co-extensive with, or else a proper subset of, cases of testifying.[4] And something similar can be said of the connection between giving one's word and asserting: if one takes knowledge to be the norm of assertion, then any case of assertion is a case of giving one's word; whereas if one takes the norm of assertion to be epistemically weaker than knowledge, then to give one's word that *p* would require a *strengthened* form of assertion.

Before I consider how blame attaches in cases in which one falsely gives one's word, it is interesting to ask whether assertion (or strengthened assertion) is the *only* way to give one's word. Can one give one's word that *p*, for example, by implicating that *p*? Although the case I will be presenting in this chapter for public linguistic norms does not require that we address this issue (see below), I address it since it is of some independent interest in its own right.

Reflection on the speech-act potential of implicatures and other indirect speech acts might seem to suggest a negative answer to our question. There are various imaginable circumstances in which it would be perfectly in order for a speaker to implicate *r*, without presenting herself as *knowing* (or otherwise being in an epistemically privileged position with respect to) *r*.[5] You ask whether Smith is having an affair; I reply, "Well, he sure has been spending a lot of time with a certain woman in New York." Let it be common knowledge – something you know, and I know you know, and

---

[4] The two appear to be co-extensive on the conception of testimony in Coady 1992. However, it is worth noting that there are defensible conceptions of testimony on which one can testify without giving one's word. Consider a conception on which one counts as having testified whenever one has performed a speech act that is apt for the transmission of knowledge of the content presented-as-true in the speech act. On such a conception, a person can testify without giving her word: perhaps she reports *p*, under conditions in which she knows *p*, but fails to know that she knows *p*, and so refrains from representing herself in the way appropriate to 'giving her word.' Alternatively, consider a conception of testimony on which one counts as having testified whenever one asserts anything, but where asserting is seen as governed by an epistemic norm that is less demanding than the knowledge norm. On such a conception, one can assert *p*, and so testify that *p*, without representing oneself in the way appropriate to 'giving one's word'.

[5] Indeed this may be so for reasons having nothing to do with epistemology. Such cases can be generated by the need for politeness in our speech exchanges. See Adler (1997: 447–9) for the relevance of politeness to the issue regarding the norms of speech.

you know I know you know, etc. – that I said what I did because I believe that Smith *is* having an affair. And let us suppose that I did in fact intend to communicate to you my belief to that effect – a case of implicature. Even so, I need not have presented myself as being in an *epistemically privileged position* with respect to the truth of the implicated proposition (the pro-position that Smith is having an affair). On the contrary, it would seem that, assuming everything was in epistemic order with my testimony and your acceptance of it, once you accept my testimony you are in the same epistemic position I am with respect to the truth of the implicated content. Precisely so, since, in having spoken as I did, I gave you the very evidence I have for thinking that the implicated content is true. (At this point you don't need to take my word for it, you can judge for yourself whether he's having an affair.) In such a case, it is clear that in speaking as I did I did *not* present myself as in an epistemically privileged position regarding – still less as *knowing* – the truth of what I implicated. However we describe this case, it is not a case of my giving you my word.

Indeed, the indirect speech act of implicating *p* might well be the *perfect* way for me to signal that I am *not* in an epistemically privileged position regarding the truth of the implicated content.[6] If I believe that Smith is having an affair and take my evidence to be good but not decisive, then implicating that Smith is having an affair, by giving you my reason for thinking he is, appears to be a very efficient (and effective) way to signal my epistemic position on the matter. The choice of implicature over explicit assertion here is crucial: it involves the desire to give you my reasons even as I make it manifest that I recognize that these reasons, though good, do not amount to the sort of epistemic standing called for in making a warranted (normatively acceptable) assertion. I could achieve the same effect by being very explicit in my response: "I believe he is, here's my evidence, yet I recognize that this does not establish what I believe" etc. etc. Or, alternatively, I could do so by asserting "Well, he sure has been spending an awful lot of time with a particular woman in New York." Here the fact that I have *implicated* that Smith is having an affair, rather than directly *asserted* it, itself signals that I am *not* in a particularly privileged position, epistemically speaking, regarding the matter at hand.

---

[6] In what follows what I say of implicature would hold, *mutatis mutandis*, for any case in which the speaker performs an indirect speech act in which the relevant content is conveyed.

The lesson of the foregoing has to do with assertion vs. implicature *as a species*: whereas assertion carries with it the pragmatic significance of presenting oneself as in an epistemically privileged position regarding the asserted content, conversational implication, as such, does not carry the same significance *vis-à-vis* the implicated content. This leaves open whether there are particular cases in which (given the context and the speaker's intentions) the act of implicating has the epistemico-pragmatic significance of outright (strengthened) assertion.[7] If so, it would not be in virtue of having *implicated* p that the speaker so presented herself; but perhaps there are cases in which the speaker has additional communicative intentions in virtue of which, in performing the speech act she did, she presented herself as knowing the content she implicated. (Consider the *knowing wink*, for example.)

Happily, for my purposes in this chapter, we need not settle this issue. The question before us is: given a case in which a speaker gave her word, what content(s) is/are such that, were a hearer to acquire a belief in those contents through accepting what she took to be the speaker's word on this occasion, the hearer would be entitled to regard the speaker as responsible for the falsity of those contents (should they turn out to be false or otherwise unreliable)? Now let it be granted that, with certain sorts of stage-setting, one can give one's word that p by implicating p. Even so, given what is involved in a hearer's taking a speaker to have given her word regarding p through implicating p, if a hearer is to be entitled to so regard a speaker, in standard cases she must also be entitled to regard the speaker as having given her word regarding the truth of the content (literally) asserted.

Consider what is involved in a hearer's being entitled to regard a speaker as having given her word that p through implicating p. To be so entitled, the hearer must satisfy both of the following conditions: (one) she must be entitled to regard the speaker as having implicated p in the first place; and (two) she must be entitled to regard the speaker's having implicated p as a case of her having given her word regarding p. Now take the first condition. A hearer is entitled to regard a speaker as having implicated p only if the derivation of that implicature – including the representation of the literal content of the speech act, needed for the derivation – is itself acceptable. The result is that, in cases in which the speaker's having given her word regarding p is a matter of her having implicated p, the hearer can

---

[7] I thank Jennifer Lackey for raising this issue (in private discussion). However, she is not responsible for the barbaric expression I am using ('epistemico-pragmatic significance').

blame the speaker for the falsity of p, in the way appropriate to cases of falsely giving one's word, only if the hearer is entitled to hold the speaker responsible for having produced a speech act whose literal content was that q. Consider now what is involved in the satisfaction of the second condition. A hearer is entitled to regard a speaker's having implicated p as a case of her having given her word regarding p, only if the hearer is entitled to regard the speaker's having implicated p as a case in which the speaker presented herself as knowing p. Now suppose (for *reductio*) that the hearer is not entitled to regard the speaker as presenting herself as knowing (the truth of) the content literally expressed in her speech act. Then it would seem that the hearer is not entitled to regard the speaker as presenting herself as knowing (the truth of) the *implicatum*. At least this will be so in cases like the above example, where the speaker's saying what she did presents evidence for thinking that the *implicatum* is true. (If one can give one's word through implicature, presumably this will be the standard case.)

To illustrate: if in response to the question whether Jones is having an affair I remark that he has been seeing a good deal of a certain woman in New York, and if in so doing I can be seen as giving my word that Jones is having an affair, this is only because I can *also* be seen as giving my word regarding what I literally said (namely, that he has been seeing a good deal of a certain woman in New York). If you take me not to know whereof I speak regarding Jones' visits to a certain woman in New York, you have no grounds for regarding me as presenting myself as knowing that Jones is having an affair – your regarding me in this way being only as warranted as the evidence you take me to have given (for the hypothesis that Jones is having an affair) is strong.[8] In this way we see that, whether or not a speaker can give her word regarding what she merely implicates, those interested in the sort of blame that attaches to giving one's word can restrict their attention to the literal case – this sort of case being part of the standard implicature case as well.[9]

---

[8] This is not to deny that one can implicate p by way of asserting something one does not know. Of course such cases exist. Indeed, there are ordinary cases where one implicates p by asserting something one *knows to be false* – as in cases of irony and sarcasm. In such a case the speaker might succeed at communicating the content in question, but it is not clear whether it would be correctly assimilable into a case in which she has given her word in the sense above.

[9] A further question of interest is this: in situations where p is false, what are the conditions under which S can be blamed for implicating (or even just making-as-if-to-implicate) p, when she does so by way of an assertion that is both true and reliable? Considerations of space prevent me from discussing this here; I hope to return to it at a later time.

Given this account of what is involved in giving one's word, I turn now to the issue of blame. But before I do it is worth noting that what goes for cases of giving one's word that p goes, more generally, for any case in which a speaker presents herself as in an epistemically privileged position regarding the truth of p. So long as a speaker performs a speech act in which she both presents p as true and presents herself as in an epistemically privileged position regarding p, then the falsity of another's belief in p, when this belief was formed through accepting her testimony, will be something for which she (the speaker herself) bears responsibility. This is so whether she presented herself as knowing p, or as standing in some weaker-but-still-privileged epistemic position regarding the truth of p. (The case of giving one's word just makes the point especially vivid.)

In what follows my claim will be that, when it comes to determining the content(s) regarding whose truth the speaker has presented herself as in some epistemically privileged position or other, the blame to which she thereby is susceptible – the contents for whose falsity she can be blamed if another person comes to believe such contents on the basis of accepting what they take to be her word – will be determined in part by the public linguistic norms in play.

3.4 WHO IS TO BLAME? AND FOR WHAT?

Given a case in which the speaker gave her word, what determines *the content* regarding whose truth she thereby presented herself as in an epistemically privileged position? Alternatively: what content is such, that with respect to that content the speaker, in speaking as she did, bears the sort of epistemic responsibility appropriate to giving her word?

I begin with some programmatic comments about the connection between these two issues. To present oneself as *knowing p* – which is part of what one does in giving one's word regarding p – is an instance of presenting oneself as in an epistemically privileged position regarding the truth of p – which is part of what one does in asserting p. In the first instance, the issue of blame arises in these testimony cases because one can present oneself as having something one does not, in fact, have. We might develop the point in terms of rule-governed activities more generally: if there is a rule requiring those who perform a certain act to have a certain property, with the result that (given that the rule is common knowledge) an agent who performs the act generates the expectation in others that she has the property in question, then she can be faulted for performing the act without having the property in question.[10] This would explain why someone who asserts p without being in the relevant epistemically privileged position regarding the truth of p could be faulted for doing so. What is more, if, on the basis of observing that assertion, a hearer comes to believe p on the strength of the speaker's assertion, that hearer could blame the speaker for having presented herself as occupying an epistemic position she did not in fact have. This is the sort of blame that attaches to cases of normatively deficient asserting, as well as to cases of falsely giving one's word.

We can now see that the two questions with which I began this section are actually two sides of a coin. In particular, whatever it is that determines the propositional content regarding whose truth a speaker has presented herself as in an epistemically privileged position *thereby* determines the contents regarding which the speaker has opened herself up to blame in the manner just indicated.

What is it that determines the content(s) in question? It will be helpful to formulate this issue in categories inherited from speech act theory: where p is the content regarding whose truth one has given one's word, can we identify p with what the speaker *meant*, or with what she *actually said*? (I don't rule out that a variant answer might be correct). The advantage of this speech-act-theoretic way of addressing the present issue is that it connects the semantic issue before us – What is it that determines the content(s) regarding whose truth one gave one's word? – with the issue of public linguistic norms. To a first approximation, if the answer to our question invokes nothing beyond *speaker meaning*, then (absent further argument) public linguistic norms are not to be regarded as relevant to the issue regarding the sort of blame to which a speaker is susceptible in cases of misunderstanding. On the other hand, if the answer to our question invokes *sentence meaning*, then – given the plausible claim that the determination of sentence meaning depends on public linguistic norms (more on which below) – such norms are relevant to the issue regarding the sort of blame to which a speaker is susceptible in cases of misunderstanding. At any rate this is precisely how I will try to motivate the existence of public linguistic norms in cases of miscommunication: by

---

[10] See also Ross 1986, where a similar point about blame is made. As here, Ross also sees blame in testimony cases generated by the rule-governed nature of language. However Ross goes further and defends a particular account of the epistemology of testimony from this appeal to the rule-governed nature of language. Aiming to be neutral on substantive epistemological issues here, I beg off this part of his argument.

adverting to the need to invoke sentence meaning in determining speaker blameworthiness.

The expressions 'what the speaker meant' and 'what the speaker said' are technical expressions. So even if it is true that these categories provide a helpful way to frame the issue before us, they also introduce certain complexities into the discussion; their use needs to be carefully regimented. One question that must be confronted is whether a speaker can count as having said that p when she didn't mean that p (in the sense that this was not something she intended to get her audience to believe, or to believe that she believes). Arguably, Paul Grice – whose work has had the most profound impact on our understanding of these notions – held that 'S said that p' entails 'S meant that p,' with the result that if S did not mean that p, then S did not say that p (see Saul 2002 for discussion). Another question is whether a speaker can count as having meant p when p itself bears no interesting semantic or pragmatic relation to the meanings of the words she used. Here we do well to recall a celebrated example in Searle (1965), in which an American soldier, hoping to get his Italian captor to believe that he (the American) is a German officer, utters the German sentence, "*Kennst du das Land, wo die Zitronen blühen?*"[11] Searle's use of the example was meant to illustrate that the meanings of the words one uses constrain what one can mean in using them. Searle concludes his discussion by crediting Wittgenstein with having made essentially the same point:

At one point in the <u>Philosophical Investigations</u> Wittgenstein says "Say 'it's cold here' and mean 'it's warm here'." The reason we are unable to do this is that what we can mean is a function of what we are saying. *Meaning is more than a matter of intention, it is also a matter of convention.* (Searle 1965, as reprinted in Martinich 2000: 134. Italics mine.)

Although I am most sympathetic to Searle's conclusion here, it would be patently question-begging in the present context to build into my use of 'what the speaker means' the assumption that what a speaker can mean is constrained by the conventions of language. For as I seek to use it, 'what the speaker means' is supposed to leave open whether there are any public linguistic norms at play in determining the content to whose truth she gave her word. Since Searle's language conventions might well be thought to constitute public linguistic norms, it will not do to assume Searle's conclusion from the start.

---

[11] Knowest thou the land where the lemon trees bloom?

We can avoid both controversies by replacing the categories of *what was said* and *what was meant* by categories that are less theoretically loaded. Thus let us replace the category of *what was said* by the category *what the speaker made as if to say*, where what the speaker made as if to say is what the speaker would have counted as having said, had she meant it. (What a speaker would have counted as having said, had she meant it, is determined by the linguistic conventions in place.) Similarly with respect to the notion of *what was meant*, we can avoid the controversy noted in connection with Searle's example by replacing it with the category of *what the speaker avowedly meant*. Roughly, what a speaker avowedly meant is what she avows having meant, where this is expressed in her avowals of the form, 'What I meant was . . .'[12] Circumstances are imaginable in which Searle's American soldier can avow having meant something which, in Searle's sense of 'what was meant,' he (the soldier) could not have meant – the idea being that in such cases 'what was meant' is being used much more loosely than Searle's own usage.

With these preliminary remarks out of our way, we can return to the question at hand. When what a speaker avowedly meant differs from what she made as if to say, which of these, if either, is needed to determine the content regarding whose truth she gave her word? More to the point: when these diverge, regarding the falsity of what content can a speaker be *blamed* in the way appropriate to having (falsely) given her word?

Consider the following example. McSorley wants to know where President Bush is today, and so she asks Jones. (McSorley knows that Jones tends to read the morning paper, and that the morning paper tends to have articles on the President and his whereabouts.) Jones replies by

---

[12] Admittedly, the sentence expressing the avowed meaning – the one figuring in the place of '. . .' above – will have to be interpreted to capture what was avowedly meant. If we assume that the proper interpretation of (the speaker's present use of) the sentence in question is also determined by what the speaker avowedly meant, we are off and running towards a *reductio ad infinitum*. This is a problem for those who think that we can get at assertoric content without invoking public linguistic norms. (This point is noted in Goldberg 2002a: 616–17.) However, at this point in my argument I don't want to assume that such a theorist is in trouble on this score – my concessiveness here reflecting my desire to reach the hypothesis of public linguistic norms as the conclusion of an argument everyone should accept. So at this point I want to allow that something like (for example) radical interpretation might help the theorist in question break into the 'hermeneutic circle' here. (In this regard it is worth noting that Davidson-style Radical Interpretation does not presume the existence of public linguistic norms. See Goldberg 2004a for a discussion.)

asserting, "President Bush is in Galveston, Texas, today." On the basis of McSorley's trust in Jones, McSorley acquires a belief whose content is *that President Bush is in Galveston, Texas today*. But it turns out that Bush is *not* in Galveston today; he's in Houston. On being apprized of this by the local TV news, McSorley blames Jones for having testified falsely. But Jones replies that he did not testify falsely – and he backs this up by asserting that he used 'Galveston' to refer to the city that Jones refers to as 'Houston.' McSorley's reaction (as well as our own) might well be that, though Jones might have *meant* that Bush is in Houston, what he *said* – or at least what he made as if to say – was that Bush is in Galveston.

In a case like this one, it is a vexed question whether Jones should count as having "given his word" that Bush is in Galveston, Texas, today. In particular, Jones did not believe (and so did not take himself to know) that Bush is in Galveston. Quite the contrary, Jones took himself to know that Bush is *not* in Galveston: Jones knew that Bush is in Houston and that Houston is not in Galveston. (This is a comment about *the content* of Jones' knowledge: *that Bush is not in Galveston today* is a content he knows to be true – though his linguistic expression of that content would be idiosyncratic and misleading.) For this reason it can seem wrong to describe Jones as having *given his word* that Bush is in Galveston. Yet even as the legitimacy of such a description is in some doubt, intuition is quite clear regarding the legitimacy with which McSorley might *blame* Jones for her (McSorley's) false belief. Here we want to say that even if Jones does not count as having given his word that Bush is in Galveston today, in speaking as he did he *made as if* he gave his word. And in any case McSorley would be entitled to blame Jones *as if* Jones had given his word that Bush is in Galveston.

If this verdict stands – if McSorley *is* entitled to blame Jones as if he had given his word that Bush is in Galveston – then we would have the basis for drawing a more general conclusion. The more general conclusion would be that hearers are entitled to regard speakers as responsible, in the way appropriate to giving one's word, for the content that the speaker made-as-if-to-say. This is because our verdict in the McSorley–Jones case does not depend in any crucial way on the specifics of the case. In particular, it does not depend on the idiosyncratic use of a proper name – any expression that has a standard meaning would do the trick. What is more, it would appear that the intuition supporting our verdict is perfectly systematic: an analogous intuition would be elicited in any case involving the use of an expression that has a standard meaning. If a speaker uses such an expression idiosyncratically, in that she means to be expressing something other than the standard meaning associated with the term, and does so under conditions in which context does not make her idiosyncratic usage clear, it is she we would hold responsible should a hearer form a false belief in the content capturing what she made-as-if-to-say. Of course, what a speaker makes-as-if-to-say is determined by the relevant sentence meaning, rather than by speaker meaning; and in this way we see that, if the intuitive verdict in the McSorley–Jones case stands, we have the basis of a case for thinking that it is sentence meaning, not speaker meaning, that is relevant to the issue of blame in cases of miscommunication.

In what follows, I want to argue that the intuitive verdict in the McSorley–Jones case – that McSorley is entitled to blame Jones *as if* Jones had given his word that Bush is in Galveston – is indeed correct. There are several reasons supporting this contention, beyond the intuitiveness of the verdict itself.

An initial supporting consideration comes from the nature of the process of comprehension involved in this case, and the role that this process plays in considering whether it is the speaker or the hearer who is/are to blame. In cases of (ordinary) Successful Communication, the process of comprehension involves at most two sorts of inference: those involved in the process whereby the hearer came to represent (what she took to be) the force and propositional content of the speech she observed; and those inferences (if any) involved in the processes whereby the hearer determined the acceptability of the testimony so construed. Now if the process of comprehension in the McSorley case involved inferences beyond one of these two types, then it might be argued that McSorley can be held responsible for having made these further inferences – in which case she bears part of the blame for having come to acquire a false belief. But it seems doubtful that the process in question did involve any such further inferences. Any alleged inferences McSorley made in the course of recovering the content in question – *that President Bush is in Galveston, Texas, today* – would be implicated in the process by which she recovered (and subsequently assessed) what she took to be the explicit content of Jones' assertion. And yet the recovery and assessment process here was no different from what it would have been had Jones actually asserted what he made-as-if-to-say. That is, even if we agree for the sake of argument that the recovered content was not the one Jones attested to, even so the process by which McSorley recovered that content was no different from what transpires in ordinary, everyday cases of Successful Communication, where the content recovered *is* precisely the content attested to. The result is that even if it is granted for the sake of argument that subcognitive inferences are being made in the process of comprehension,[13] these sub-cognitive inferences are not of the sort that would differentiate the present case from a case involving a hearer recovering the content regarding whose truth the speaker *explicitly gave her word*.

The foregoing establishes that, from the perspective of the process of comprehension, this case is no different from a case in which Jones does give his word to the effect that Bush is in Galveston today. But the verdict I aim to support is that McSorley is *entitled* to so regard Jones. Here the desired entitlement claim is supported, I submit, by reflection on how comprehension mediates between (the hearer's observation of) testimony and (her formation of) reliable testimonial belief. Take a case in which a piece of testimony is (on its literal construal) unreliable. From the per-spective of the hearer's aim to acquire a reliable testimonial belief, it is immaterial whether the unreliability of the testimony on its literal con-strual is owed to the fact that the speaker meant what she said but failed to have the knowledge in question, or because the speaker had the knowl-edge in question but failed to say what she avowedly meant. From the hearer's perspective these come to the same thing: the hearer can't rely on the speaker's word. Either way, such a speaker would fail to be a reliable radical communicator.

We have before us, then, an initial (albeit still superficial) point in defense of the claim that, insofar as our interest is in knowledge transmis-sion through speech, there are good reasons to construe the reliability of testimony in terms of the reliability of testimony *on its literal* (sentence meaning) *construal*. The superficial point is that, given that testimony must be typed by semantic, representational content if it is to be typed the way appropriate to the acquisition of testimonial knowledge, we have reason to type it according to sentence meaning (unless there are positive reasons for not doing so in a particular case – more on which below).

We can deepen this superficial point by noting that there are good, social reasons for construing testimonial reliability in this way. Suppose (with Davidson 1986) that we had to relativize our 'theory of interpreta-tion' to each new speaker we encountered (worse yet: on each occasion),

---

[13] See Recanati (2002) for a discussion of the extent to which the process of linguistic understanding is an inferential affair. This paper is of interest here insofar as it takes place against the backdrop of an interest in knowledge communication.

and that, for the purpose of doing so, we were not entitled to make any assumptions about the language our interlocutor is speaking.[14] In that case, the testimonial spreading of knowledge would be much less efficient, and arguably much less prevalent, than it actually is. It has already been noted that understanding a piece of testimony (in the rather demanding sense involving 'reliable comprehension' of their speech) is a necessary condition on Successful Communication. As a result, to the extent that the requirement of understanding itself places great demands on hearers – as it does on any theory on which a hearer's 'interpretation manual' must be tailored to each individual speaker, and no substantive presumption about the language being spoken is in epistemic order – it will be correspondingly difficult to attain the sort of understanding required by the acquisition of knowledge through another's say-so.

Essentially the same point can be made in terms of the sort of blame to which a speaker is susceptible when she offers testimony. In acquiring beliefs through your testimony, I am relying epistemically on you. In the first instance I am relying on your having reliably gotten things right. But I do not have unmediated access to how you have gotten things, to how you have represented things as being. Instead, I must recover how you represent things as being. I do so, of course, through comprehending your speech. But suppose that your speech does not enable me to recover how you represent things as being, in the following sense: the sentences you use elicit certain characteristic states of comprehension amongst your co-linguals (myself included), where it is often the case that the state attained by your audience does not correctly capture how you have represented things as being on that occasion. On any particular occasion on which this is so, you are far from being the sort of person who can be relied on epistemically. This is not for being unreliable in getting things right, but rather for being unreliable along the dimension whereby you put others in a position to recover how you have gotten things – how you have represented things as being – in the first place.

---

[14] No doubt, we sometimes use our words non-standardly; but to treat this as the kind of case on which to base claims about the nature of the process of interpretation as such strikes me wrongheaded *in the extreme*. Better we should focus on cases of successful R-communication and regard non-standard uses as deviant (and hence to be explained away). See Burge 1999 for an argument against Davidson making a similar claim; but see also Davidson 1999, where he disavows this reading, and Goldberg 2004a, where I give the evidence for thinking that this reading is faithful to the way Davidson originally formulated his method of Radical Interpretation.

Now it is a fact about out interpretational practices that in the ordinary course of events, hearers typically *do* hold speakers to the literal ('face value') interpretation of their words. But this descriptive claim has an epistemic significance. This can be seen in connection with claims from the previous chapter. There it was argued that Successful RC depends on the existence of public linguistic norms, and in particular on the (implicit) reliance on such norms in the processes whereby testimony is both produced by speakers and comprehended by hearers. Now if the practice whereby knowledge is efficiently spread through a community depends on a speaker's having implicitly relied on public linguistic norms, then a speaker who produces the sort of speech act apt for such knowledge transmission, and whose aim is such transmission, has a practical reason to conform in her speech to those norms. Of course, if a hearer aims to acquire knowledge from such a speech act, she too has a practical reason to conform to those norms in her interpretation of that speech. And both sides, it would seem, have practical reasons to reinforce such norms more generally: as speakers we have a practical reason to ensure that the pre-conditions for the efficient spreading of knowledge are in place, as we will want to spread knowledge in the future; and as hearers we have a practical reason to ensure that the preconditions for the efficient attainment of knowledge through speech are in place, as we will want to benefit from the spread of such knowledge. Of course, such practical reasons bear on speakers who violate these preconditions: idiosyncracy in a co-lingual's speech can erode both the efficiency and the prevalence of knowledge communication.

At the very least, then, our practical interests in participating in the practice whereby knowledge is spread through speech – an interest shared by all, since epistemic impoverishment awaits those who do not so parti-cipate – rationalize the move to interpret others' words at face value. In saying that our practical interests 'rationalize' this move, I do not mean that these interests give hearers the reasons they themselves would cite in defense of their move to interpret co-linguals' speech at face value. For whether or not a hearer would cite these reasons, they form the basis of a proper theoretical account of how Successful Communication can be as widespread and efficient as it is. Ordinary hearers need not formulate this account for themselves in order for their interpretational practices to be rationalized in this way. (Insisting that they do is tantamount to inviting skepticism about the justification with which we interpret and compre-hend each other at face value.) At the same time, ordinary hearers may well implicitly grasp these considerations. After all, such an implicit grasp might well explain why it is that hearers react in very characteristic and systematic ways when it is revealed that a given sincere speaker did not mean what she made-as-if-to-say, on a given occasion when others relied on her epistemically. In such cases blame will invariably be placed on the speaker. My claim is that this is appropriate – that the hearer is *entitled* to impose community standards in her interpretation of others' speech – since the standard against which the speaker is being assessed is one required for the practice whereby knowledge is efficiently spread through speech.

I conclude, then, that hearers are (presumptively but defeasibly) entitled to hold speakers to the 'face value' interpretation of their words. This entitlement is *presumptive*, in that, absent determinate reasons bearing on the correct interpretation of a given speech act by an apparent co-lingual, the hearer is entitled to interpret the speech act in a way that maximizes the chances of Successful Communication – such communication being central to the role language plays in our life more generally.[15] At the same time, the presumption is *defeasible* in that speakers can 'opt out' on occasion; but given the positive presumption of face value interpretations, a speaker who 'opts out' must make manifest her intention in this regard, if she aims to avoid the sort of blame associated with having given her word.

I conclude, then, that it is the 'face value' interpretation of another's words that determines the content regarding which the hearer is entitled to regard her as having given her word. But the 'face value' interpretation is the interpretation yielded by the relevant norms of the public language. So there must be such norms if we are to have a adequate account of the "blame game" in cases of unsuccessful communication owing to misunderstanding.

---

[15] Of course, this presumption will bear on the interpretation of speech acts not aiming to communicate knowledge, at least insofar as language used for other aims must be seamlessly interwoven into a linguistic practice one of whose central aims is the communication of knowledge.

4

From public linguistic norms to anti-individualism regarding language and thought

4.1 OVERVIEW OF THE ARGUMENT

In the present chapter, my aim is to use the results of the previous two chapters to argue for three anti-individualistic doctrines in the philosophy of mind and language. These doctrines express anti-individualistic theses regarding speech content, linguistic meaning, and mental content/attitude individuation.[1] The arguments themselves all share their basic structure: appealing to a thought experiment in which we vary the public linguistic norms in play while leaving intact all individualistic facts regarding the participants in a speech exchange, it is argued that these three properties – the content of the speech, the linguistic meanings of the expressions used, and the contents of the beliefs acquired in the exchange – will vary in a way reflecting the change in public linguistic norms. The result, of course, will be that the instantiation of the determinate properties in question is not fixed by the individualistic facts regarding the participants in a speech exchange. The facts regarding speech content etc. do not supervene on the set of individualistic facts regarding the speaker and hearer, respectively. (Putting the point in terms of supervenience connects our result with the standard way of formulating anti-individualistic doctrines.)

---

[1] The label 'anti-individualism' is usually associated with a doctrine (owed to Tyler Burge) regarding *attitude individuation* rather than speech content or linguistic meaning: it is the doctrine that "the mental natures of many of an individual's mental states and events are dependent for their individuation on the individual's social and physical environments" (Burge 1986: 697). I will be offering an argument for attitude AI; but, as the theses for which I will be arguing in connection with speech content and linguistic meaning are very much in the spirit of Burge's work, I label these doctrines 'anti-individualist' as well.

This sort of argument for anti-individualism will be familiar to readers of Putnam and Burge. But it is worth highlighting what I see are the three main differences.

First, the present argument motivates its anti-individualistic conclusions without appeal to the various premises used by Putnam and Burge. Their arguments have appealed – or, more neutrally, have typically been taken (by commentators) to appeal – to one or another premise regarding the semantics of speech- or attitude-individuation (Putnam 1975;[2] arguably Burge 1979),[3] the objectivity of perception (Burge 1986b and 1988), the possibility of non-standard theorizing (Burge 1986), or the possibility of incomplete grasp (Burge 1989). The present argument makes no use of considerations of these sorts. Rather, it appeals to what I argued in chapters 2 and 3 are the presuppositions of knowledge communication.[4]

Second and relatedly. Not only does the present argument avoid using considerations regarding the semantics of speech- or attitude-reports, or the possibility of incomplete grasp or non-standard theorizing; what is

---

[2] Arguably, Putnam's reflections on the division of linguistic labor establish an anti-individualism regarding linguistic meaning. The matter is vexed, however, by Putnam's 1975 appeal to a demonstrative component in reference-fixation. (This affects Putnam's account of linguistic meaning as, on his 1975 view, differences of reference make for differences of meaning.) However, Putnam recants in his 1996, making clear that he came to view as a mistake his earlier allegiance to the demonstrative analysis. In any case, since my main aim is not Putnam exegesis, I will leave this matter off to the side.

[3] Burge's (1979) argument has also struck many readers as appealing to one or another doctrine regarding the semantics of attitude-reports, although Burge has been at pains to deny that it does – even as he acknowledges that some of his formulations (see for example his 1979: 538) were misleading in precisely this way (see Burge 2003: 436–38; see also Goldberg 2002a). People who have read Burge in this way include Bach 1988, Loar 1988, Patterson 1990, Elugardo 1993, McKinsey 1994 and 1999, Ebbs 1997, and Jackson 2005.

[4] The argument that I am offering for this bears some interesting similarities with the argument in Gauker 1994, chapter 3 (an early version of which was Gauker 1991). Gauker's focus is slightly different in its aim. In particular, Gauker 1994 is taking aim at what he called the Lockean theory of communication (on which our utterances are taken to express some mental object distinct from the speaker's words), whereas I am taking aim at individualistic accounts of speech content and linguistic meaning. In addition, Gauker makes his argument in connection with the effect of speech acts on a hearer's having *practical reasons* to do certain things, whereas my focus is on the effect of speech acts on a hearer's acquisition of a certain distinctive kind of knowledge – testimonial knowledge. This said, I should say that my central thesis, that anything other than an anti-individualistic account of speech content will be unable to explain how the phenomenon of testimonial knowledge transmission has the features we take it to have, bears a close resemblance to Gauker's central thesis, that anything other than an anti-individualistic account of speech content will render the epistemic division of labor inexplicable or otherwise irrational. (I take my account of the nature of testimonial knowledge to be an account of the relevant aspects of what Gauker calls the epistemic division of labor.)

more, it suggests that the role of these considerations in the case for AI is actually derivative. In particular, whatever support these considerations give to AI, this support derives from considerations relating to the conditions on the spread of knowledge through speech. Thus I will be arguing that anti-individualistic intuitions regarding reported speech (which, as we will see, are widely shared even among the critics of AI) are sensitive to what a hearer can come to know through observing the speech act being reported; and that anti-individualistic intuitions regarding the phenomena of incomplete grasp and non-standard theorizing can be taken to reflect an implicit recognition that the semantic conditions on acquiring testimonial knowledge are liberal, as they allow that a hearer can count as having 'understood' testimony in the required sense even when she does not completely grasp all of the concepts in the attested content (and even when she has a non-standard theory of the subject-matter in question).

Third, the present argument makes clear that the cost of rejecting anti-individualism is greater than what the traditional arguments would suggest. The traditional arguments for AI make clear that there are at least two costs associated with rejecting AI: opponents of AI must reject a certain (*de dicto*) account of the semantics of speech- and attitude-reports; and opponents of AI must also come up with an individualistic account of perceptual content. But both of these are costs many critics of AI appear ready to bear: in connection with the costs incurred in connection with the semantics of speech- and attitude-reports, see Bach 1988 and 1997a; Loar 1988; Patterson 1990; McKinsey 1994 and 1999; and Jackson 2005; and in connection with the costs pertaining to perceptual content, see Segal 1989; Egan 1991; 1992, 1995; and 1999; and Morton 1993 (but see also Shagrir 2001 for a critical discussion). Here I claim that there is an additional, heretofore unacknowledged cost of rejecting AI: opponents of AI must reject the only plausible account we have of communication as we (take ourselves to) know it. At the very least, individualists have more explaining to do.

4.2 OUTLINE OF THE ARGUMENT

The argument I will be giving has various premises and conclusions. I begin by making these explicit.

Premise 1. There are two possible worlds, w (with speaker S and hearer H) and $w^\star$ (with speaker $S^\star$ and hearer $H^\star$), where the only difference in the instantiated (non-haecceitic) properties in w and $w^\star$ concerns the public linguistic norms in play (and those properties whose individuation depends on such norms). In particular, S and $S^\star$ instantiate the same individualistic (non-relational) properties, as do H and $H^\star$.

Premise 2. If (i) S assertorically utters U and $S^\star$ assertorically utters $U^\star$, (ii) U and $U^\star$ are utterances of the same form of words (morphologically individuated), (iii) there are no semantically context-sensitive expressions involved in either form of words,[5] (iv) the norms governing S's utterance differ from those governing $S^\star$'s utterance, and (v) both S and $S^\star$ intend their words to be taken at face value, then the content asserted by S differs from the content asserted by $S^\star$.

Conclusion 1. (Therefore) Speech content does not supervene on the individualistic facts regarding the speaker [*Anti-individualism regarding speech content, AI–S*].

Premise 3. Speech content is exhaustively determined by (a) the linguistic meaning of the sentence uttered and (b) relevant contextually supplied values, where these are determined by (b1) reference assignment to semantically context-sensitive expressions used and (b2) more broadly pragmatic considerations (if any) relevant to the propositional (truth conditional) content of the speech act.

Premise 4. But there are no indexical or other more broadly pragmatic differences between U and $U^\star$ that can account for the difference in their respective speech contents.

Conclusion 2. (Therefore) The linguistic meaning of the sentences uttered in U and $U^\star$ differs.

Conclusion 3. (Therefore) Linguistic meaning does not supervene on the individualistic facts regarding the speaker [*Anti-individualism regarding linguistic meaning, AI–M*].

Premise 5. If (i) on occasion O speaker S knowledgeably asserts p (where p is the content asserted), (ii) hearer H understands (in the sense of *reliably comprehends*) S's testimony on O, (iii) H is epistemically entitled to rely on S's word on O, and (iv) H accepts this testimony on the basis of (ii) and (iii), then H comes to know p through the testimony she accepted (where p is the content that is testimonially known).

---

[5] The point of condition (iii), asserting that no semantically context-sensitive expressions figure in the sentences asserted, is not actually needed at this point in the argument, but its satisfaction here simplifies the transitions made later in the argument.

Premise 6. S and H, and $S^\star$ and $H^\star$, respectively, satisfy each of (i)–(iv).

Conclusion 4. (Therefore) H and $H^\star$ thereby come to know different things – p and $p^\star$, say.

Premise 7. Knowledge of p (where p is the content known) entails belief in p (where p is the content believed).

Conclusion 5. (Therefore) H and $H^\star$ believe different things. (Alternative formulation: their beliefs differ in their contents.)

Conclusion 6. (Therefore) Psychological properties such as *believing that p* do not supervene on the individualistic facts regarding the subject. (Alternative formulation: the mental contents of an individual subject's attitudes do not supervene on individualistic facts regarding the subject.) [*Anti-individualism regarding the attitudes, AI–A*].

The three conclusions that interest us, of course, are Conclusions 1, 3, and 6. Several comments about this argument are in order.

First, it is worth noting that the foregoing argument does not make any appeal whatsoever to subjects' ignorance or otherwise incomplete knowledge of the application conditions of the concepts figuring in their thoughts – considerations typically taken to be central to the case for anti-individualism. At the same time (and as I will argue in section 4.11 below), the argument would lead us to expect that (and explain why) such ignorance or incomplete knowledge is wide-spread. In this way the present makes good sense of, but does not itself rely on, a phenomenon long noted by anti-individualistic theorists.

Second, it might be wondered why the argument runs through testimonial knowledge. Couldn't the same argument be given without any appeal to the epistemic dimension of communication at all? The answer is that it cannot, since that dimension plays a key, if implicit, role in the argument. It is worth making this clear at the outset. My argument will turn on the idea that communication involves the hearer's coming to believe *the very content* expressed in the speaker's testimony. Having established this, the case for AI–A will be quick indeed. The result is that opponents of AI–A will be under some pressure to deny the claim that communication is (typically) content-preserving; and, correspondingly, my argument will be under some pressure to provide a compelling motivation for that claim. It is this that is provided by the argument's epistemic orientation.

In this regard it is worth noting that, when it comes to what can be *believed* in communication cases, there would seem to be no principled reason to hold that communication is (typically, and perhaps paradigmatically) content-preserving. To be sure, we might try to defend the content-preservingness thesis by insisting that communication involves the acceptance of another's speech contribution, where what is 'accepted' is the very content attested to. However, those who wish to resist the content-preservingness thesis could respond that it is simply question-begging to assume that communication involves acceptance in this sense. And in addition they might question whether all cases of accepting another's speech contribution are cases of accepting the content attested to. (Suppose *H*, a monolingual English speaker, knows that *S* is a highly reliable monolingual Greek mathematician who is presently asserting mathematical claims. Arguably *H* could accept *S*'s speech contributions, in the sense of regarding *S*'s say-so, *whatever it amounted to*, as true – despite the fact that *H* does not know what propositions *S* is expressing.) This suggests that the content-preservingness of communication cannot be established merely by appeal to the notion of acceptance and its role in communication.

However, once we introduce the epistemic dimension, there is a straightforward case for the thesis that, for at least one subdomain of communication (that bound up in the practice of knowledge transmission), communication is content-preserving. As I have characterized it in chapter 1, testimonial knowledge is that unique sort of knowledge grounded on hearer *H*'s epistemic reliance on speaker *S* to have reliably gotten things right,[6] where *H*'s entitlement to rely on *S* in this way *ipso facto* entitles *H* to regard *S* as in an epistemically privileged position regarding the truth of the very content *H* herself came to believe through that reliance, and where this has the added effect that, in happy cases, there is a characteristic expansion in the epistemic support enjoyed by *H*'s belief. But, as I also argued in chapter 1 (and in greater detail in chapters 2 and 3), there is a semantic condition on this sort of knowledge: to acquire this unique sort of knowledge, one must have reliably comprehended (and then subsquently have come to believe) *the very content attested to*. If this is correct then the hypothesis of content-preservingness is as strong as the hypothesis that there are cases of the sort of knowledge I have been calling 'testimonial knowledge.' Equivalently, a denial of the content-preserving nature of communication is at the same time a denial

---

[6] Here I disregard the complication I introduced there in order to accommodate cases in which the hearer accepts the testimony only after having "repaired" the epistemic defects in the testimony.

of the prevalence, and arguably even the existence, of knowledge of this sort. This is the key advantage of giving the argument an epistemological orientation. (In addition, running the argument in this way makes clear that the cost of rejecting AI–A is much greater than even its proponents suppose.)

One final comment about the argument is in order. There is an intriguing symmetry of sorts in the argument. As presented above, the argument runs, from claims regarding speech content, to claims regarding knowledge (and from there to claims regarding belief). It is *because* S and $S^\star$ asserted different things (p and $p^\star$, respectively), that H and $H^\star$ came to know (and hence to believe) different things (again, p and $p^\star$, respectively). But there might be an argumentative strategy that reverses this order, one that begins with claims about knowledge, and which uses these to establish claims about speech content (and linguistic meaning). Thus suppose that we had strong intuitions in two cases that the hearers – say, H and $H^\star$ – acquired knowledge of different things, where there is no question but that they came to acquire the knowledge in question through the testimony each observed and accepted. Then we might infer, from this difference in the pieces of knowledge the two hearers acquired, a conclusion asserting a difference in the speech content of the respective testimonies they observed. Of course, such an argument would provide an independent argument for its conclusion only if the original intuitions regarding differences in what the hearers came to know were themselves independent of intuitions regarding the content of the testimonies they observed. But so long as this condition is met, we have an argument, from descriptions of what hearers came to know, to descriptions of the content of the testimonies they observed.[7] I will be returning to the possibility of this sort of 'inverted' argument at the end of section 4.9, below.

In what follows I will defend each premise in turn, as well as the conclusions that I draw from them.

4.3 IN DEFENSE OF PREMISE I

Premise 1 is a possibility claim. It claims that there are two possible worlds, w (with speaker S and hearer H) and $w^\star$ (with speaker $S^\star$ and hearer $H^\star$), which differ (other than in the individuals each contains) only in the public

---

[7] Compare Evans (1982: 310–11).

linguistic norms in play (as well as in those properties whose individuation depends on such norms). However, the claim that these worlds are alike save for the difference in public linguistic norms is actually stronger than the claim required for the argument. The claim required for the argument is that, despite the difference in public linguistic norms, the speakers S and $S^\star$ instantiate the same individualistic (non-relational) properties, as do the hearers H and $H^\star$. As such it depends only on the idea that public linguistic norms can be varied even as we hold fixed the individualistic facts regarding a speaker and hearer.

To illustrate, consider the following, modeled on an example from Burge 1986. There are two worlds, w and $w^\star$, which are alike except for the following curious difference: in one of them, w, the norms regarding 'sofa' (as this word-form is used by a particular community in w) is such that the term correctly applies to all and only overstuffed pieces of furniture made for the purpose of seating two or more people, whereas in the other, $w^\star$, the norms regarding 'sofa' (as this word-form is used by a particular community in $w^\star$) are such that the term correctly applies to all and only religious artifacts of a certain kind. By strange coincidence, instances of the kinds in question look exactly alike: the religious artifacts – the objects that constitute the extension of 'sofa' as used by denizens of $w^\star$ – have all of the outward appearances of overstuffed pieces of furniture made for the purpose of seating two or more people – the objects that constitute the extension of 'sofa' as used by denizens of w. Next we can imagine individualistically type-identical speaker–hearer pairs in both worlds – Ethan and Nadia in w, Ethan* and Nadia* in $w^\star$. We will suppose that the hearers in these pairs – Nadia and Nadia* – are familiar with the items referred to by their co-linguals as 'sofas': each can discriminate these items from among other things, each expresses her empirical beliefs about the items in question by using 'sofa' in sentences that are taken by her co-linguals to be linguistically unexceptional, and so forth. However, neither Nadia nor Nadia* has ever once sat on one of the items in question, and neither is disposed to do so. This is because both endorse an unusual strain in the moral thinking of her community, according to which it a moral duty not to sit on the items in question. (The reason for this stipulation will emerge below.)

Now suppose that on w Ethan is speaking to Nadia, and that he tells her that sofas are less common than chairs. That is, Ethan assertorically utters the English sentence, "Sofas are less common than chairs." And suppose that on $w^\star$, Ethan* assertorically utters the sentence, "Sofas are less common than chairs," and that he does so in the presence of Nadia★. Premise 1 merely asserts that such a scenario is possible. That is, the fact that Ethan and Ethan★, and Nadia and Nadia★, respectively, are type-identical in all of the non-relational properties they instantiate, is compatible with the difference in norms on w and $w^★$ regarding the proper use of 'sofa.' I take it that this is not a controversial claim.

4.4 IN DEFENSE OF PREMISE 2

Premise 2 advances a sufficient condition on differences of speech content. It implies that in cases like that of Ethan–Nadia and Ethan★–Nadia★, the content asserted by Ethan would differ from that asserted by Ethan★. Interestingly, Premise 2 may well be stronger than what the argument actually requires: its antecedent condition (v), regarding intentions to be interpreted at face value, may be stronger than is needed. In light of my argument from chapter 3 regarding the positive-presumptiveness of face value interpretations, (v) could be replaced with

(v★) Neither S nor $S^★$ has done anything to suggest that they are not to be interpreted at face value.

The point here is that one need not have formed an explicit intention to be interpreted at face value; it suffices, if one is to be interpreted at face value, that one has done nothing to suggest that one is not to be so interpreted. (See chapter 3, section 3.4.) In any case, I will stick with (v), since at worst it is overkill.

To see the plausibility of Premise 2, then, we can reason about the case involving Ethan and Ethan★. (Since nothing will hang on the details of this case, the point we will be making will be perfectly general.) Ethan and Ethan★ both assertorically assert "Sofas are less common than chairs," and both intend to be interpreted at face value (expressing this via utterances of 'I intend to be interpreted at face value'). The case for Premise 2, then, can be clinched by showing that the face value interpretation for each differs. And what needs to be shown here follows from a claim for which I have already argued in chapters 2 and 3: public linguistic norms determine the face value interpretation of the words used. Premise 2 holds.

The truth of Premises 1 and 2 entails the following possibility. Two intrinsically indistinguishable speakers, alike with respect to their individualistic properties, might nevertheless count as having asserted different contents, for being members of linguistic communities with different public linguistic norms. This, of course, amounts to an anti-supervenience thesis: speech content does not supervene on the individualistic facts regarding a speaker. In short, *anti-individualism regarding speech content*, AI–S.[8]

Premise 3 advances a claim about the role of linguistic meaning in the determination of speech content. It claims that speech content is exhaustively determined by (a) the linguistic meaning of the sentence uttered and (b) the contextually supplied values as determined by (b1) the semantically context-sensitive expressions used[9] and (b2) more broadly pragmatic considerations, if any, relevant to the propositional (truth conditional) content of the speech act. This claim should be uncontroversial, as it is merely identifies the various possible determinants of speech content while remaining silent on their respective contributions.

It is important that Premise 3 is neutral on the respective contributions, since there are indeed important controversies regarding the respective contributions of the various determinants of speech content. For example, does meaning merely constrain the set of candidate propositions that might be expressed by speaker's utterance, or is meaning's role more substantive than that of a constraint? We might wonder, too, about the scope of what

---

[8] The foregoing argument might be thought to be committed to the doctrine of incomplete grasp. For if Ethan and Ethan★ are intrinsic duplicates despite the fact that each asserts something different with their respective 'sofa'-utterances, this can only be because neither one has an explicit (non-trivial) mental representation of the application conditions of the 'sofa'-concept she expressed. And this is just to say that both exhibit an incomplete grasp of their own 'sofa'-concept – and this, despite my advertising the argument as one not relying on the phenomenon of incomplete grasp. Against this, however, it should be noted that the argument could easily be recast so as not to depend on this phenomenon. Let Ethan and Ethan★ each have exhaustive knowledge regarding the application conditions of their respective 'sofa'-concepts. Even so, since Nadia and Nadia★ reliably comprehend the respective reports each observes – I will argue below that one denies this at the cost of holding Successful Communication hostage to a requirement of complete grasp – the result is that Nadia and Nadia★ each acquire a belief involving a concept only incompletely grasped. Only in this case the doctrine of incomplete grasp is not something that the argument needs to *assume*, but rather an *implication* of the argument. (Then we can run the argument again using Nadia and Nadia★ as the speakers – both go on to assert their new knowledge – and hearers who, like them, satisfy the conditions on reliable comprehension without complete grasp of the respective 'sofa'-content.)

[9] Roughly put, we can say that an expression is *semantically context-sensitive* just in case its semantic value – that is, its contribution to the propositional, truth-conditional content expressed by sentences containing that expression – can systematically vary by context of use.

111

I am calling more 'broadly pragmatic' considerations relevant to speech content. Is there more to speech content – something that must determine the truth conditions for an assertoric utterance – than linguistic meaning plus reference assignment to semantically context-sensitive expressions such as indexicals and other demonstratives? This is a very large question, and one regarding which there is little consensus in the philosophy of language community.[10] But Premise 3 is neutral on these matters: it merely points out that speech content is exhaustively determined by linguistic meaning, reference assignment to semantically context-sensitive expressions, plus whatever widely pragmatic considerations are relevant[11] – it being left to the side whether there are such widely pragmatic considerations that are relevant, and if so, what they are.

4.6 IN DEFENSE OF PREMISE 4

Whereas Premise 3 was unproblematic because it provides a merely schematic distinction between the three major determinants of truth conditional content, Premise 4 is slightly more controversial in that it assumes how these determinants can be factored in particular cases. It claims that in at least some cases, differences of asserted content can be uniquely traced to differences in linguistic meaning. At the same time, endorsing Premise 4 need not be controversial, so long as we have plausible ways to rule out differences along the other two dimensions (context-driven reference assignment to semantically context-sensitive expressions, and more broadly pragmatic considerations).

In the cases of Ethan and Ethan*, we do indeed have plausible ways to rule out differences along these dimensions. Consider the dimension of reference-assignment to semantically context-sensitive expressions. Since the only relevant difference between the sentence that Ethan utters and the one Ethan* utters pertains to each's use of 'sofa', we can restrict ourselves to that word-form, as it was used by each. And I submit that it is not the case that 'sofa' is context-sensitive in either Ethan's or Ethan*'s mouth. Some might be tempted to deny this. But, as many (including Burge himself) have pointed out, denying this flies in the face of the

---

[10] For an affirmative answer, see Sperber and Wilson 1986; Recanati 1989; Bach 1994 and 1997b; Bezuidenhout 1997 and 1998; Wilson and Sperber 2002 (see especially 605–13); Carston 1988 and 2002. For a negative answer, see Stanley 2000 and 2002.

[11] I borrow the notion of 'narrow' vs. 'wide' pragmatic processing from Bach 1997b.

semantic data: uses of 'sofa' do not exhibit the sort of context-sensitive variation in semantic value[12] that uses of 'I' or 'now' do. (See Burge 1982a.)[13] Consider next whether there is any broadly pragmatic difference between Ethan's and Ethan★'s utterance which would affect the truth conditional content of the respective speech acts themselves. (There may well be pragmatic differences whereby the set of contents that Ethan's utterance communicates to his hearers differs from the set of contents that Ethan★'s utterance communicates to *his* hearers. These are irrelevant to the present issue, which pertains to the *truth conditional content* of their respective utterances; broadly pragmatic differences are relevant only if they affect such contents.) But the hypothesis of a difference of a broadly pragmatic sort that affects the truth conditions of their respective utterances would appear to be ruled out by the fact that the respective pairs – Ethan and Ethan★, Nadia and Nadia★ – are dopplegängers. Given that Nadia and Nadia★ are doppelgängers, Nadia has a belief if and only if Nadia★ has what I will call the 'corresponding' belief. The correspondence relation here is that of identity of content save for the ways in which their respective contents incorporate elements from their distinct environments. (This includes differences traceable to public linguistic norms, since such a difference affects each's *linguistic* environment.) Now their environments are alike save for differences pertaining to the difference in public linguistic norms. So unless this difference in public linguistic norms makes for an environmental difference, where the environmental difference itself will alter the context involved, the result will be that there are no relevant broadly pragmatic differences between the cases. What is more, we can stipulate that Nadia and Nadia★ are ignorant that there is a difference between the norms, and that they are otherwise alike as regards their attitudes and behavior towards the relevant objects. (This was the point of having both of them subscribe to the somewhat idiosyncratic moral doctrine regarding the objects in question.) With these points in place, it would appear that there are no relevant differences of context that might make for a difference in the sort of broadly pragmatic considerations relevant to the propositional (truth conditional) content of their respective speech acts.

---

[12] Let the semantic value of an expression on an occasion of use be that expression's contribution to the proposition expressed on that occasion.

[13] The argument convinced Putnam, who in his 1975 regarded his argument as showing that natural kind terms such as 'water' had a hidden indexicality. See Putnam 1996 for his recantation of this view.

I conclude that Premise 4 is true. But if Premises 1–4 are true, then we have the following possible situation: two speakers, alike with respect to all intrinsic (non-relational) features, nevertheless assert two different contents, under conditions in which there are no relevant differences involving semantically context-sensitive expressions or other broadly pragmatic considerations. Given Premise 3, the difference in content asserted is traceable to a difference in linguistic meaning. Given that this difference occurs in a case with intrinsic duplicates as speakers, the result is an anti-supervenience thesis: the linguistic meanings of one's words do not supervene on the individualistic facts regarding the speaker herself. *Anti-individualism regarding linguistic meaning*, AI–M, has been established.

(A side note, for those not convinced by the foregoing. My real interest in this chapter is in establishing anti-individualism regarding attitude-individuation. This conclusion will not depend in any way on anti-individualism regarding linguistic meaning; it depends only on the prior result, anti-individualism regarding speech content. My foray into considerations of linguistic meaning was merely to suggest how considerations pertaining to the conditions on knowledge communication might be used to establish a thesis regarding lexical semantics. I regard the case for such a view to be strong; but as the result I am most anxious to establish does not turn on this, I push on without further ado.)

4.7 IN DEFENSE OF PREMISE 5

Premise 5 makes a claim about knowledge transmission. It states that knowledge is transmitted from S to H when (i) S knowledgeably asserts p, (ii) H understands (that is, reliably comprehends) S's assertion, (iii) H is epistemically entitled to rely on S's word, and (iv) H accepts this assertion on the basis of (ii) and (iii). Such a thesis is neutral on all of the flash-points in the epistemology of testimony. As a sufficient condition pertaining only to those cases where the speaker is knowledgeable, it takes no position on cases in which S does not know whereof she speaks, and so is neutral on the question whether testimony can only transmit pre-existing knowledge or whether it can generate new knowledge. (See chapter 1, section 1.4 for further discussion.) Similarly, it takes no position on the conditions on being entitled to accept another's testimony: it merely specifies that, whatever these conditions come to, their satisfaction is part of a set of jointly sufficient conditions on knowledge transmission. Given that it is entirely schematic, Premise 5 should be eminently acceptable no matter one's background views in the epistemology of testimony.

Premise 5 presents a set of jointly sufficient conditions on knowledge transmission; Premise 6 asserts that all of these conditions are satisfied in both the Ethan/Nadia case, and in the Ethan★/Nadia★ case. This claim will be less controversial with respect to the satisfaction of some of these conditions, than it will for others. But I will take each of the four conditions, (i)–(iv), in turn.

Condition (i) asserts that the testimony in question was knowledgeable. At this point in our argument we have already established that Ethan and Ethan★ (S and S★) have asserted different things, so we need only stipulate, as part of the thought experiment, that both of these assertions are knowledgeable. It follows that condition (i) is satisfied in both cases.

Skipping condition (ii) for the moment – establishing the satisfaction of this condition will be the most controversial part of the present argument – we move on to condition (iii). This condition asserts that each of the hearers, Nadia and Nadia★ (H and H★), is entitled to rely epistemically on the word of the say-so she observes. Again, we can tell the story of the two cases in such a way that this condition holds in both. Suppose that Nadia and Nadia★ both know their respective interlocutors very well, and know in addition that they are very reliable assertors; and imagine as well that the respective assertions of Ethan and Ethan★ are both characterized by the speakers' authoritative tone, confidence, etc. – in short, by the trappings of authoritative testimony. Finally, let us also suppose that both Nadia and Nadia★ are such that, with respect to what each took her respective interlocutor to have asserted, there are no other relevant defeaters for their respective testimony-based beliefs in those contents. (We can imagine this to be so even as we bracket precisely what each takes their respective source testimony to have asserted: for any plausible account of what each took her interlocutor to be asserting, there are no relevant defeaters.) Given this background, it would seem that both Nadia and Nadia★ are entitled to rely epistemically on the testimony each observes. The satisfaction of condition (iii) is thus unproblematic.

Turn then to condition (iv), according to which each accepts the testimony on the basis of the satisfaction of (ii) and (iii). Although I have not yet given an argument for thinking that (ii) is satisfied, the following conditional statement should be uncontroversial: if (ii) is satisfied in both cases, then there is no further problem for imagining these cases so that condition (iv) is satisfied in each as well. (Again, we can build the satisfaction of this condition into the way we tell the story in each of the cases.) In this way we have reduced the burden of establishing Premise 6, to that of establishing that condition (ii) holds with respect to both Nadia and Nadia★. In what follows I want to offer both a positive argument, and a *reductio* argument, for the thesis that the reliable–comprehension condition holds in the cases of both Nadia and Nadia★. (Although the positive argument will appeal to the role of acceptance in communication cases, and although the dialectical strength of this sort of move was questioned in section 4.2, we will see that the *reductio* argument bolsters these claims about acceptance.)

Bracketing for the moment the issue of the *reliability* of Nadia's comprehension, various factors support the hypothesis that Nadia has *correctly* comprehended Ethan's testimony (and the same points hold, *mutatis mutandis*, for Nadia★'s comprehension of Ethan★'s testimony). For one thing, in acquiring a belief through Ethan's testimony, Nadia herself explicitly claims to have "accepted what Ethan said" (or so we can stipulate, as part of the thought experiment). What is more, we can imagine that, were she asked what it was that Ethan said – which, if she did succeed in accepting what Ethan said, will also be what it was that she came to believe – Nadia would respond by using the very same form-of-words that Ethan himself used in the testimony, with the avowed intention to be using these words so as to preserve the content of Ethan's saying. (I hasten to note, though, that as we saw in chapter 2, we should not assume that this intention was part of what Nadia *meant* when she used these words.) These aspects of the semantic dimension of the testimonial exchange make sense only on the hypothesis that Nadia has correctly comprehended Ethan's testimony. Here it is worth pointing the cost of denying this hypothesis. For one thing, one would be committed to an error-theory with respect to Nadia's claim to have accepted what Ethan said.[14] Relatedly, one will have to hold that Nadia's re-use of the word-forms Ethan used, with the explicit intention of preserving the content of Ethan's own use, fails in this task – and this, despite the fact that Nadia and Ethan are co-linguals in the sense that their linguistic exchanges have all

---

[14] Here I am taking "what Ethan said" to designate the propositional content of the saying.

the outward trappings of communication. (Are there any independent reasons supporting such an ungenerous construal?)

Perhaps it will be said in response that the foregoing considerations do not establish that Nadia has correctly comprehended Ethan's testimony. For even if Nadia claims to have accepted what Ethan said, and even if she expresses the content in question by re-using the same sentence-type used by Ethan with the avowed intention to be saying the same thing, even so, perhaps she is merely parroting him – in which case she does not correctly understand his words after all. But this reply would show too much. For in all other relevant respects, Nadia is like many of us. As noted above, regarding the objects referred to as 'sofas' by her peers, she can distinguish them from virtually all other sorts of object; she expresses her empirical beliefs about the items in question by using 'sofa' in sentences that are taken by her co-linguals to be linguistically unexceptional; and so forth. It is true that she cannot articulate in an illuminating way the application conditions for the predicate 'x is a sofa.' But even in this she is like most people: it is typical to accept the say-so of others without being in a position to articulate the application conditions of the predicates used in the sentence(s) uttered by our interlocutor. If the envisaged objection succeeds at showing that Nadia is a mere parrot, then it succeeds at showing that most of us, most of the time, are mere parrots. This is too high a price to pay. (I return to this below.)

I have just defended the hypothesis that Nadia has correctly comprehended Ethan's testimony. Let us now move from the *correctness* to the *reliability* of Nadia's comprehension of Ethan's testimony. The hypothesis that Nadia's comprehension is reliable can be defended by generalizing the considerations supporting the correctness hypothesis. Consider that when one's belief is formed through "accepting another's testimony," the hearer will avow having come to believe what the speaker said. (Nadia is no exception here.) If we take this talk seriously – and I see no reason why we shouldn't – then we can regard the hearer as implicitly using her words with the intention to preserve the content of the testimony she observed.[15] But this supports the general hypothesis that her lexical recycling of the words used by her source speaker succeeds in capturing what the source speaker said, in this *and every other case*. Nadia is no different: regarding the

---

[15] Note that at this point in the dialectic, no problem is generated on the score of the social calibration problem of chapter 2. This is because the content of the testimony is itself determined by public linguistic norms.

content she took Ethan to have asserted, in each and every (non-indexical) case she would express that content via lexical recycling, as informed by a content-preserving intention. But then Nadia would take Ethan to have asserted that *p*, only if Ethan did assert that *p*. And this just is the hypothesis that Nadia's comprehension is reliable. In this way we see that we have some strong positive grounds for thinking that condition (ii) is satisfied in the case of Nadia (and, *mutatis mutandis*, in the case of Nadia★).

It is worth remembering as well that the claim, that condition (ii) is satisfied in the cases of Nadia and Nadia★, has also been supported indirectly, by way of a *reductio* argument. It seems that the only way to resist the hypothesis that Nadia satisfies condition (ii) is by appeal to the idea that Nadia doesn't *completely understand* Ethan's testimony. The claim might be that, absent complete grasp of all of the concepts involved – something that might be manifested by the hearer's ability to articulate (non-trivial) application conditions for the concepts themselves[16] – the hearer does not count as having attained such understanding. And if she doesn't count as having attained such understanding (the objection concludes), she does not reliably comprehend the testimony she observed. But, as noted above, this objection comes as a steep epistemic price. Complete grasp – or at least complete grasp of the concepts expressed in one's public language – is a rare phenomenon indeed. So if complete grasp is required in order to satisfy the reliable comprehension condition, then, since the satisfaction of the reliable comprehension condition is a necessary condition on acquiring testimonial knowledge (as argued in chapter 2 section 2.4), the result is that testimonial knowledge will be correspondingly rare as well. I need not repeat here why this implication is not an attractive one.[17]

To be sure, those who are forced to hold such an unhappy position might try to soften the blow a bit by saying that, even though Nadia and Nadia★ cannot be represented as having acquired *testimonial* knowledge in these cases, still they might have acquired knowledge. But this would appear to be small solace, since in that case the knowledge in question would not have the epistemic features characteristic of testimonial knowledge. So even if the hypothesis of knowledge acquisition can be preserved, the present position has unhappy epistemic implications. I conclude that the case for thinking

---

[16] See Goldberg 2002a for a discussion of the distinction between trivial and non-trivial articulation of a concept's application conditions.

[17] I only note that here is a point at which we see the benefits of pitching the argument in distinctly epistemological terms. See also my comments against the 'hybrid view,' in section 4.10.

that condition (ii) is satisfied in both cases is quite strong. And since I reduced the burden of establishing Premise 6 to that of establishing this very claim, I conclude further that the case for Premise 6 is quite strong as well.

Before moving on to complete my argument for attitude anti-individualism, however, it is worth pausing at this point to draw out one important implication of the argument so far. Given that Nadia and Nadia* are doppelgängers, they instantiate the same non-relational properties. Yet the foregoing argument establishes that they come to know different things through their acceptance of the testimony each observes. But for this very reason, the foregoing argument establishes that there is a difference in how each *comprehends* the testimony she observes. Since Nadia and Nadia* are alike with respect to all non-relational properties, this means that *the state of comprehension itself cannot be understood in non-relational (individualistic) terms*. This is an important corollary of the argument through Premise 6.[18]

<h3 style="text-align:center">4.9 IN DEFENSE OF PREMISE 7</h3>

Premise 7 is the familiar doctrine that knowledge entails belief. More formally – since we want a version of this doctrine to specify the content

---

[18] At this point one final objection may occur to some. If one's comprehension of another's utterances reflects the public linguistic norms in play, then a variant on the evil demon argument could be used to generate a new form of scepticism about content. For if, unbeknownst to one, the evil demon switched the relevant norms, then how one understood one's interlocutor would be affected; and since we could multiply these switching cases, the result would appear to be that one would have lost one's grip on the contents of one's understanding altogether – a skeptical conclusion. But this objection is without warrant. Indeed, there is a substantive literature on what in all relevant respects is essentially the same topic. I refer here to the literature on so-called world-switching cases, presented as objections to anti-individualist approaches to the mind. (Relevant papers include Burge 1987, 1996, and 1998; Brueckner 1997; Boghossian 1989; Falvey and Owens 1994; Gibbons 1996; Goldberg 1997; Heal 1998; Ludlow 1995; McLaughlin and Tye 1998; Tye 1998; and Warfield 1995.) In such cases, an Earthian subject is unwittingly world-switched to Twin Earth, in a way that is parallel in all relevant respects to the evil demon case in which the norms of one's language are 'switched' without one's knowledge. Now in response it has been widely noted (by those defending anti-individualism) that switching by itself will not shift the contents of the subject's mental states – to get a shift one needs extensive history in the new locale (or with the new norms). (For my own comments on how world-switching affects one's semantics, see Goldberg 2005c; but see also Goldberg 1999, 2000b, 2003a, 2007a, and 2007c, where I have also talked about the 'semantics of switching'.) In any case, since the worry assumes that a mere shift in linguistic norms makes for a content-shift, it is groundless.

of the belief entailed by knowledge – it states that knowledge of p (where p is the content known) entails belief in p (where p is the content believed). Two things can be said in defense of Premise 7. First, it is eminently plausible, and has been assumed by most people in epistemology. While there are those who have denied this view, the examples proffered are all a bit strained. In any case – and this is the second point – Premise 7 is actually stronger than what the argument needs. What the argument needs is simply that, *in the case described in the thought experiment*, the subjects believe the content that they came to know through their sources' testimony. And indeed this much can be built into the thought experiment itself: we need only stipulate that the thought experiment does not involve the sort of strained cases that some epistemologists have used to call into question whether knowledge entails belief.

Of course, if Nadia and Nadia★ do believe what they came to know through the respective testimonies each observed, then they believe different things: Nadia believes p, whereas Nadia★ believes p★. This is to say that these beliefs differ in content. But it is part of the thought experiment that Nadia and Nadia★ are doppelgängers: they do not differ in any of their individualistic (non-relational) properties. The result is our last anti-supervenience thesis: mental contents do not supervene on the individualistic facts regarding the subject. Mental contents can vary, even as we hold fixed the individualistic properties of a subject. Alternatively, we might formulate our anti-supervenience thesis in terms of the individuation of the attitudes: the instantiation of particular attitudes – in this case, believing that p (equally: believing that p★) – does not supervene on the individualistic facts regarding the subject. Fixing these individualistic facts does not determine whether a subject instantiates the property of *believing that p* (as opposed to *believing that p★*). In short, we have *anti-individualism regarding mental contents and attitude individuation*, AI–A.

4.10 CAN THE HYBRID VIEW BE USED TO RESIST ATTITUDE ANTI-INDIVIDUALISM?[19]

Can the foregoing argument for attitude anti-individualism be resisted by endorsing a 'hybrid' view on which we treat the level of language differently than we do the level of thought? The sort of hybrid view I have in mind is one which combines an anti-individualist position regarding

---

[19] I thank Nick Zangwill for raising this issue.

language (speech content and linguistic meaning) with an individualist position regarding mental content. The hybrid view is worth considering for two reasons. First, it has been endorsed in print by several people, including some of those who have contributed to the debate on individualism and anti-individualism (Loar 1988; Patterson 1990; Elugardo 1993; McKinsey 1994 and 1999; Bach 1988 and 1997a; Byrne and Thau 1995). But second, the hybrid view holds out the prospect of a middle position – one that can concede that Ethan's and Ethan★'s respective assertions assert different things, while denying that Nadia and Nadia★ succeed at coming to know different things through their 'acceptance' of these testimonies. As others have argued against such 'hybrid' views elsewhere (for an example, see Heck 1995, 1996), here I will restrict myself to indicating the costs of endorsing such a hybrid view in connection with the domain of communication.

A first cost is this. The hybrid view will be committed to holding the following unhappy combination: while a person's knowledgeable testimony puts a hearer who understands the testimony in a position to know the attested content, hearers rarely succeed in acquiring the knowledge in question. To bring this out, let us say that a person 'is in a position to know p (at time t)' when the following two conditions hold: first, she does not (at t) believe that p; but second, given her actual belief-forming mechanisms, there is a route to believing p which is such that if (holding everything else about her cognitive situation at t fixed) she forms the belief that p through the relevant route, she would satisfy all of the conditions on knowing p. In the case in which the knowledge in question is testimonial, the route in question is via the testimony. To be in a position to know p through testimony, the hearer's situation must be such that (a) she observed what was in fact a reliable piece of testimony, (b) she attained a reliable comprehension of the testimony she observed, and (c) were she to accept the testimony, she would do so on the basis of a reliable capacity to discriminate reliable from unreliable testimony. We might add for good measure that the hearer must be entitled to regard the speaker's testimony as reliable.

Now the hybrid view will deny that Nadia and Nadia★ succeed at coming to know different things through their respective reactions to the testimonies each observes. For, given the hybrid view, the fact that Nadia and Nadia★ are doppelgangers ensures that they are mental duplicates. So even if they each 'accept' the respective testimonies they observe, in the sense that each forms a belief in the content she takes to have been asserted in that testimony, even so, their status as mental duplicates, together with the claim that Ethan and Ethan★ asserted different things, ensures that neither Nadia nor Nadia★ has succeeded at coming to believe the content expressed in her interlocutor's testimony. But if neither Nadia nor Nadia★ has succeeded at coming to believe the content expressed in her interlocutor's testimony, then neither has succeeded at coming to know that content. This leaves the proponent of the hybrid view with no choice but to deny that Nadia and Nadia★ can attain a reliable comprehension of the respective testimonies each observes: as long as they are mental duplicates, reliable comprehension of these testimonies is out of the question. I have already argued that such a result is unhappy on its face.

What is more, this result leads to other unhappy implications. We just saw that the hybrid view will deny that reliable comprehension is out of the question in the cases of Nadia and Nadia★. At the same time, the proponent of the hybrid view will want to soften the blow by granting that Nadia can re-express the content in question *in her speech*. (The idea is that, though Nadia can't mentally represent the content of Ethan's statement, she can make the same statement, given that she speaks the same language.) But this position is unhappy. For – putting the two claims together – the hybrid view would then hold that Nadia does not reliably comprehend *her own statement*. Stronger still, it holds Nadia *cannot* do so while still remaining a physical duplicate of Nadia★. In this way the hybrid view appears to have worked itself into a curious position, concluding (as it must) that cases are possible in which a speaker cannot represent the semantic features of her own speech, and so cannot think what she can say!

Still other unhappy implications follow. For one thing, it would now seem that a dilemma awaits the proponent of the hybrid view. Either it is denied that there are ever cases of Successful Communication (in which the content that the hearer comes to know is the very content reliably attested to), or it is allowed that there are such cases. I have already argued that the first horn is deeply implausible on its face (see chapter 2). But it is unclear whether the proponent of the hybrid view can endorse the second horn. To do so is to allow that hearers sometimes succeed at coming to know (through the testimony) the very thing attested to in the testimony. But then we can ask: under what conditions does this transpire? In answering this, the proponent of the hybrid view must keep in mind that any case involving a hearer coming to know (through testimony) the very thing attested in the testimony will be a case in which the hearer reliably comprehended – and so was in a position to mentally represent – the content of the testimony itself. So in attempting to answer the question just raised, the hybrid theorist faces pressure from two distinct sources. On the one hand, the answer will have to make the conditions (on content-preserving, knowledge-transmitting communication) demanding enough so that it is impossible for internal duplicates to come to know different things through accepting different (internally indistinguishable but content-distinct) testimonies; but, on the other, the answer ought to avoid making these conditions so demanding that normal human beings rarely satisfy them. I don't have a knock-down argument for thinking that there is no independently plausible way to meet these two conditions simultaneously; I merely note that doing so will be difficult at best.

And there is yet another related difficulty that a hybrid view faces in connection with communication. Given that reliable comprehension is a necessary condition on testimonial knowledge, the hybrid view's implication, to the effect that most people will not attain such comprehension, implies in its turn that most people will not attain the unique sort of knowledge I characterized in chapter 1. Perhaps the proponent of the hybrid view can preserve the idea that in such cases the hearer does come to acquire a piece of knowledge through her understanding of the speech she observed; but even assuming that this could be shown, the knowledge which (according to the hybrid view's reconstruction) the hearer would then have attained will not have the trappings of knowledge through testimony.

It would appear, then, that the hybrid view has some deeply revisionary epistemic implications in connection with the communication of knowledge. (Compare Heck 1995 and 1996.) Those who are antecedently convinced of the truth of the hybrid view may not be convinced by such considerations to abandon the view; but these considerations ought to sway those not already committed, against the hybrid view.

4.11 THE UNIQUENESS OF THE COMMUNICATION-BASED ARGUMENT FOR AI-A

This officially concludes my argument, from the conditions on knowledge communication, for anti-individualism about the attitudes. However, it is my sense that the virtues of the argument are not fully appreciated if our attention is restricted to the argument itself. For part of what makes this argument worth taking seriously, I submit, is the way that it differs from traditional arguments for anti-individualism. In this section I focus on these differences.

It is clear that the argument I have used to establish the various anti-individualistic theses borrows from the sort of thought experiment that Burge used to motivate AI–A. However, we use the thought experiment to highlight different things. For Burge, a key consideration in the case for AI–A is that human speakers exhibit a high degree of semantic deference to (some subset of) our co-linguals. Indeed, some of Burge's most familiar arguments for AI–A, and especially his 1979 and his 1986, appeal either explicitly or implicitly to the phenomenon of semantic deference. The foregoing argument makes no such appeal.

What is more, the foregoing argument highlights that the phenomenon of semantic deference is itself to be traced to our epistemic reliance on others: human speakers exhibit a high degree of semantic deference to (some subset of) our co-linguals *precisely because we exhibit a high degree of epistemic reliance on the say-so of our co-linguals*. It is because each of us relies pervasively on others for what we *know* of the world, that each of us relies on (a subset of) others for the proper explication of the concepts figuring in *what* we know of the world.

We can bring this out in two steps.

The first step involves noting what is required, in order to acquire testimonial knowledge, in the way of understanding the testimony. I have formulated the relevant condition as requiring *reliable comprehension*. To satisfy this condition, it suffices that the process generating one's representations of the (force and) contents of others' speech acts is reliable – that is, that the hearer *H* is such that she would apprehend a speech act as having the content, *p*, only when it does have the content *p*. It is noteworthy that this condition says nothing whatsoever of *H*'s ability to explicate the concepts figuring in the content *p*. And indeed it would seem that one can be reliable in the sense indicated even if one is not in a position to explicate the concepts involved. For the capacity to represent the (force and) content of another's speech act is one thing, the capacity to explicate the concepts involved would appear to be another. Where the former merely involves a capacity to reliably map the speaker's words onto their semantic values (on this occasion of use), the latter involves the capacity for a great deal of conceptual explication that, at least on the surface of it, is simply irrelevant to the former.

The first step made clear that satisfying the comprehension requirement on knowledge through testimony does not require the hearer to be knowledgeable with respect to the application conditions of all the concepts figuring in the proposition attested to; the second step involves making clear why, as a matter of fact, satisfying the former requirement will typically not involve satisfying the latter. Here we connect the point above to facts about speakers. We do so by noting (what should be obvious in any case) that, while it may be that in taking S's word H inherits or sustains the public-language concepts expressed therein, it is not true that in taking S's word H also inherits S's (or anyone else's) grasp of the application conditions of those concepts. So if H was deficient in her grasp of the concepts in the first place, she will remain so after the linguistic exchange.[20] In that case she must look elsewhere for a proper articulation of the application conditions of the concept(s) in question. And here it is natural that she defers to others to do so: after all, it is from others that she acquired the concept(s) in the first place (through consuming their testimonies involving the concept(s) in question). It is in this sense that the phenomenon of semantic deference can be traced to our epistemic reliance on the other members of our linguistic community.

Indeed, the foregoing also makes clear how we might similarly trace the prevalence of the phenomenon of *incomplete grasp* to our epistemic reliance on the say-so of others. There can be little doubt that our earliest knowledge includes knowledge acquired through our acceptance of the say-so of our adult guardians. Indeed, many philosophers have remarked that without credulous acceptance of others' words, young children would not even be in a position to learn language. (See Coady (1992: 91–3) and Stevenson 1993.) But it is implausible that, prior to consuming a given piece of testimony, the young child already has a complete grasp of the concepts figuring in the testimony; and it is equally implausible to think that her consumption of the testimony *confers* such grasp on her (how could it?). A better description is that the young child comes to know things through testimony prior to having a complete grasp of the concepts that figure in the propositional content of her testimonial knowledge. And there is no reason to think that this stops in early childhood: on the contrary, throughout our lifetime we continue to acquire a good deal of very specific (and very useful) pieces of knowledge, in advance of having a complete grasp of concepts that figure in the propositional content of that knowledge. For even though we lack the relevant grasp, the knowledge we acquire in this way remains of great value to us, practically speaking. Although I can't

---

[20] So long, of course, as her grasp is not affected by the exchange itself.

articulate the application conditions of '*x* is a diamond' enough to differ-entiate the extension of this predicate from that of predicates for several other precious stones, even so learning of an apparent gem that it is (or is not) a diamond is of obvious practical and epistemic value to me. In this way the pervasiveness of the phenomenon of incomplete grasp is owed in large part to our epistemic reliance on the say-so of others.

(It is worth noting, parenthetically, that the foregoing explanation answers a question that proponents of AI–A should want to be able to answer but which would otherwise appear to be difficult to answer. The question is this: what is the point of a subject's having concepts whose application conditions regularly outstrip her abilities to articulate? Seen from an engineering/evolutionary perspective, the question is: what selective advantage might there be to creatures who evolved to employ such concepts, over those who have not so evolved? The explanation of the previous paragraph offers an answer: creatures who have evolved to employ such concepts are in a position to acquire very useful pieces of knowledge in an efficient way from their conspecifics, even when they have little background knowledge of their conspecifics. But suppose that a human-like species were such that its members could only acquire knowl-edge whose conceptual contents could be fully articulated by the member herself. In that case, either each member would be massively restricted in the contents she could know efficiently through accepting the word of a conspecific; or else each member would be bogged down with the cognitively expensive machinery that a repertoire of fully articulable, publicly shared concepts would require. It would thus appear that incom-plete grasp is itself the by-product of a very well-designed cognitive system, one geared to participate in the communal spreading of knowledge through speech.)

The foregoing reflections on the source of semantic deference and incomplete grasp suggest that the present argument from knowledge communication is importantly different from Burge's argument for AI. In particular, the present argument explains, but does not rely on, the phenomena of incomplete grasp and semantic deference. But even given this difference, it might continue to seem that the present thought experi-ment is open to an objection that many have raised against Burge's thought experiments. It has struck many that Burge's thought experiments (espe-cially as presented in his 1979, 1982b, 1986, and 1989) rely on an implicit assumption regarding the semantics of speech- and/or attitude-reports. Disregarding for the moment that Burge has explicitly repudiated this reading of his arguments, it might seem that my argument, too, trades on an implicit assumption to the same effect.

Whether or not Burge's versions of the argument for anti-individualism are susceptible to this criticism (as many appear to think),[21] the present argument is not. In arguing for this, I will argue for a point of more general interest. My claim will be that speech and attitude reports about what the speaker said and what the hearer came to believe reflect still deeper points about knowledge communication – points that can be established without appeal to any assumptions about the semantics of speech- or attitude-reports.

It will help to have another doppelgänger case in front of us. Imagine two worlds that are type-identical, save that in one of the worlds (Earth) people speak English, and so use 'arthritis' to refer to (and so to express the concept for) a disease of the joints only, whereas in the other (Twin Earth) people speak Twin English, a language just like English except that 'arthritis' is used to refer to (and so to express a concept for) a disease of the joints and ligaments. Now we can present my case for anti-individualism in a nutshell in terms of the following twin cases. Jim is a life-long Earthian who is informed about a particular disease by a doctor whom he has justifiably grown to trust; the doctor asserts 'Arthritis is more common in men than in women.' In accepting the doctor's testimony, Jim thereby comes to know through the testimony something whose content is *that arthritis is more common in men than in women*. Twin-Jim is a life-long Twin-Earthian who is molecule-for-molecule type-identical to Jim; Twin-Jim is informed about a particular disease by a doctor whom he has justifiably grown to trust; the doctor asserts 'Arthritis is more common in men than in women.' Twin-Jim, too, accepts his doctor's testimony. However, in so doing, Twin-Jim does not thereby come to know what Jim came to know; rather, Twin-Jim comes to acquire testimonial knowledge of something else, which we might render in English as the content *that arthritis is more common in men than in women*. Once again, on the assumption that knowledge that *p* entails belief that *p*, Jim and Twin Jim differ in their beliefs (since one but not the other has a belief with the content *that arthritis is more common in men than in women*). Since Jim and Twin Jim are molecular duplicates, we conclude that

---

[21] See Bach 1988 and 1997a; Loar 1988; Patterson 1990; Elugardo 1993; McKinsey 1994 and 1999; and Jackson 2005. But see my 2002a, where I argue that Burge's argument is not susceptible in this way.

at least some of the mental natures of their mental states depend for their individuation on their respective social and physical environments.

Does the conclusion I have drawn, to the effect that the mental natures of their mental states depend for their individuation on their respective social and physical environments, itself depend on any implicit semantics for speech or belief reports? On the contrary, the case depends on the conditions on the transmission of knowledge through testimony. That is, it turns on the idea that Jim and Twin-Jim are not in a position to acquire the very same piece of testimonial knowledge. The first point to note here is that the doctors' respective training makes them experts *regarding different diseases.* The Earthian doctor is an expert in the recognition, characterization, and treatment of a disease of the joints only, whereas the Twin-Earthian doctor is an expert in the recognition, characterization, and treatment of a disease of the joints and ligaments. Since it is precisely this expertise that is drawn on in their respective testimonies – it is their respective expertise that makes their respective testimonies *reliable* – the result is that their testimony differs along an epistemic dimension: the Earthian doctor's testimony puts a hearer in a position to learn something about (what his expertise covers) a disease of the joints only, whereas the Twin-Earthian doctor's testimony puts a hearer in a position to learn something about (what *his* expertise covers) a disease of the joints and ligaments. To make this vivid we can even imagine that the Earthian doctor would not be a reliable guide to the recognition and treatment of a disease of the joints and ligaments, whereas the Twin-Earthian doctor would not be a reliable guide to the recognition and treatment of a disease of the joints only. On the assumption that you can learn (in the sense of *come to know*) only through reliable testimony,[22] the result would be that what can be learned (known) through the respective doctors' testimonies differs. What is more, to make this point *we need not assume anything about the semantics of attitude- and knowledge-ascriptions of the form 'S φs that p.'*

Note, too, that the foregoing suggests that the argument from communication does not depend on any contentious assumptions regarding the semantics of speech reports either. The difference in the knowledge that Jim and twin-Jim acquire has its source *in the difference in the expertise of the doctors on whom they are relying.* It is true that the doctors are manifesting their respective expertise linguistically; but it is the expertise itself that grounds what can be known through their respective speech acts. Indeed

---

[22] I ignore 'repairing' cases of the sort described in chapter 1.

we might even say that it is their respective expertise that grounds the differences in what they say, when they say something by way of assertoric utterances involving the word-form 'arthritis.'

At this point it is worth recalling the kind of 'symmetry' that I claimed (in section 4.2) for the argument I am offering. There I said that one could argue *from* claims about what was asserted in the testimony *to* conclusions about what the hearer came to know, and hence what she came to believe; or else one could reverse this and argue *from* claims about what the hearer came to know, *to* conclusions about what the speaker asserted. It is at this point that I am exploiting the latter, 'reverse' direction. For the present claim is that the thought experiment can be used to bring out differences in what is known in the Jim/Twin-Jim cases, which difference can then be used to account for or explain our intuitions about how we ought to report the various subjects' speech acts. In particular, it is *because* the Earth-doctor's speech act puts Jim in a position to acquire knowledge whose content is *that arthritis is more common in men than in women*, that we are disposed to report that testimony as testimony to the effect (or as a saying to the effect) that arthritis is more common in men than in women. Similarly, it is *because* Jim has learned through testimony something whose content is *that arthritis is more common in men than in women*, that we are disposed to report his doxastic state as one of 'believing that arthritis is more common in men than in women.' (In both cases, what is known through the testimony can be taken to be explanatorily prior to how the knowledge, belief, and testimony-constituting speech are reported.)

I do not pretend that this argument can be used in conjunction with the argument in sections 4.3–4.8, as a distinct argument. Rather, the point I am making now is simply that, if one comes at matters from the 'reverse' perspective, reasoning from what the hearer can come to know through the testimony, to what the testimony 'says', one sees that it is our intuitions regarding speech reports that are supported by our intuitions about the knowledge that is transmitted, rather than vice versa.

Having spent some time trying to establish that the foregoing argument is novel in the way it uses the Burge-style thought experiment, it is perhaps worth ending on a note suggesting continuity with the Burgean tradition. In particular, although I think that nothing like the foregoing argument for AI can be found in the literature, the idea behind an argument of this sort is itself not entirely novel. Indeed, one finds the suggestion of the possibility of such an argument in a recent passage from Burge himself. In a very suggestive passage (already quoted in chapter 2) he writes,

Comprehending standing, conceptual aspects of one's own thought and idiolect is itself, as a matter of psychological and sociological fact, normally dependent on having comprehended thoughts (one's own) *that were shaped and expressed through the words of others*. Even innate nonlinguistic concepts are commonly associated with one's words only via understanding them as expressed by others' words. So homophonic comprehension of one's own words is normally interwoven with homophonic understanding others. (1999: 243; italics mine)

I think that Burge is exactly right about this point; my aim in the foregoing has been to develop the sort of argument that this point suggests, to the point where we can see clearly that the argument is importantly different from the (traditional construal of the) standard arguments for AI. Such is my proposed contribution to the Burgean tradition.

With this, I conclude Part I of this book, in which I tried to argue that communication as we know it depends on various anti-individualistic doctrines in the philosophy of language and thought. In Part II I will be assuming as unproblematic that hearers typically do achieve a reliable comprehension of speakers' testimonies. I will focus instead on the factors that are more commonly regarded in connection with the *epistemic dimension* of knowledge communication – the testimonial reliability condition, and the reliable discrimination condition. Focusing on what it takes to satisfy these conditions, I will be arguing that a proper account of testimonial knowledge will yield various epistemically externalist doctrines pertaining to the epistemology of testimony. Here the contribution I will be seeking to make is that these doctrines amount to a kind of *epistemic* anti-individualism: they make claims that go *beyond* standard forms of externalist epistemology. In making out the case for this, I am trying to show that the mind is more deeply social, and is social along more dimensions, than has traditionally been appreciated.

PART II

Epistemic anti-individualism

5

The epistemic dimension of knowledge communication: towards an anti-individualistic approach

In chapter 1 I presented three conditions as necessary conditions on testimonial knowledge: the hearer must rely epistemically on what in fact was reliable testimony; the hearer must reliably comprehend the testimony; and the hearer's acceptance of the testimony must be grounded in her capacity for reliably discriminating reliable from unreliable testimony. Chapters 2–4 then focused on the reliable comprehension condition, as a way to motivate several *semantically* anti-individualistic results. Here I begin the first of four chapters that will explore factors more standardly discussed in connection with the *epistemological* dimension of knowledge communication. In particular, I will be focusing on the testimonial reliability and reliable discrimination conditions. In doing so, I will be assuming that the subjects I discuss have attained a reliable comprehension of the testimony they observed. The question, rather, will be: What else must be the case, if such subjects are to count as having attained *justified belief* and/or *knowledge* through their acceptance of the testimony?

In addressing questions such as these, my ambition in Part II is two-fold. Narrowly, I want to argue that the three conditions, presented so far as *necessary* conditions on testimonial knowledge, are also *sufficient*. Here I drop the pretense of epistemic neutrality, as I aim to endorse and defend something like a reliabilist account of knowledge and justification in connection with testimonial belief. As a reliabilist account, the position is an instance of epistemic externalism regarding both knowledge and justification. But the particular details of the externalist account are of less importance to me than what I take to be the upshot of such an account. This is because, no matter how we formulate the externalist condition on

133

knowledge, an adequate account of the epistemology of testimony will have us endorse a particularly *strong* version of epistemic externalism. The version in question will be one on which the ascription of justification and knowledge to a subject *S* sometimes depends on factors pertaining to *the cognitive lives of subjects other than S*. Establishing this sort of 'anti-individualistic' externalism is the second, more ambitious objective in Part II.

As I noted in the Introduction of this book, 'anti-individualism' is not a label that is typically applied to epistemic positions. However, the bundle of views I will be advocating under such a label is not entirely new. What I have to say here will be very much in the spirit of some of the work that is sometimes advanced under the generic label 'Social Epistemology.'[1] My reasons for preferring the label 'epistemic anti-individualism' over that of 'Social Epistemology', however, will give some insight into the sort of position I aim to occupy and defend in Part II.

First, using the 'anti-individualism' label in connection with the epistemic dimension of communication signals this book's overarching agenda, which is to show that the conditions on knowledge communication, which (I argued in Part I) provide the basis for an argument for anti-individualism regarding mind and language, also provide the basis for an argument in support of regarding one's social environment as relevant to the *epistemic statuses* enjoyed by the beliefs one forms through accepting the word of one's co-linguals. Using 'anti-individualism' in both connections signals the doctrinal affinities I see on this score between epistemology, on the one hand, and the philosophy of mind and language, on the other.

But I also prefer 'epistemic anti-individualism' to 'social epistemology' for a second reason. Some theorists use 'social epistemology' as a label under which to challenge central epistemological assumptions pertaining to the locus of knowledge ascriptions. On such a 'social epistemology' view, it is communities, rather than individuals, that are the proper subjects of such ascriptions.[2] Now it is no part of my present project to

---

[1] Of those who contribute to this field, several stand out. Perhaps the most prominent is Alvin Goldman (see Goldman 1992, 1999, 2002a, 2004). But see also Welbourne 1986; Schmitt 1994 and 2006; and a volume of the 2005 edition of the *Southern Journal of Philosophy* devoted to the Spindel Conference on Social Epistemology. It is worth noting as well that there is an new journal entirely devoted to social epistemology (*Episteme: A Journal of Social Epistemology*).

[2] Such a view is presented in Welbourne 1986 and Kutsch 2002b, among other places. But see Goldman 2002 for a defense of the individual as the primary locus of knowledge.

endorse such a view.[3] Rather, the anti-individualistic flavor of the position that I will be advocating comes out in another idea: various epistemic properties ascribed to individuals – in particular, the properties of *knowledge*, *warrant*, *justification*, and *rationality* – are ascribed on grounds that involve an ineliminable reference to factors in the individual subject's social environment. Once again, the factors are 'social' in that they regard the cognitive lives of subjects *other than* the one of whom the properties hold.

Some of the views I will be endorsing under the rubric of 'anti-individualism' regarding the epistemic dimension of communication, and in particular those views pertaining to testimonial knowledge and warrant, are relatively uncontentious. But I anticipate that the whole package will be controversial indeed. For one thing, I will be rejecting the idea, motivated by internalist epistemology[4] and endorsed by reductionism in the epistemology of testimony (more on which below), that all of the materials that make for one's being justified in accepting a piece of testimony are discernible through one's searching reflection. What is more, my move to endorse a version of epistemic externalism will be a move to endorse a particularly strong (anti-individualistic) version of epistemic externalism. The implications of such a position, I will claim, go far beyond what is often associated with epistemic externalism as such.

It is worth bringing this last point out. Let epistemic internalism regarding an epistemic status *e* be the thesis that all of the materials in virtue of which a subject's belief has *e* are discernible through the subject's searching reflection alone; and let epistemic externalism regarding *e* be the denial of this claim.[5] Then we can call an externalism *individualistic* when its focus on

---

[3] But see chapter 8, where I do enter one significant point of agreement with those who question whether individuals are the proper subjects of knowledge ascriptions. Even there, however, I will not call into question that it is the *single subject* who believes and knows. Rather, my point will pertain more to *the process* that eventuates in reliable belief and knowledge in a single subject: my thesis is that sometimes this process is itself non-individualistic.

[4] See Alston 1986 for an inventory of various traditional internalist positions; and see also Conee and Feldman 2004, for a variant on traditional internalism.

[5] This, of course, is not the only way to characterize the internalism/externalism debate. Some have characterized epistemic internalism as the conjunctive thesis that (a) only states that are first-personally accessible can be epistemic justifiers and (b) epistemic justification, so understood, is a necessary condition of knowledge. (This characterization, which I will call the *traditional conjunctive characterization*, can be found for example in Feldman 2004 and arguably Pritchard 2005.) Another (less popular) view regards epistemic internalism as the conjunction of the claim that (a*) only mental states can be epistemic justifiers, and (b). This

external factors is restricted to the functioning of the agent's own cognitive system and its relations to her non-social environment. (That is, an epistemically externalist position is individualistic when it does not include factors pertaining to the cognitive lives of subjects other than the one currently under epistemic assessment.) Although nothing in the doctrine of externalism *per se* suggests such a narrowing of focus, it is interesting to

position, known as *mentalism*, has been endorsed by Conee and Feldman 2004, as well as by Conee 2007. However, I believe my own formulation is to be preferred to either of these two.

For one thing, both of these alternative characterizations of epistemic internalism endorse (b), and there are reasons for thinking that (b) should not be part of our characterization of epistemic internalism as such. For where (b) entails that epistemic justification is a necessary condition of knowledge, the necessity view is one that is rejected (or otherwise goes unendorsed) by some self-described internalists. It is rejected, for example, by Audi 1993, and Foley 2004 wants to remain neutral on it (even as he formulates his own – what most would regard as an internalist – account of epistemic justification). It thus seems that perspicuous taxonomy would have us characterize the internalism/externalism debate, as I have, in a way that is neutral on whether justification is a necessary condition of knowledge.

For this reason, my characterization enjoys a methodological advantage over both the traditional conjunctive characterization and mentalism. In particular, my characterization can allow what they cannot, namely, a methodology according to which the epistemic internalist can pursue inquiry into the nature of justification without making any assumptions about the relation between epistemic justification and knowledge. This is a methodological virtue since several epistemic internalists have proposed to do just that, arguing that we detach inquiry into the nature of justification from that into the nature of knowledge. In this respect I cite Foley's (2004) proposal for a 'trial separation' between 'the theory of knowledge and the theory of justified belief.' But I also cite the arch-internalist Larry Bonjour, who has recently urged that serious epistemology should pursue the issue of justification *and ignore the issue of knowledge completely*. (See Bonjour's contribution to Bonjour and Sosa 2003: 21–3.)

It is of course true that my characterization of epistemic internalism has at least one implication that might seem objectionable. As will become clear in the text, my characterization will have the implication that virtually everyone in epistemology is an externalist about knowledge. This might seem objectionable. After all, the labels 'internalism' and 'externalism' were originally introduced into the epistemology literature by David Armstrong, and he was characterizing a debate about the nature of knowledge (see Armstrong 1973: 157). If we assume that there was a serious debate in the air, that there really were 'internalists' in his sense, then my characterization's implication, that nearly everyone is an externalist when it comes to knowledge, is objectionable. But this line of reasoning does not withstand scrutiny. 'Internalism' and 'externalism' have become technical terms characterizing contemporary disputes in epistemology, and I have already given good reasons to think that my characterization of the divide provides the more fruitful taxonomy of these disputes.

To the reasons I have already given in support of this latter contention, I add one final, defensive reason. While my taxonomy suggests that virtually everyone is an externalist about knowledge, it gives the right verdicts on the matter of justification, where the real action lies. The one notable exception to this is the 'mentalist' position of Conee and Feldman 2004: my taxonomy will regard this view as externalist, while they advance it as an

note that a good many externalist theories are narrowly focused in just this way. Such a restricted focus is evident when we understand the externalist property in question – whether this be the sensitivity, safety, proper functionality, epistemic virtuousness, etc., of the subject's cognitive processes – without reference to factors pertaining to any subject other than the one under assessment. The views I will be defending under the rubric of 'anti-individualistic epistemology' are versions of externalism, but they are versions of an externalism that extends its focus to include factors regarding other subjects. My main ambition in Part II is to show that such an extended focus is essential, if we are going to have an adequate account of the epistemic dimension of knowledge communication. Such a view brings with it some bracing implications – implications asserting a social dimension to epistemic justification (chapters 5 and 6) and rationality (chapter 7), as well as the non-individualistic nature of some cognitive processing (chapter 8).

My strategy is as follows. I begin in this chapter by arguing that there are certain epistemically anti-individualistic theses that *everyone* should accept in connection with testimony-based belief. In presenting an argument for the theses in question, I make no assumptions about the conditions on justified acceptance of testimony – the main flash-point in the epistemology of testimony debate. Given its neutrality, my argument on this score is one that everyone can and should accept, and its anti-individualistic conclusions are above serious doubt. The remainder of the chapter is then devoted to arguing that, once one accepts these uncontroversial anti-individualistic conclusions, we have at least one reason to endorse an anti-individualistic conclusion regarding the conditions on the justified acceptance of testimony. This reason stems from the connection between epistemic justification and the expansion of epistemic support that (I argued in chapter 1) is characteristic of testimonial belief and knowledge. If the anti-individualistic thesis regarding justification is otherwise adequate, this sort of consideration gives us a reason to prefer such an anti-individualistic thesis over its individualistic and internalist rivals. (Chapters 6 and 7 are then devoted to arguing that the anti-individualistic thesis

internalist theory. However, I am not alone in questioning whether mentalism is internalist, given that it surrenders the core of what motivated internalism (in all of its varieties) in the first place. For this reason it is best to regard the question of the proper taxonomic category for mentalism as up in the air – as something that should be determined by what is on other grounds our best characterization of the internalism/externalism controversy – in which case it is no strike against my account that it considers that theory to be externalist regarding justification.

regarding justification *is* otherwise adequate – or at the very least, that reasons to suppose that it is not do not themselves hold up to scrutiny.)

5.2 KNOWLEDGE AND WARRANT IN TESTIMONY CASES

I begin with an initial argument for two prosaic anti-individualistic theses regarding the epistemological dimension of communication. I will be presenting an argument for them despite their obviousness, since they play an important role in my subsequent argument for more controversial results, and I want to nip in the bud any thought of rejecting the more controversial results by rejecting the prosaic claims.[6] The argument I will offer on their behalf involves reflection on a variant of the cases with which I began chapter 1.

The first case is as follows. Fred and Wilma have been married for more than three decades, having known each other since they were little kids. Wilma knows that Fred is a highly reliable reporter: he has very high epistemic standards and to date has never said anything unless he took himself to have ample evidence for it. One day Wilma and Fred and are conversing with one another about a stone-cutters' conference Fred just attended, in the course of which Fred assertorically utters

(1) Professor Swinegarten was in attendance at the conference.

Fred is speaking from knowledge; he saw Swinegarten at the conference. And for her part, Wilma accepts Fred's testimony (knowing Fred to have a long track record of reliable testimony, and discerning nothing unusual about Fred's assertion on this particular occasion).

Now consider a slight variant on this case, involving Fred★ and Wilma★. (Our subjects here can be thought of as Fred and Wilma in a counterfactual context.) This case is just like the other one, with the following difference. Fred★ has begun to suspect that Wilma★ has recently shown a certain (by his lights, unnatural) interest in Professor Swinegarten. So when Fred★ utters (1), he does so not because he wants to transmit knowledge regarding Swinegarten's presence at the conference – he had no idea whether Swinegarten was actually there – but rather because he wants Wilma★ to form a negative impression of the good professor (Fred★ knows that

---

[6] Compare Russell's (1924/93) dictum: "The point of philosophy is to start with something so simple as not to seem worth stating, and to end with something so paradoxical that no one will believe it."

Wilma★ has nothing but disdain for those who go to stone-cutters' conferences). Of course, Fred★ has expertly concealed his suspicions; Wilma★ noticed nothing abnormal in his testimony. As a result Wilma★ comes to accept Fred★'s testimony, and so acquires the belief that Professor Swinegarten was in attendance at the conference. Fortuitously, it turns out that Swinegarten *was* in fact at the conference.

There are two natural things to say about these cases. First, Wilma but not Wilma★ counts as acquiring knowledge through the testimony she accepts. Second, though both Wilma and Wilma★ acquire beliefs through the testimony they accept, these beliefs do not enjoy the same degree of epistemic support. Let us introduce the term 'warrant' to designate the total truth-conducive (knowledge-relevant) support enjoyed by a belief, where this includes considerations pertaining not only to the reasons the subject has for holding the belief, but also any other factors bearing on the likelihood that the belief is true.[7] The second claim, then, is that Wilma's and Wilma★'s beliefs differ along the warrant dimension as well.

If knowledge differs from merely true belief at least along the dimension of warrant, then my second claim (asserting a difference in the degree of warrant) follows from the first claim (asserting a difference along the dimension of knowledge). But it may be worth noting that we could equally well have argued for the difference along the warrant dimension directly, without appeal to a prior difference along the knowledge dimension. To do so, suppose that, though Fred's testimony was based on observation, he saw Professor Swinegarten from a distance, in less than perfect lighting, and under conditions in which Swinegarten's appearance was similar in many respects to the appearance of many others who were present. In that case, Fred's judgment that it was Swinegarten he saw was less than fully reliable – there were many other situations in nearby possible worlds in which Fred would have mistaken someone with similar appearances for Swinegarten – even as this judgment was much more reliable than chance – there are a good many situations in nearby possible worlds in which he would not have mistaken someone at the conference for Swinegarten. In this case we might say that Fred's judgment that it was

---

[7] This usage of 'warrant' is thus not the same as that found in Plantinga 1993a and 1993b, where 'warrant' is used to designate the property (whatever it is) that epistemicizes true belief, rendering it knowledge. On my view, one can have warrant for one's belief in *p* even in a case in which one fails to know *p*.

Swinegarten was based on perceptual evidence that, though good, ultimately fell short of the kind of conclusiveness we expect from knowledge-sufficient warrant: he did not speak from knowledge. But even so, surely his testimony enjoys more warrant than does the testimony of Fred* (who just made it up). The result would then be that the beliefs Wilma and Wilma* acquire through their acceptance of the respective testimonies of Fred and Fred* differ along the warrant dimension, even though neither one of these beliefs amounts to knowledge.

This said, it will be helpful to imagine that the cases differ along both the warrant and knowledge dimensions. Now I submit that these differences hold even if we hold fixed all of the facts of the two cases, as these pertain to Wilma and Wilma*. Thus we suppose that Wilma and Wilma* would offer precisely the same reasons for accepting the testimony of their respective spouses, and that their cognitive processes were working equally well.[8] And we suppose as well that Fred* was excellent at keeping his suspicions to himself: these never manifested themselves in any of the behavior he exhibited towards Wilma*. In fact, we can imagine that the entire course of behavior Fred* exhibited in the presence of Wilma* (up to and including the point of the testimony) would be indistinguishable from the entire corresponding course of behavior Fred exhibited in the presence of Wilma. Even so, Wilma knows and Wilma* does not; and Wilma's belief enjoys a higher amount of warrant than that enjoyed by Wilma*'s corresponding belief. But now Wilma and Wilma* can be taken to be doppelgängers, type-identical so far as all of their non-relational (and non-epistemic) properties go. It follows that their case is one in which the knowledge and warrant properties of their respective beliefs depend on factors regarding their social environment, and in particular on factors

---

[8] In saying that they would *offer* the same reasons, I do not intend to be taken to mean that they *have* precisely the same reasons for accepting the testimony. To address this would require a clear sense of what it is to 'have a reason' bearing on whether to believe *p*. On some conceptions, it may turn out that a fact can count as a reason bearing on whether to believe *p*, even when the subject in question is not aware of the fact in question. If so, Wilma and Wilma* do *not* have the same reasons: the fact that Fred* is just making things up is a reason (a defeater) that bears against Wilma*'s belief in what he attests to, whereas no corresponding reason (defeater) obtains in the case of Wilma's belief in what Fred attests to. Be this as it may, the reasons that Wilma and Wilma* would offer (on behalf of accepting their respective spouse's testimony) are the same. And this is all that I need in order to establish what I am trying to establish here. Below, as well as in various parts in chapters 6 and 7, I return to the issue of defeaters of which the hearer is unaware.

pertaining to (the cognitive processes implicated in the respective testimonies of) Fred and Fred★.

I do not imagine that the foregoing argument will be very controversial. Surely whether one *knows* through testimony – and, more generally, how well-supported, epistemically speaking, one's testimonial belief is – will depend on epistemically relevant features of the testimony one has consumed. And the presence of these features, in turn, depends on factors regarding the cognitive processes of the testifiers, since these processes underlie the reliability of the testimony itself. (Was the content to which the speaker attested one that she came to believe through reliable belief-forming and -sustaining processes, and that she succeeded at expressing through her competence in the language?) So whether one knows through the testimony etc. will depend on factors pertaining to one's social environment. This result would appear to be independent of any particular theory of knowledge one endorses; and the corresponding claim regarding warrant would appear to be independent of any particular theory of warrant one favors. We thus would appear to have a straightforward case for two epistemically anti-individualistic doctrines, as follows:

AI–K When *S*'s belief that *p* is formed through testimony, whether *S* counts as knowing (as opposed to merely truly believing) *p* depends on facts regarding one (or more) of *S*'s social peers.

AI–W When *S*'s belief that *p* is formed through testimony, the warrant (= total truth-conducive support) enjoyed by *S*'s belief that *p* depends on facts regarding one (or more) of *S*'s social peers.

5.3 METHODOLOGICAL INTERLUDE: KNOWLEDGE, WARRANT, AND JUSTIFICATION

As I said, I do not suppose that either of these two anti-individualistic doctrines, in themselves, will be very controversial. This is for two reasons: first, the case for them appears unassailable; and second, and perhaps more importantly, neither AI–K nor AI–W, by itself, makes or entails any claim regarding differences along the dimension of *epistemic justification* – and it is here, I suspect, that the real controversy emerges. Now below, in section 5.6, I will be arguing that the corresponding anti-individualist doctrine regarding justification, AI–J, holds *if* a certain view about justification in testimony cases, *anti-reductionism*, holds. Since anti-reductionism about testimonial justification is by most accounts the dominant view these days,[9] it would be possible to rest my case for AI–J on the argument from that section, together with the arguments others have offered for anti-reductionism itself (for which see footnote 12). However, in what remains of this chapter I will be offering an additional case for AI–J.

The argument proceeds as follows. I begin by noting that, on the assumption of a view known as *reductionism*, AI–K and AI–W have no direct bearing on the conditions on the justified acceptance of testimony. On the other hand, on the assumption of a view known as *anti-reductionism*, there is a straightforward argument from AI–K and AI–W to an anti-individualistic result regarding these conditions. So the case for an anti-individualistic result regarding justification is as strong as the case for anti-reductionism. Next I introduce a *desideratum* on accounts of the epistemological dimension of communication, and I claim that this *desideratum* is satisfied by anti-reductionism but not by reductionism. The result is that, if anti-reductionism is otherwise satisfactory as an account of the conditions on the justified acceptance of testimony, our anti-individualistic thesis regarding such conditions would be established. Finally, I will argue that, while there are some grounds that have been offered for thinking that anti-reductionism is not otherwise satisfactory, these ultimately do not compel. (I respond to one such ground in section 5.8 of this chapter, and two other such grounds in the following two chapters.)

Two comments about my argumentative strategy are in order. First, it will be the burden of the argument to show – not something that the argument assumes – that there are important connections between justification, on the one hand, and warrant and knowledge, on the other. (I will leave to the side the question whether these connections are conceptual or metaphysical.) Second, the dialectic I am pursuing in defense of this aim will be familiar from the debates between epistemic internalists and externalists. While I will be pursuing this dialectic in connection with epistemic justification in testimony cases, the very same sort of dialectic could be played out in other epistemic domains as well. One might wonder, then, why it is worth playing out this well-worn dialectic in the domain of testimonial belief and knowledge: isn't it sufficient that we have seen how it goes in the domains of perception, memory, and reflection (for example)? My answer was anticipated above: it is in the domain of testimony that we find reasons for endorsing a particularly strong version of epistemic externalism. Here I refer to the anti-individualistic conclusion

---

[9] This point is noted in Schmitt (2006: 194).

I seek to draw: whether a person's belief is justified depends in part on features of *the cognitive lives of other individuals*. This sort of thesis is not one that appears reachable merely on the basis of considerations from the domains of perception, memory, and reflection.

5.4 THE JUSTIFIED ACCEPTANCE OF TESTIMONY: REDUCTIONISM VS. ANTI-REDUCTIONISM

As noted, the aim of the subsequent argument will be to establish a view I will call anti-individualism about justification (AI–J) by appeal to AI–K and AI–W. However, it is a vexed matter to move from considerations of knowledge to considerations of justification. The situation is even more complicated in testimony cases, given the terms in which the issues surrounding justification have been debated. The main issue has been to characterize the conditions on the justified acceptance of testimony,[10] and the main competing positions in contemporary literature are two. On the one hand there is the Reductionist position, according to which

RD A hearer is not epistemically justified in accepting (does not have the epistemic right to accept; is not epistemically entitled to accept) another's testimony unless she has (inductive or *a priori*) reasons, ultimately not themselves based on still further testimony, for regarding the testimony she confronts as credible.[11]

Such a view is 'reductionist' in the sense that one's justification for accepting testimony ultimately reduces to a kind of (inductive or *a priori*) justification having nothing in particular to do with testimony. Opposing this position is the Anti-Reductionist position, according to which

---

[10] There are many debates that fit under the rubric of 'the epistemology of testimony.' The two main ones concern knowledge and justification. As I will note below, most of those who call themselves 'reductionists' are offering a thesis about justification, not knowledge. However, the argument that I will be offering can be formulated whether reductionism is construed as a thesis regarding knowledge, or one regarding justification. I return to this below.

[11] Reductionist views are sometimes presented (by Fricker 1987 and 1994) as views which deny any 'presumptive right to trust'. (See chapter 6 for my discussion of this point.) For a defense of a reductionist view, see Fricker 1987, 1994, and 1995; Adler 1994; Lyons 1997 (where it is argued that some arguments against reductionism are not successful); and Shogenji 2006.

AR A hearer is justified in accepting (has the epistemic right to accept; is epistemically entitled to accept) another's testimony so long as there are no undefeated good reasons *not* to accept the testimony.[12]

This view is regarded as an 'anti-reductionist' view in the sense that it regards the justification involved in the acceptance of testimony as not reducible to other, allegedly more basic kinds of epistemic justification.

I begin with my claim that, on the assumption of RD, AI–K, and AI–W have no direct bearing on the conditions on the justified acceptance of testimony. This is because proponents of RD conceive of matters of testimonial justification as independent of matters of testimonial warrant and knowledge. As evidence for this I cite two of the more prominent recent defenders of RD: Elizabeth Fricker and Paul Faulkner.[13]

Fricker's view is this. The sort of evidence that renders a hearer *H*'s testimonial belief *knowledge* involves the reasons or evidence that supported the testimony *H* has consumed. However, this is not a sort of reason or evidence that *H* herself can be said to possess. Fricker explains:

> knowledgeable belief based on trusted testimony implicitly refers back to the existence of a non-testimonial ground or warrant for what is testified to: the ground or warrant in virtue of whose possession the original teller spoke from knowledge . . . **When I know that P solely from trust in testimony, I do not possess the evidence for P**. Instead, my knowledge is premised on the existential supposition that there is non-testimonial evidence for P, although I myself do not possess it. I suppose that **a person or persons upstream in the chain of informants between them possess that evidence** – the grounds for believing P true. [Such] epistemic dependence on others . . . extends one's knowledge base so enormously . . . (Fricker 2006: 241; **boldface** added)

---

[12] Anti-reductionist views are sometimes presented (by Burge 1993) as views which assert a 'presumptive right to trust.' For a defense of anti-reductionist views, see Reid 1872/1993; Welbourne 1979, 1981, 1986, and 1994; Evans 1982: 210–11; Hardwig 1991; Coady 1992 and 1994; Burge 1993 and 1997; Webb 1993; Dummett 1994; Foley 1994; McDowell 1994; Stevenson 1993 (which argues for a conclusion asserting a moderate kind of anti-reductionism); Strawson 1994; Millgrim 1997 (which defends a restricted version of AR); Schmidt 2002; Insole 2000; Davis 2002; and chapter 6 of this book. For something claiming to be a 'hybrid' of RD and AR, see Faulkner 2000.

[13] The case of Faulkner is somewhat complicated by the fact that his (2000) is presented as a 'hybrid' position, one that combines reductionism with anti-reductionism. However, my characterization of his position as 'reductionist' is still fair, and (I imagine) would be acceptable to him, given that I am construing reductionism as a thesis about justification – which thesis Faulkner explicitly accepts. (His 'anti-reductionist' element concerns warrant and knowledge.)

In this way Fricker's position acknowledges AI–K and AI–W. At the same time, when it comes to the justified acceptance of testimony, Fricker conceives of this in terms of the reasons one has for accepting the testimony – one's reasons for thinking that the testimony was credible or trustworthy (see Fricker 1987 and 1994: 128). The result is that the considerations on which the question of knowledge turns, having to do with the adequacy of the evidence *the (original) testifier* has in support of the testimony she offered, swing free from those on which the question of justification turns, having to do with the adequacy of the reasons *hearer H herself* has for accepting the testimony.

It is worth noting that, on such a view, there would appear to be a kind of double dissociation. (Fricker herself does not make the point explicit, but it is implicit in what she says.) On the one side, there can be cases in which a hearer has the sort of evidence that justifies her in accepting what she is told, but none of the sort of evidence that would render such a belief knowledge. (Indeed, this is how the proponent of RD will describe the case of Fred* and Wilma*, above.) And on the other, there can be cases in which a hearer does not have the sort of evidence that would justify her in accepting what she is told, even though there is plenty of evidence "upstream in the chain of informants." Just imagine a case in which one has no compelling reasons for regarding a particular piece of testimony as trustworthy, when in fact the testimony is highly reliable (based on excellent evidence). Fricker would describe such a case as one in which the hearer's own lack of positive reasons prevent her from justifiably accepting a piece of testimony which, had she possessed such reasons, would have enabled her to acquire knowledge through her acceptance of the testimony. If we use the label 'distinctly testimonial support' to describe the support provided by the testimony itself (as opposed to the hearer's reasons for accepting the testimony), we get the double dissociation in question: there can be cases of justified testimonial belief without any further distinctly testimonial support; and there can be cases of unjustified testimonial belief with distinctly testimonial support that would have been sufficient for the acquisition of testimonial knowledge (had the hearer possessed positive reasons for accepting the testimony).

A similar position can be found in the reductionist position of Paul Faulkner. Faulkner's conception of the conditions on justified acceptance of testimony is like Fricker's: he holds that "it is our reasons for accepting testimony which provide the justification for our testimonial beliefs" (2000: 593), and that in the 'fundamental' case the hearer's reasons are "his experience of what testimonies are credible" (2000: 591–2). But Faulkner, again like Fricker, regards these reasons – the reasons that underwrite one's justification for accepting what one was told – as distinct from the reasons that bear on whether one's true testimonial belief amounts to *knowledge*. He writes that "in accepting testimony an audience frequently believes propositions *whose warrant could not possibly be equated with whatever justification the audience has for its acceptance*" (Faulkner 2000: 592; italics in original, boldface added).[14] The result is that, on Faulkner's view, as on Fricker's, we can doubly dissociate the two sorts of reasons or evidence: that which bears on whether one's acceptance of what one was told is justified, and that which is found 'upstream' in the chain of communication.

The take-home point is this. Given the reductionist's dissociation of justification and warrant, there are cases in which a hearer is RD-justified in accepting a piece of testimony, but where her resulting testimonial belief enjoys no distinctly testimonial support (in the sense defined above). This, I submit, is a *prima facie* weakness of RD views. For our present result indicates that RD views fail to square with what I will now argue is a *desideratum* on theories of the epistemic dimension of communication.

In chapter 1, I argued that what was distinctive of testimonial belief and knowledge is the characteristic expansion in the epistemic support for testimonial beliefs that obtains in 'happy' cases. Indeed, it would appear that this is precisely what hearers aim for when they accept testimony: they aim to acquire a belief whose epistemic (truth-conducive) support outstrips the support provided by the reasons they have for accepting the testimony. It would be nice, then, if an account of justified acceptance could be squared with the claim that

JES one who is justified in accepting a piece of understood testimony *ipso facto* acquires the sort of belief that enjoys the expanded (distinctly testimonial) epistemic support characteristic of testimonial belief and knowledge.

I do not say that the preservation of JES is an *adequacy* condition on an account of justified acceptance: perhaps it will turn out that JES cannot be accommodated by any account that hopes to be adequate to the remaining

---

[14] I note that Faulkner uses 'warrant' here, not as Plantinga does (roughly: *that which epistemicizes true belief, rendering it* knowledge), but rather as I do – as something akin to 'total epistemic support.'

demands on a theory of justification. My claim is rather that the preservation of JES is a *desideratum*. More specifically, if two views are otherwise adequate, the fact that one of them preserves JES and the other does not gives us a reason to prefer the former to the latter. This is so for considerations of theoretical simplicity: views that preserve JES can regard justified acceptance as tracking the warrant enjoyed by the resulting testimonial belief. For if a view preserves JES, the ascriptions of justification it sanctions will go hand-in-hand with the presence of a non-negligible degree of the sort of warrant that is characteristic of testimony cases. To be sure, ascriptions of justification must also be sensitive to considerations regarding (e.g.) rationality: one who irrationally accepts what in fact is normatively acceptable testimony is not thereby justified in so doing. But assuming two competitor accounts of testimonial justification are *otherwise adequate*, one that preserves JES is to be preferred to one that does not.

Those who are justification internalists may well deny that the preservation of JES should be seen as a *desideratum* in theorizing about the epistemology of communication. They will reply that the justified acceptance of testimony should go hand-in-hand, not with the *de facto* presence of distinctly testimonial support, but rather with the subject's *having good reasons to think* that distinctly testimonial support is present. However this is a weak reply in the current dialectical situation. To see this, suppose there is an account of the conditions on justified acceptance of testimony that *both* preserves JES *and* is otherwise adequate to the demands on a the theory of justification. My claim is that such an account is to be preferred to one that, though otherwise adequate, fails to preserve JES. To be sure, the justification internalist is betting that there will be no such account forthcoming: she will offer reasons to think that the adequacy demands on a theory of justification will preclude any account that preserves JES. Below, and in the subsequent two chapters, I will be arguing that these reasons do not hold up to scrutiny. But if they did, then we might opt to settle by replacing the proposed *desideratum* with the internalist variant. My present point is only that such a move is premature at this point of the dialectic.

Returning then to our examination of RD, it is easy to see that RD fails to satisfy the proposed *desideratum*. Given that it conceives of justified acceptance in terms of the hearer's reasons for accepting testimony, and given that these can be in perfectly good order even in cases in which the testimony is not normatively acceptable, the result is that one can be RD-justified in accepting testimony in a case in which the resulting testimonial belief enjoys no distinctly testimonial support. (This is precisely the way that the Fred★-Wilma★ case would be described by RD's proponent.) In this way we see that, given RD, JES is false.

We have seen that RD fails to satisfy the proposed *desideratum*; here I argue that AR satisfies it. My main claims will be two: the rationale behind AR is reliabilist (in a suitably broad sense of 'reliabilist'); and given its broadly reliabilist motivation, AR preserve JES.

AR tells us that, absent reasons not to do so, a hearer is entitled (or has the epistemic right) to accept what she is told. How can it be reasonable for an epistemologist to advance such a claim? I submit that the anti-reductionist's thesis, to the effect that there is a presumption of trust, is itself advanced against the backdrop of two particular empirical assumptions. The first is that testimonial belief-fixation involves (subcognitive) processes whose job it is to enable the recipient to discern cases in which trust is to be extended, from those cases in which it is not. And the second is that these processes are in fact highly reliable in that, in cognitively mature and well-functioning adults, they issue in acceptance in most of the cases where the testimony is both true and reliable, and they issue in non-acceptance in most cases where the testimony is false or otherwise unreliable.

These two empirical assumptions are in keeping with externalist accounts of justification more generally. Consider an account of perceptual justification according to which we are presumptively but defeasibly justified in taking the perceptual appearances at face value. Such a proposal might be defended (as in Burge (2003) and Peacocke (2004a; 2004b, chapter 3)) by invoking the idea that the processes that subserve the formation (and sustainment) of perceptual belief are themselves *highly reliable*. If these processes weren't reliable – say, if they yielded true belief with the same ratio as is yielded by *guesses* – no one would think to offer a presumption-to-trust thesis in the domain of perceptual experience. This makes it clear that any plausible presumption-to-trust thesis in connection with perceptual experience will incorporate empirical (reliability) presuppositions. The key presupposition is that, whatever they are, the processes that mediate between perceptual experience and perceptual belief – the processes that subserve the production of perceptual belief from the perceptual experiences – operate in such a way as to amount to a *reliable belief-producing process*. Any sub-process that contributes to this reliability should be seen as part of the background presuppositions of the presumption-to-trust thesis itself. So it is not at all *ad hoc* to suppose that e.g. the mechanisms ensuring the reliability of the subject's recovery of the 3-D properties of the world from the retinal projection are themselves part of the story regarding the subject's presumptive entitlement to take the perceptual appearances at face value. Precisely not, since these mechanisms are among the mechanisms that make for reliability in this domain in the first place.

Now I submit that precisely the same thing can be said with respect to whatever processes subserve the formation of testimonial belief. I will have much more to say about the nature of these processes in chapter 6. For now, I will be content with saying this: a presumption-to-trust thesis here, as in the case of perception, is plausible only against the background of certain empirical (reliability) presuppositions. The key presupposition is this: the processes that serve to mediate linguistic input and testimonial belief-fixation work together to constitute a reliable belief-forming process. Again, it is not at all *ad hoc* to suppose that the mechanisms ensuring the reliability of the subject's testimonial beliefs, whatever these mechanisms are, are themselves part of the background presuppositions of the presumption-to-trust thesis.

Return now to the 'no good reasons' condition in AR. Given the reliabilist motivation for postulating a presumption to trust in the first place, it stands to reason that the proper way to read this condition is as designating those factors whose presence tells against the likely truth of the testimony. Such a factor may be 'internal' to the hearer, as when the hearer herself believes something that suggests that the testimony is false or otherwise not credible; or it may be 'external' to the hearer, as when there are facts of which she is unaware but which make it likely that the testimony is false.

Given this construal of the 'no good reasons' condition of AR, it is easy to see how AR preserves JES. The claim is simply that, in the absence of such reasons (whether 'internal' or 'external'), the testimony itself will possess the epistemic good-making properties that make it justifiable for the hearer to accept it. (Compare the corresponding claim about the perceptual appearances.) And if this is so, then in any case in which a hearer is AR-justified in accepting a piece of testimony, the testimony itself will be based on some non-negligible degree of epistemic support. In such cases the AR-justified belief, formed through accepting the testimony, enjoys a non-negligible degree of distinctly epistemic support. But then any belief formed through AR-justified acceptance of testimony will *ipso facto* enjoy the sort of 'expanded' epistemic support characteristic of testimonial belief and knowledge. In short: if the 'no good reasons' condition in AR is read as I have proposed, then AR is not merely compatible with JES, it *entails* JES.

5.6 AR IMPLIES AI−J

I just argued that AR but not RD preserves JES, and so preserves the idea that justified testimonial belief is testimonial belief enjoying the sort of (distinctly testimonial) support that is characteristic of testimonial belief and knowledge. The result is that if AR is otherwise adequate to the demands on a theory of justification, then the foregoing considerations offer grounds for preferring it to RD. I will return to the adequacy of AR below, and in chapters 6 and 7. Here however I want to draw out another implication AR has for the nature of justified acceptance of testimony. In particular, I want to argue from AR to an anti-individualistic conclusion regarding such acceptance, to the effect that

AI−J Whether S counts as justified in accepting a piece of testimony – as having the epistemic right or entitlement to accept the piece of testimony – depends on facts regarding one (or more) of S's social peers.

The claim here is simply that once one endorses AR, AI−J can be seen to follow by reflecting on the reliabilist considerations that motivate AR's postulation of a defeasible right to trust in the first place.

Let us say that a subject S's belief that p, formed on occasion O via method M, was formed in a manner that is *locally reliable* when the following counterfactual holds: if S were to believe that p via M in a situation relevantly like O, p would be true. The local reliability of hearer H's testimonial belief that p, formed on an occasion O, would then require the following: if the hearer H were to believe that p through testimony in a relevantly similar situation, p would be true. Such a requirement is met when the process through which H forms the belief is sensitive to indications of the reliability and unreliability of testimonies relevantly like the testimony she actually observed. If H is sensitive in this way, then her testimonial belief-forming process would indeed be such that, were she to have formed the testimonial belief in situations similar to this one, the belief would have been true.

What would ground the truth of such a counterfactual? It should be uncontroversial to suppose that part of H's sensitivity on this score involves her sensitivity to signs of unreliability in interlocutors relevantly like the present one. That is, part of *H*'s sensitivity resides in her sensitivity to those empirical signs – of incompetence, lack of confidence, malice, and so forth – that are reliable indications that a piece of observed testimony is not to be trusted.[15] But – and this is the all-important point – whether what *H* takes to be such signs *really are* such signs, as opposed to signs of (say) indigestion or some other epistemically neutral condition in her interlocutor, *will depend on facts about the cognitive and speech dispositions of interlocutors like her current one.*[16] If sweating and an inability to look one's audience in the eyes were not a reliable (if imperfect) indicator of deceitful intention in a speaker, then *H*'s sensitivity to those indications would not be a sensitivity to unreliable testimony. Similarly, if authoritative tone and apparent confidence were not a reliable (if imperfect) indication of competence – where competence in an interlocutor involves her having formed and sustained the belief in question through reliable mechanisms – then *H*'s sensitivity to those indications would not be a sensitivity to reliable testimony. Thus we see that whether *H* is sensitive to indications of the reliability and unreliability of testimonies relevantly like the testimony she actually observed, and so whether *H*'s present testimonial belief was formed in a locally reliable way, depends on facts about the linguistic and cognitive make-up of interlocutors like her current one. Given AR and the thesis that justification is or involves local reliability, AI–J holds.

We can reach the same conclusion on the assumption that justification is or involves *global* reliability. Let us say that a subject *S*'s belief that *p*, formed on occasion *O* via method *M*, was formed in a manner that is *globally reliable* when the following counterfactual holds: if *S* were to believe that *p* via *M*, in any of a range of counterfactual situations corresponding to the range of situations in which *M* might be employed by subjects like *S*, *p* would be true. Applied to the case of testimonial belief we

---

[15] Part, but only part: *H* will also use her background information to reach a verdict about the *prima facie* plausibility of the attested content. This is so even in cases where there is no question of *H*'s 'repairing' testimony that otherwise fails to meet the norm of assertion (for which see chapter 1). Thus you will automatically scrutinize my testimony about today's weather by appeal to your background beliefs about the normal weather patterns during this time of year in Lexington, Kentucky. For more on the (typically subcognitive) nature of this scrutiny see chapter 6.

[16] In the sense I intend, *H* can be said to be 'taking something' to be a sign of reliability if the processes that subserve belief-fixation in this case are causally sensitive to such signs, preventing the formation of belief when certain signs are detected. None of this need be conscious. See chapter 6 for further details.

get: *H*'s testimonial belief that *p*, formed on an occasion *O*, is globally reliable if, were *H* to believe that *p* through testimony, *p* would be true. The only difference here from what was said in the preceding paragraph is that we have expanded the set of possible situations we are considering: they need not be sufficiently like *O*. But once we see that this is the only difference, we see that whether *H* satisfies this condition depends on whether what he takes to be signs of reliability and unreliability, in the host of testimonies he confronts, actually *are* such – and this depends on facts about the linguistic and cognitive make-up of *H*'s co-linguals. Once again, AI–J holds.

In a nutshell: on the assumption of AR, whether hearer *H* is justified in accepting a piece of testimony is a matter of whether *H*'s acceptance is the output of processes that reliably discriminate reliable from unreliable testimony; and whether *H*'s acceptance is the output of such processes will depend on facts pertaining to the cognitive and linguistic make-up of at least some of *S*'s peers. If AR holds, AI–J holds.[17]

5.7 A WORRY ABOUT EPISTEMIC RESPONSIBILITY

The reasoning up to this point might be put as follows. All else equal, we should want to hold that the justified acceptance of testimony goes hand-in-hand with the presence of a non-negligible degree of distinctly testimonial support on the part of the testimony itself. My claim has been that the AR view but not the RD view squares with this *desideratum*. Of course, this sort of consideration provides the basis for preferring AR over RD, and so provides the basis for endorsing AI–J (which follows from AR), *only if* AR is otherwise adequate. There are at least three considerations that a reductionist might offer against AR's adequacy. Two of these are of sufficient interest to warrant independent treatment; I will do so in chapters 6 and 7. In this section here, however, I want to address a third consideration. The allegation is that anti-reductionist views are inadequate because they sever the important connection between *epistemic justification* and *epistemic responsibility*.

---

[17] This argument from AR to AI–J proceeds in terms of the idea that reliability is the core of the notion of epistemic justification. For an alternative argument from AR to AI–J, see Schmitt 2006. (Schmitt's argument proceeds in terms of the idea that *being based on good reasons* is the core of the notion of epistemic justification.)

We can bring out the nature of this charge by returning to the two cases from section 5.2. As I have been developing them here, AR and AI–J imply that the *de facto* unreliability of testimony constitutes a flaw in the grounds the hearer has for accepting testimony, even under conditions in which the hearer's exemplary scrupulousness uncovered nothing suggesting that the testimony was unreliable. On such a view, being epistemically responsible in accepting testimony does not suffice for being justified in accepting testimony. Thus it would appear that proponents of AR who understand the 'no good reasons' condition as I have suggested are precluded from endorsing the following:

RESP One has the epistemic right to accept a piece of testimony, in the sense that one is justified in accepting the testimony, if it would be epistemically responsible of one to accept the testimony.

The problem is that many will regard RESP as a truth regarding justification in testimony cases. Those who do accept RESP might ask us to return to the case of Wilma★, who was in the position of accepting what in fact was an unreliable piece of testimony despite her epistemic scrupulousness in accepting it. No one should doubt that Wilma★ was epistemically responsible in accepting Fred★'s testimony; the defender of RESP will go on to argue that *for this very reason* Wilma★ ought to be seen as having had epistemic right to accept – as having been justified in accepting – that testimony. Since an anti-reductionist view of the sort I am describing delivers the wrong verdict here – it regards the unreliability of Fred★'s testimony as a "good reason not to accept" that testimony, and so regards Wilma★ as unjustified in her acceptance – such a position ought to be rejected.

Or so a reductionist might argue. In response, the anti-reductionist should concede the point regarding RESP but deny that it is grounds for regarding AR as inadequate. The situation is as follows. Given the sort of anti-reductionism I am advocating, the following must be denied:

(Int1) Wilma★ has the epistemic right to accept Fred★'s testimony.

Admittedly, denying (Int1) is counter-intuitive. But when we look at its source we see that the intuitive acceptability of (Int1) derives from the still-deeper intuition that

(Int2) Wilma★'s acceptance of Fred★'s testimony was an instance of *responsible* acceptance.

Since (Int2) supports (Int1) only given RESP, the anti-reductionist should conclude that, since (Int2) is non-negotiable, RESP is false. To draw this conclusion is to hold that accepting testimony in a responsible way is not *sufficient* for having the epistemic right to accept the testimony. Two points can be made in defense of taking such a position. First, responsible acceptance of testimony is still regarded as *necessary* for having the epistemic right to accept testimony. (Indeed, this is what motivates the inclusion of a 'no defeaters' clause in anti-reductionism; see chapter 6, where the point is discussed at length.) And second, responsible acceptance *suffices* for the (anti-reductionistically construed) epistemic right to accept testimony, *modulo* the sort of case in which there is a warrant failure, indiscernible to the hearer's searching reflection, 'upstream' in the chain of communication.

All in all, the position on offer is one for which the anti-reductionist ought to hold out. Although I can sympathize with the desire to preserve (Int1), in chapter 6 I will be arguing that any anti-reductionist position that preserves (Int1) will do so at the cost of inviting other problems – in particular, problems on the score of sanctioning gullibility. This is because what is needed to preserve (Int1) is a restriction on what counts as a "reason not to accept testimony" – such "reasons" must be restricted to reasons of which the subject herself is aware – and yet once one makes such a restriction, one risks leaving oneself without resources to answer the charge that anti-reductionism sanctions gullibility. (Or so I will be arguing in the next chapter.) Of course, at this point the critic of anti-reductionism might think to argue that, if the best version of anti-reductionism would have us reject (Int1), then this is so much the worse for anti-reductionism itself. But as we will see in the next chapter, the sort of anti-reductionist position that implies the falsity of (Int1) enjoys a good deal of independent motivation: it is recommended by parallels with the epistemology of memorial and perceptual belief.

Admittedly, the move to reject (Int1) has the implication that hearers cannot determine by reflection alone whether they have the epistemic right to accept a piece of testimony. But is it really plausible to insist that such a right be determinable by reflection alone? This of course is a familiar issue between internalist and externalist positions on epistemic justification; so it will not do, as a way to settle this debate, simply to insist that whether one has such epistemic rights is something that is accessible to reflection. If the AR view is to be rejected on this score, further argumentation is needed.

In this connection the anti-reductionist's dialectical position is quite good. The issue before us concerns the relation between epistemic responsibility and epistemic justification. The track record of accounts of justification that honor something like RESP are not good. In particular, as various authors have argued, it would appear that any notion of epistemic justification that is linked (in the manner of RESP) to the notion of epistemic responsibility will face difficulties in connection with the link between justification and truth (see Goldman 1980, 1999; Kornblith 1988; and Sosa (in Sosa and Bonjour 2003), to name just a few). As a result, the objection from epistemic responsibility (as it might be called) is on dialectically unstable grounds.

I cannot pretend that these several points themselves serve to silence the objection from epistemic responsibility. But they do suggest that the objection itself need not be decisive, and in any case does not by itself warrant the charge that AR is inadequate. This said, much more can and should be said in connection with epistemic justification and epistemic responsibility. For example, it is clear that no account of justified acceptance is adequate if it cannot condemn (as unjustified) the gullible acceptance of testimony; and perhaps the worry about responsibility might take the form of an allegation that AR will fail on this score. Further, it is equally clear that no account of testimonial justification is adequate if it sanctions (as justified) patterns of consumption and sustainment that are clearly irrational; again, the worry about epistemic responsibility might take the form of an allegation that AR will fail on this score. Then again, the tables might be turned: we might put to rest the worry over epistemic responsibility by showing that neither allegation succeeds. Showing precisely this will be the aim of chapters 6 and 7, respectively. Doing so will enable me to descend from the heights of the internalism/externalism controversy regarding epistemic justification, to consider the details of the debate as they pertain to testimonial belief-fixation in particular.

6

The objection from gullibility

6.1 INTRODUCTION

In the previous chapter I began my case for several anti-individualistic doctrines regarding the epistemic dimension of communication. After arguing for two doctrines that should be conceded by all sides – AI–K, pertaining to the knowledge dimension of communication, and AI–W, pertaining to the warrant dimension – I went on to argue for a decidedly more controversial anti-individualistic doctrine, regarding the dimension of justification. The anti-individualistic doctrine in question, AI–J, is an implication of the anti-reductionist (AR) approach to the conditions on justified acceptance of testimony, according to which one is justified in accepting testimony in the absence of any defeating reasons. I argued that a particular *desideratum* favors AR over its reductionist (RD) rivals. In particular, AR but not RD squares with the idea that justified acceptance of testimony makes for a testimonial belief that enjoys a non-negligible degree of distinctly testimonial warrant.

In this chapter I aim to address an objection, owed to Fricker 1994, which aims to show that AR is not ultimately acceptable. According to the objection, AR will regard as justified certain cases in which testimony is *gullibly accepted*. Since such cases are not cases of justified acceptance, AR should be rejected. Or so Fricker contends.

It is clear that a proper response to this objection will require descending from the heights of the generic and rather abstract considerations presented in chapter 5, to address considerations specific to testimonial belief-fixation. Here I will have the opportunity to fill in more details of my case for both anti-reductionism and for AI–J. In the course of doing so I will be returning to the reliable discrimination condition on testimonial knowledge. In particular I will be arguing that it is legitimate to regard this condition as part of an anti-reductionist account, and that, so understood, anti-reductionism is not a recipe for gullibility (Fricker's objection notwithstanding).

I will proceed as follows. I begin, in section 6.2, by outlining Fricker's argument from gullibility. In 6.3 I note that her argument addresses itself only to a particularly strong (and implausible) form of anti-reductionism – one that, to the best of my knowledge, is endorsed by no one. After formulating a version of anti-reductionism more in keeping with the AR position formulated and developed in chapter 5, I move on, in 6.4, to consider whether her objection might apply to that version. Here I argue that Fricker's gullibility objection can score points against AR only if it appeals to reliability considerations. I suggest that this spells trouble for Fricker's objection: insofar as anti-reductionism's presumption-to-trust thesis is itself motivated by reliabilist considerations – a claim I developed in chapter 5 – a natural fix, if one is required, is to so modify AR that its presumption-to-trust thesis is advanced in connection with whatever empirical conditions make for reliable testimonial belief-fixation. After suggesting that this can be achieved by adding a monitoring requirement to AR, I move on in section 6.5 to argue that the consumption of testimony by mature humans does indeed appear to incorporate the sort of credibility-monitoring process I incorporate into my modified anti-reductionist view. In 6.6 I reiterate that the postulation of such monitoring still leaves room for a substantive presumption-of-trust thesis.

6.2 FRICKER'S ARGUMENT FROM GULLIBILITY

Polyanna is notoriously naive. She is optimistic in the face of cogent evidence that things are not going well. She maintains her faith in the goodness of humanity in spite of numerous examples of human perfidy and malice. She has no imagination when it comes to the vicious motives that often inspire people's behavior. Here I focus on another epistemic shortcoming: her gullibility. Polyanna is easily deceived insofar as she is ready to accept whatever she is told, merely in virtue of being so told. This is not admirable. The effects of her gullibility are both practical – she is easily manipulated by others – and epistemic – she comes to believe many things which could easily be the results of epistemically undesirable processes in others, and which she would not believe but for the testimony. An adequate epistemology of testimony must see Polyanna as unjustified in the way that she acquires beliefs through testimony. The burden of Fricker's 1994 argument is that anti-reductionist accounts fail this adequacy requirement.

In order to appreciate Fricker's contention, it is important to appreciate how Fricker characterizes the anti-reductionist view. The "problem to be solved" by the epistemology of testimony, she writes, is that of "showing how it can be the case that a hearer on a particular occasion has the epistemic right to believe what she is told – to believe a particular speaker's assertion" (1994: 128). She goes on to claim that there are only two possibilities:

It may be shown that the required step – from 'S asserted that p' to 'p' – can be made as a piece of inference involving only familiar deductive and inductive principles, applied to empirically established premises. Alternatively, it may be argued that the step is legitimised as the exercise of a special presumptive epistemic right to trust, not dependent on evidence. (1994: 128)

The second of these options is the anti-reductionist position. On her reconstruction, such a view is motivated by the claim that "the first, *reductionist* route to justifying testimony is closed." On this reconstruction, the characteristic anti-reductionist thesis asserting a positive presumption to trust is the only non-skeptical solution to the epistemological problem presented by testimony.

It is against anti-reductionism, understood to be advancing such a positive-presumption thesis, that Fricker raises the objection from gullibility. Her objection begins by noting that

The notion of a presumption to trust testimony ... seems only to make sense when it is interpreted as giving the hearer the right to believe without engaging in epistemic activity; when there is no requirement to be on the alert for defeating conditions ... (1994: 143)

Fricker then suggests the following as the proper formulation of anti-reductionism:

PR: An arbitrary hearer H has the epistemic right, on any occasion of testimony O, to assume, without investigation or assessment, of the speaker S who on O asserts that P by making an utterance U, that S is trustworthy with respect to U, unless H is aware of a condition C which defeats this assumption of trustworthiness. (p. 144)

The "clear and sharp difference" between the account she advocates and the PR account, is that

on [the reductionist] account, but not on a PR thesis, *the hearer must always be monitoring the speaker critically*. This is a matter of *the actual engagement of a counter-factual sensitivity*: it is true throughout of the hearer that if there were any signs of untrustworthiness, she would pick them up. (154; italics mine)

She reiterates this point in her (1995), writing that "a PR principle worthy of the name must dispense a hearer from the requirement to monitor and assess a speaker for trustworthiness" (404). The argument, then, appears to boil down to two matters. The first is Fricker's contention that, given AR, *H*'s having the epistemic right to accept a piece of testimony is compatible with *H*'s failure to have monitored the testimony for its trustworthiness. The second is the inference that Fricker draws from this first claim, to the conclusion that AR is "an epistemic charter for gullibility" (1994: 143).

6.3 AR'S 'GOOD REASONS' CONDITION, REVISITED

An initial point must be made in connection with Fricker's formulation of anti-reductionism as PR. This formulation amounts to a significant strengthening of the doctrine over how it was formulated in chapter 5. I repeat that formulation here:

AR A hearer is epistemically justified in accepting (has the epistemic right to accept; is epistemically entitled to accept) another's testimony so long as there are no undefeated good reasons not to accept the testimony.

The key point is that Fricker's PR restricts the "no defeaters" condition to defeaters of which the subject herself is 'aware,' whereas AR introduces no such restriction in connection with its "no good reasons not to accept the testimony" condition.

Two things can be said in the connection.

First, Fricker is correct to think that there are serious difficulties facing any version of anti-reductionism that, with PR, restricts defeaters to those of which the hearer is 'aware.' Indeed, as stated PR seems obviously false. Take the case of Polyanna, as gullible as can be: she is never aware of any defeaters, even under conditions in which her environment teems with them. Presumably this does not make for justified acceptance of testimony. At the very least it does not make for acceptance that will give rise to reliable testimonial belief (as per chapter 1, section 6.4). Since such a view is so obviously mistaken, it is hard to take seriously the idea that any epistemologist ever held such a view. It would seem, then, that if Fricker is to have a serious opponent, we must have a more charitable reading of anti-reductionism.

A second point regarding PR reinforces this need for a more charitable reading. Few (if any) actual proponents of anti-reductionist positions endorse such a narrow conception of defeaters. As standardly conceived defeaters need not be known about, or even believed in, to play a defeating role: in addition to doxastic defeaters (which function by being believed), there are also *factual* and *normative* defeaters.[1] (Below, in 6.4, I will argue that the acknowledgment of these types of defeaters has a clear reliabilist rationale; see also chapter 5 section 6.5.) In any case it is clear that characteristic formulations of anti-reductionism contain no such "awareness" restriction. In this respect my formulation of anti-individualism as AR, in chapter 5, was not idiosyncratic in the least. Take for example Burge's Acceptance Principle, which is perhaps the paradigmatic formulation of an anti-reductionist thesis: "*a person is entitled to accept as true something that is presented as true and that is intelligible to him, unless there are stronger reasons not to do so*" (1993: 467, italics in the original). Although it is formulated in terms of reasons rather than defeaters, it is noteworthy that there is no 'awareness' restriction put on the 'stronger reasons' condition. (Nor is Burge's formulation of AR idiosyncratic in this respect: compare Evans (1982: 310–11) and Stevenson (1993: 448–9).)

In light of the foregoing, we might well wonder why Fricker imposed this 'awareness' restriction on defeaters. Her claim is that "the notion of a presumption to trust testimony ... seems only to make sense when it is interpreted as giving the hearer the right to believe without engaging in epistemic activity; when there is no requirement to be on the alert for defeating conditions ..." (1987: 143). This is not an adequate defense of her move to impose such a restriction on defeating conditions. Those who formulate epistemic principles in terms involving defeaters regularly acknowledge all three sorts of defeaters (doxastic, normative, and factual). Consider the thesis that there is a defeasible presumption that one's own perceptual experience is trustworthy. An epistemologist who advanced such a thesis would clearly want to acknowledge all three sorts of defeaters. The need for doing so is evident as early as Goldman's (1976) recognition that knowledge requires that one's grounds rule out any 'relevant' alternatives. To be sure, Goldman was speaking of perceptual *knowledge* rather than *justification*; but so long as one is endorsing a broadly reliabilist outlook regarding epistemic matters, the same point would appear to hold with respect to justification. In particular, if reliability is the core of the notion of justification, then any considerations affecting reliability are *ipso facto* relevant to justification. And, as Goldman's barn-facade case itself made clear, 'external' conditions about which the subject herself is unaware can

---

[1] See Lackey (1999: 474–6) for a discussion of defeaters in connection with testimony cases.

affect the reliability of her belief. It would thus seem that, insofar as AR's presumption-to-trust thesis is backed by reliabilist considerations, there are clear grounds for *not* restricting the 'no defeaters' condition to defeaters of which the subject is aware. Since Fricker has not provided any reason to think that the presumption of trustworthiness regarding testimony is any different, her 'awareness' restriction is unjustified.

Suppose, then, that we formulate anti-reductionism as I did in chapter 5, with no 'awareness' restriction on defeaters. Does anti-reductionism, so formulated, remain susceptible to Fricker's objection from gullibility? Clearly, if 'gullible' means nothing more than "ignoring good reasons not to trust testimony," then AR is not guilty of sanctioning gullibility: after all, AR conditionalizes justification on the *absence* of "good reasons not to trust testimony." But it remains to be seen whether there is some other sense of 'gullibility' on which AR sanctions gullibility. In pursuit of this question we do well to recall that Fricker raises the gullibility charge in connection with her call for some monitoring-for-truthfulness in the reception of testimony.[2] It is natural, then, to wonder whether Fricker's charge is best pursued in connection with AR's implications regarding the alleged need to monitor testimony for truthfulness.

As noted, the charge that anti-reductionism sanctions gullibility is made on the basis of Fricker's prior claim that anti-reductionism dismisses the hearer from the need to monitor testimony for trustworthiness. But once we move to endorse AR rather than PR as our formulation of anti-reductionism, we are regarding the presumption-to-trust principle as defeasible by *any* relevant defeater (i.e., whether or not the hearer is aware of the presence of the defeater). This places a special burden on Fricker to motivate her monitor-for-trustworthiness requirement.[3] For if there are any relevant defeaters which the hearer cannot defeat, then, even by the lights of AR, the hearer will not count as having the epistemic right to accept the testimony – *whether or not* she has monitored for testimony. This shows that the alleged requirement to monitor-for-trustworthiness cannot be motivated by the need to uncover defeaters. From this vantage

---

[2] In Goldberg and Henderson 2007, we distinguish various gullibility-properties as part of an argument against Fricker's gullibility objection. However, in the time since that paper was completed, I have begun to think that the crucial points can be made without such distinctions.

[3] Here, and throughout the rest of this chapter, talk of a monitoring 'requirement' is to be understood as amounting to the claim that credibility-monitoring is a necessary condition on being justified in accepting a piece of testimony.

point, it can seem that even if Fricker is correct to think that AR dispenses with the need for the hearer to monitor a piece of testimony for trustworthiness, even so her case against anti-reductionism fails, since in that case AR will not sanction as justified any acceptance in which defeating conditions are present.

Despite this, I think that Fricker's call for a 'monitoring' condition on justified acceptance can still be motivated – albeit in a way that will ultimately prove harmful to her case against anti-reductionism. To see how we might motivate the claim that some 'monitoring for trustworthiness' is a necessary condition on the justified acceptance of testimony, let us return to Polyanna. Take a case in which, gullible as always, she accepts a piece of testimony through her credulity, but where she does so under conditions in which there are no defeaters. Is she *ipso facto* justified in so doing? It would appear that she satisfies the conditions set forth by AR; and yet, intuitively, we do not want to regard her as justified in accepting the testimony.

What is the basis of this intuitive verdict? I submit the following reconstruction (which I think is faithful to Fricker's own position). The actual world involves a good deal of false or otherwise unreliable testimony. The result is that, even in a case in which *in fact* there were no defeaters, *had* there been such, Polyanna would not have been sensitive to their presence. (In Fricker's own words: Polyanna is not "counterfactually sensitive to the presence of defeaters.") On this reconstruction, the proponent of the gullibility objection concedes that, had there been defeaters, AR itself would not have sanctioned Polyanna's acceptance, since in that case the 'no good reasons' condition would have been violated. But (the objection's proponent maintains) this is small solace in the *actual* case in which there are no defeaters: in this case AR, as formulated above, would appear committed to the claim that Polyanna *is* justified in her acceptance. And it is this result that is problematic: what the Polyanna case makes clear is that there are cases in which AR regards as justified a hearer's acceptance of testimony, yet where the hearer herself is counterfactually insensitive to the presence of defeaters.

Fricker is correct on this point: there would appear to be something wrong with an account of justified acceptance on which a gullible hearer such as Polyanna counts as justified in accepting a given piece of testimony, under conditions in which, had there been defeaters whose presence would have prompted any reasonable adult human being not to accept the testimony, she still would have accepted it. Interestingly, Fricker's point here would appear to be backed by reliabilist considerations. Indeed, it is at this point in the theory of *justification* that we see the need for the 'reliable discrimination' condition (introduced in chapter 1 in connection with testimonial *knowledge*). Consider that Polyanna was not properly sensitive to the presence of defeaters, with the result that her testimonial belief, though based on her acceptance of what in fact was reliable testimony, was nevertheless unreliably formed. After all, had the testimony been false (or otherwise unreliable), she would have accepted it anyway, and so would have formed the corresponding belief anyway – even though the belief in that case would have been false. Thus her actual belief was unreliably formed, through no 'fault' in the testimony itself: the 'fault' was hers (or rather it was that of the subcognitive processing implicated in her formation of the belief).

It seems, then, that Fricker can motivate the monitoring require-ment on justified acceptance by appeal to reliabilist considerations. On this motivation, the sort of gullibility that involves failing to monitor testimony for trustworthiness is an epistemically bad thing – is something incompatible with justified acceptance – as it conduces to unreliable testimonial belief. (At least such gullibility will so conduce in any world, such as ours, in which one regularly encounters false or otherwise unreliable testimony.)[4] But I am under no illusions here: such reliabilist overtones will not sit well with a reductionist like Fricker. After all, her epistemology of testimony is couched in epistemically internalist terms, where pride of place is given, not to reliability considerations, but rather to the hearer's having positive rea-sons for accepting the testimony (see Fricker 1987, 1994, 1995, 2003, and 2006).

Might Fricker then have another way to motivate her 'monitoring' condition, one that does not essentially rely on the reliability implications of the failure to monitor? The challenge she faces on this score is to establish what I will call the *independence thesis*:

---

[4] Since the reliability of the gullible hearer's testimonial beliefs is a function of the amount of false or unreliable testimony in her environment, it would appear that one can be gullible without acquiring unreliable testimonial belief. This is the case if H's sources are themselves invariably reliable, and where any possible world in which there are false reports is far enough away so as to be irrelevant to an assessment of the beliefs H forms through testimony in the invariably reliable-reporting world. See chapter 8, where I use this idea to suggest how we might model the acceptance of testimony by very young children.

Being gullible, in the sense of failing to monitor testimony for trustworthiness, is inconsistent with being justified in accepting a piece of testimony, on grounds that *do not essentially depend on* whether or not such gullibility conduces to false or unreliable belief.

Unfortunately, the independence thesis is controversial, and if Fricker's argument from gullibility depends on it, it is correspondingly contentious. For one thing, it is doubtful that the independence thesis can be established by appeal to the gullible subject's violation of epistemic norms: even if the existence of such norms is conceded, the very legitimacy of the epistemic norms themselves, as *epistemic* norms, appears to depend on the role that the satisfaction of such norms plays in conducing to the twin epistemic objectives of acquiring (interesting) truths and avoiding falsehoods.[5] And a similar point can be made in connection with the more contentious matter of epistemic duties.

It would seem, then, that if Fricker's gullibility argument is to make a non-question-begging case against AR, it must be read as advancing the claim that AR is an 'epistemic charter' for a form of gullibility that leads, or is likely to lead, to unreliable (testimony-based) belief. There is a certain irony here. As I have been presenting the view (and see also section 6.4, to follow), anti-reductionism itself is supposed to be motivated by reliabilist considerations. But Fricker's argument can be taken to indicate that AR is *not reliabilist enough*. This is a curious result from an argument that is supposed to be motivated by (and to give support to) a more internalist approach to justification.

6.4 ANTI-REDUCTIONISM, RELIABLE TESTIMONIAL BELIEF, AND THE MONITORING REQUIREMENT

The dialectical situation is this. If Fricker's gullibility objection is to have a serious version of anti-reductionism in its crosshairs, it must address itself to AR rather than to PR. Once this is seen, however, Fricker's objection faces a difficulty, as it is no longer clear why hearers need to monitor testimony for credibility, in order to count as being justified in accepting the testimony. Fricker can respond to this difficulty, but only by appeal to reliabilist considerations. In this section I begin my case for thinking that

---

[5] This point is common ground among epistemologists who otherwise disagree on many basic issues: see Bonjour (1985: 7–8) and (Bonjour and Sosa 2003: 5); Chisholm (1977: 14); Goldman 2001a; Haack (1993: 203, 220–1); and Lehrer (1981: 87) and (1989: 143).

this spells doom for Fricker's challenge to AR. The upshot of Fricker's argument can be taken to be that, if it is to remain sensitive to reliabilist considerations, a broadly anti-reductionist account regarding the justified acceptance of testimony – one that regards acceptance as presumptively but defeasibly justified – must embrace a monitoring requirement. In this section I argue that a slightly modified version of AR is *compatible* with such a requirement; and in the section following I present reasons to think that mature humans monitor testimony in ways described here as compatible with a broadly anti-reductionist approach to the conditions on justified acceptance.

First, a word of motivation is in order. *Prima facie*, it can seem simply *ad hoc* to build in a monitoring requirement into an otherwise anti-reductionistic account of the conditions on justified acceptance. After all, if the point of anti-reductionism is to say that hearers are presumptively entitled to accept testimony, why then go on and require that hearers monitor the testimony they are presumed entitled to accept? But we have already seen how such a requirement can make good anti-reductionist sense. In chapter 5 I suggested that AR can be motivated generically, as a version of an externalist – and in particular a reliabilist – account of justification. But for precisely this reason it is no more *ad hoc* to suppose that the mechanisms ensuring the reliability of the subject's testimonial beliefs, whatever these mechanisms are, are themselves part of the background presuppositions of the presumption-to-trust thesis regarding testimonial belief-fixation, than it is to suppose that the mechanisms ensuring the reliability of the subject's *perceptual* beliefs, whatever these mechanisms are, are themselves part of the background presuppositions of the presumption-to-trust thesis regarding perceptual belief-fixation. If credibility-monitoring processes are among those mechanisms in the testimony case – and below, in 6.6, I will give reasons for thinking that they are – then these processes, far from being an *ad hoc* postulation, are part and parcel of any account that postulates a presumption-to-trust in connection with testimony.

Still, one might have some reservations regarding whether a presumption-to-trust thesis can be happily combined with a call for monitoring-for-trustworthiness. In this respect it is not enough to point out the parallel with the perceptual case, for here it is not to the point to note how reliabilist presuppositions are built into the very postulation of a presumption-to-trust thesis regarding perceptual experience. Rather, what we want to know is this: what content can a presumption-to-trust-testimony thesis have, given a requirement on trustworthiness-monitoring?

In addressing such a question, it is important to recognize at the outset that there is a difference between *being on the lookout* for defeaters, and *going out and looking* for them.[6] At most, only the former can legitimately figure as a necessary condition on (the avoidance of gullibility, and hence on) justified acceptance. This much is conceded by Fricker herself, when she notes that "in claiming that a hearer is required to assess a speaker for trustworthiness" it would be 'absurd' to "insist ... that [the hearer] is required to conduct an extensive piece of MI5-type 'vetting' of any speaker before she may accept anything he says as true" (1994: 154). Rather, as Fricker herself formulates it, the monitoring requirement on justified acceptance is merely that of having something like a 'counterfactual sensitivity' (1994: 154) to the presence of defeaters, such that "[it is] true throughout of the hearer that if there were signs of untrustworthiness, she would register them, and respond appropriately" (Fricker 1987: 149–50).

I believe that a broadly anti-reductionist view – one endorsing a presumption-to-trust thesis – can incorporate this sort of monitoring requirement into its account of the conditions on a subject's having the epistemic right to accept what she is told. In order to make vivid the content of the presumption-to-trust thesis on such a position, I will speak here in terms, not of a realistic subcognitive monitoring system, but rather of an unrealistic buzzer system designed to exploit testimonial regularities. I indulge in this science fiction in order to work my way towards an understanding of a kind of 'monitoring' that is compatible with a defeasible presumption to trust.

Consider, then, the following illustration. Smith has a buzzer that is always by her side and which goes off whenever anyone tells her something that is not reliable. For present purposes, it does not matter whether Smith herself knows how the buzzer works, nor whether she even knows or reasonably believes that the buzzer is highly sensitive to the reliability of proffered testimony. All that matters is that, as a matter of fact, Smith never accepts any testimony that elicits a buzz from her buzzer. (We can think of the buzzer as the contemporary version of Socrates' *daimon*, applied to the case of received testimony.) In that case, her testimony based beliefs are reliable – in fact, they're *perfectly* reliable. True, this reliability is sustained by the role her buzzer plays in the system that mediates her acceptance of testimonies. But the point remains that a (reliability sustaining)

---

[6] I owe this way of putting the point to an anonymous referee of Goldberg and Henderson 2007.

monitoring-based sensitivity to trustworthiness is not, by itself, incompatible with the anti-reductionist's assertion of a defeasible presumption to trust. In 'buzzer-theoretic' terms: Smith enjoys a presumptive entitlement to accept testimony, which presumption is cancelled when a piece of testimony elicits a buzz. Here the presumption-to-trust thesis is underwritten by the fact that the buzzer system is part of a reliable belief-forming process in connection with Smith's testimonial beliefs. We might say that the existence of this system, together with the role it plays in enabling reliable testimonial belief, are empirical presuppositions of the presumption-to-trust thesis itself.

Those sympathetic to the claim that anti-reductionism sanctions gullibility might respond by insisting that Smith *is* objectionably gullible – if you take away her buzzer she would be easily deceived by false or unreliable say-so – albeit fortunate that she happens to form testimonial beliefs in accordance with a buzzer of this sort. But we can vary the story. Suppose that the buzzer cannot be easily detached from her, and attempts to do so have appreciable effects on her cognitive and practical life beyond those in connection with her dispositions to accept proffered testimony. And suppose as well that Smith's possession of the buzzer is not an idiosyncratic feature of her condition, but rather is a 'natural' endowment possessed by all normal adult human beings. In that case, the charge that Smith is gullible after all, in a way that would make for unreliability in her consumption of testimony, is simply unreasonable.

The foregoing aims to show that if "engaging in the epistemic activity [of monitoring]" (Fricker 1994: 143) merely requires a 'counterfactual sensitivity' (156) to the presence of defeaters, then such a requirement can be easily accommodated within – and indeed is a natural part of – a view endorsing a presumption to trust. Consider then the following, strengthened presumption-to-trust thesis:[7]

---

[7] Some anti-reductionists will not see the need to modify AR as proposed. This is because, while my modification will involve adding to AR a condition requiring a "counterfactual sensitivity to defeaters," some proponents of AR will regard such a condition as an empirical presupposition of AR. It should be clear from my discussion in chapter 5 section 5.5 that I am sympathetic to this idea; in any case I have no axe to grind on this score. My only reason for adding this condition to the formulation of AR itself is only to make clear that anti-reductionist views like AR are naturally thought of as endorsing the need for such a 'monitoring' condition. Whether this condition is seen as part of the formulation of anti-reductionism itself, or as a background empirical presupposition of anti-reductionism, is immaterial to me. This said, I will stick with my more explicit formulation.

AR + A hearer *H* is epistemically justified in accepting (has the epistemic right to accept; is epistemically entitled to accept) another's testimony on occasion *O* so long as (i) there are no undefeated good (doxastic, factual, or normative) reasons *not* to accept the testimony, and (ii) on *O H*'s acceptance was the outcome of a process that exhibited a 'counterfactual sensitivity' to the presence of defeaters (which, given (i), turns up no such defeaters on *O*).

Of course, Fricker herself might insist on a more demanding conception of monitoring (even though the 'less demanding' characterization, in terms of a 'counterfactual sensitivity' to the presence of defeaters, is hers). But we saw above (at the end of 6.4) that this point about "counterfactual sensitivity" plays a crucial role in motivating her demand for monitoring in the first place. And it would seem that any more demanding conception would be hard to motivate. For she would have to establish that monitoring, so construed, both is a necessary condition on gullibility-avoidance (in a sense of 'gullibility' on which gullibility makes for unreliable testimonial belief), and is inconsistent with AR + . Since I have already argued that there is a kind of monitoring available to the proponent of anti-reductionism on which anti-reductionism sanctions no form of gullibility that gives rise to unreliable testimonial belief, it is hard to see how she can establish what she needs to establish.

The foregoing reasoning supports a compatibility claim: anti-reductionism's presumption-to-trust thesis is *compatible* with certain ways of realizing a monitoring requirement, and so does not *entail* the sanctioning of gullibility in any form that gives rise to unreliable testimonial belief. What remains to be seen is whether the way monitoring is actually performed by human subjects can be accommodated within a broadly anti-reductionist epistemology of testimony. On this score the sci-fi buzzer example is no help. Instead, I propose to speak to this issue by suggesting what I take to be a substantive parallel with the process of *recollection*.[8]

---

[8] If space permitted, I would have liked to develop further the parallel between testimony- and perception-based belief. I believe that this parallel is instructive. One who is perceptually competent on a given matter has learned much in the course of past training, and this learning makes for a kind of sensitivity to details then encountered. The sensitivity to trustworthiness requisite for the epistemically appropriate reception of testimony would seem to exhibit a parallel sensitivity to nuanced new information about concrete cases – a sensitivity itself borne of information antecedently acquired through ongoing experience with interlocutors.

6.5 MONITORING IN RECOLLECTION[9]

Let the *process of recollection* designate those core memory processes that generate that state of "seeming to recollect" something, where this is a state short of belief and/or acceptance. Commonly, one proceeds smoothly and automatically – without a conscious, articulate thought – from seeming to recollect *p* to accepting *p*. Still, the distinction is required by simple facts about recollection and memory: there are cases in which, having set oneself to recollect something (an acquaintance's last name, say), one finds a particular thought emerging from the process of recollection, but declines to accept the thought in question, owing to its failure to square with other things one takes oneself to know or believe on good evidence. In such cases, other pieces of information are somehow dredged out of memory and recognized to be relevantly in conflict with what one now seems to recall. In such cases, the process of forming a memory belief is inhibited by processes that check for coherence with other information antecedently possessed by the agent – *coherence-monitoring processes.*

More typical, of course, are those cases where all goes smoothly – one has no sense of an impending incoherence with antecedently possessed information – and one goes on to form the memory judgment. I submit that, in these cases, coherence-monitoring processes are operative *through-out* the process of recollection. As a result, were the agent to possess bases for not believing what is recollected in a given case, these would likely inhibit the formation of that belief. In such cases there would be a reflective moment in which the agent would give some thought to the confidence to be assigned to what was recollected. In some cases, as in the illustration above, the agent may be able to dredge up a particular ante-cedent belief for purposes of articulate reflection on the content suggested by recollection. In other cases the agent will only be able to articulate a crude basis for caution (a sense that the content in question is "not quite right," or that the memory is curiously sketchy or unsupported by asso-ciated details, etc.).

This picture is one in which the coherence-monitoring process serves as a nearly constant filter on the production of memory beliefs – although it is seen as working largely submerged from articulate or conscious thought. But why should one think that such a process is so commonly in play? In

---

[9] Special acknowledgement is owed here to David Henderson, who contributed a great deal to the argument of this section.

part the answer is that it is difficult to understand how it could be deployed intermittently in an epistemically desirable way. Ideally, the filter would be employed selectively – where it would do the most good, where it is needed. This requires that the coherence-monitoring processes be triggered. But how? Not by some sense for the importance of the matter in question: sometimes one is inhibited in the formation of a belief on which little hangs either practically or epistemically. Nor can the filter be triggered by incoherence with antecedent beliefs, for that would require that the coherence-monitoring filter be triggered by – the coherence-monitoring filter! Rather, I submit that coherence-monitoring processes serve as a near ubiquitous check on the formation of memory beliefs, but that they do so by operating in a largely subconscious fashion, and only occasionally give rise to articulate reflection.

Granting the *prima facie* epistemic desirability of such monitoring, is it plausible that humans have the capacity for such monitoring? Here a comparison with a wider set of epistemic chores and modalities is helpful. One does not need to be a coherence-theorist to recognize that there are coherence-sensitive, holistic chores to be managed by the central processes of belief-fixation. This is reflected in the literature on theory-choice and confirmation in science, and in Fodor's continuing (1983, 2002) cautions regarding the associated problems facing classical cognitive science. Employing Fodor's useful terminology, there are two holistic dimensions of confirmation and central processes of belief-fixation: such processes are *isotropic* and *Quineian*. For reasons of space, I will discuss only the first, but both have similar implications.

Central processes of belief fixation are *isotropic* – every belief or candidate belief one has is at least potentially relevant to any other belief one has. This obtains because relevance itself can be highly mediated. Beliefs about trace elements found in vats of dry-cleaning fluid can be relevant to beliefs about fusion processes at the center of a nearby star – given mediating theory. Beliefs about a politician's previous job experience can be relevant to expectations for future fuel efficiency standards for automobiles – given one's expectations regarding human nature and political organizations. But, then, in deciding whether to adopt some proposed change in belief, one must somehow manage to identify what beliefs *are* relevant, and then one must gauge the cumulative significance of these relevant beliefs. There is a daunting catch here: since any belief is potentially relevant to any other belief, all beliefs are actually relevant to relevance, and so to determine what beliefs are relevant, one must somehow automatically accommodate or be sensitive to the relevance of *all* of one's beliefs to relevance. This challenge is closely related to what has come to be called the frame problem for computational cognitive science; managing such cognitive chores does not seem to be classically computationally tractable. My suggestion is that these chores are managed by automatically and inarticulately taking into account much possessed information that is not articulately represented in the cognitive system itself.[10]

These quick remarks on the central processes of belief-fixation suggest how coherence monitoring can be tractably managed in connection with recollection/memory. Consider then the epistemic parallels with the reception of testimony. I submit that, much as the recollection/memory processes are regulated by coherence-monitoring processes throughout, so too the process by which one moves, from the reception-with-understanding of testimony, to the formation of belief through one's acceptance of that testimony, is regulated by processes that monitor for trustworthiness. As we have seen, monitoring of this sort is needed anyway, independent of considerations of testimony. What is more, many of the chores monitoring performs in connection with memory – in particular, determining the coherence of a recollected content with background belief – have clear analogues in connection with the reception of testimony. In sum, there are independent reasons to suppose that the human cognitive system employs a pervasive but largely subcognitive monitoring system in connection with the reception of testimony. Not only is anti-reductionism *compatible* with certain ways of realizing a monitoring requirement; the hypothesis that humans monitor testimony in one of these ways is itself independently plausible.

6.6 WHITHER THE PRESUMPTION TO TRUST?

How does the model of testimonial belief-fixation on offer, on which coherence-monitoring processes are constantly operating (albeit typically subcognitively), relate to the anti-reductionist's hallmark doctrine of a *default epistemic entitlement* to accept what one is told? To say that the acceptance of testimony enjoys such a default status is to say that it is epistemically appropriate for one to accept testimony – provided that certain conditions were met. The conditions advanced by AR+ are

---

[10] This suggestion draws on the work of Henderson and Horgan (2000) and Horgan and Tienson (1995 and 1996).

two: there were no defeaters, and one's acceptance was the end result of a process which itself was counterfactually sensitive to the presence of defeaters.

But what should be said of the default status AR + extends to testimony? It may help to consider epistemic channels to which no such status is to be attributed. Consider daydreaming. As her mind is wandering, the thought occurs to Smith ('out of the blue') that there are albino penguins. Although she has no strong positive reasons for thinking that there are,[11] the hypothesis itself is consistent with her background beliefs (or what she has accepted to date). For this reason, were the claim that there are albino penguins to be subject to a process of subpersonal monitoring for coherence, such a claim would pass.[12] Despite this, the musing-generated hypothesis that there are albino penguins would not be such that Smith would be entitled to believe it. A reliabilist rationale supports this verdict, as musing is not a reliable source for belief. Herein is the substance of the presumptive status that AR + ascribes to observed testimony: the fact that a proposition was *attested to* provides it with a sort of epistemic seal which generates a defeasible but presumptive entitlement to accept the proposition. This does *not* go for propositions that occur to one in one's daydreams. Musing-with-monitoring – unlike perception-, memory-, or testimony-with-monitoring – does not give rise to entitled acceptance, as musing – unlike perception, memory, and testimony – is not a reliable source of belief.

6.7 CONCLUSION

In conclusion, no one should reject anti-reductionist approaches – or, by extension, their anti-individualistic implications, and in particular AI–J – on the grounds that they are a recipe for gullibility. In the next chapter I

---

[11] The reasons that she does have are from certain general claims she accepts – the claim, for example, that for any (of the precious few) species into which she has looked into the matter, there have been albino members of the species – and from a lack of any reason to think that such general claims are restricted in scope in ways that prevent their application to the case of penguins.

[12] I am glossing over some subtle and significant questions regarding that character of the monitoring processes. Do the processes monitor not simply for consistency of what is imagined with what is antecedently known, but also for more demanding coherentist features such as explanatory unification? If so, then it becomes correspondingly less plausible that a given suggestion of imagination would pass, and correspondingly less plausible that imagination-so-checked would enjoy a default entitlement.

want to extend this defense of anti-reductionism: I will argue that no one should reject AR + (or, by extension, AI–J) on the grounds that it fails to square with claims about the *rationality* of testimonial-belief fixation and sustainment. On the contrary, I will be arguing that, given the more-or-less uncontroversial anti-individualistic theses regarding knowledge and warrant I defended in chapter 5 – AI–K and AI–W – there is an anti-individualistic aspect to the process by which we rationally police our (testimonial) beliefs. Ascriptions of rationality – like ascriptions of knowledge, warrant, and justification – sometimes turn on anti-individualistic factors.

7

The objection from rationality

In the previous two chapters I have defended three anti-individualistic theses regarding the epistemology of testimony. These were:

AI–K When *S*'s belief that *p* is formed through testimony, whether *S* counts as knowing (as opposed to merely truly believing) *p* depends on facts regarding one (or more) of *S*'s social peers;

AI–W When *S*'s belief that *p* is formed through testimony, the warrant (= total truth-conducive support) enjoyed by *S*'s belief that *p* depends on facts regarding one (or more) of *S*'s social peers;

and

AI–J Whether *S* counts as justified in accepting a piece of testimony – as having the epistemic right or entitlement to accept the piece of testimony – depends on facts regarding one (or more) of *S*'s social peers.

In chapter 5 I claimed that AI–K and AI–W should be uncontroversial, and I gave evidence that they are widely accepted by epistemologists working on testimony (no matter their views about the nature of epistemic justification). And while AI–J is controversial, I gave two distinct arguments in support of it.

My initial case for AI–J was presented in chapter 5. After showing that AI–J is true given anti-reductionist views of the conditions on justified acceptance of testimony, I went on to argue that anti-reductionism is to be preferred to reductionism in that the former but not the latter squares with a particular *desideratum* on theories of the epistemic dimension of communication. What is more, in the course of defending anti-reductionism against the charge of being a recipe for gullibility (in chapter 6), I argued that anti-reductionism is motivated as well by parallels with other domains – I focused mainly on perception and memory – involving *de facto* reliable belief-formation and -sustainment, where the reliability in question is achieved through processing that is largely subcognitive.

In this chapter I seek to address another worry that one might have in connection to the anti-reductionist approach from which AI–J follows. Where the objection from gullibility left AI–W in place, the present worry actually derives from AI–W itself, and in particular from AI–W's implications for the rationality of testimonial belief. Since AI–W is common ground in the debate over the epistemology of testimony, the worry to be discussed here is one that will have to be faced by anyone, regardless of their views about the conditions on the justified acceptance of testimony. However, as we will see, the worry from rationality might appear to put particular pressure on those views – such as anti-reductionism, at least as I am presenting it – that link justification to the materials that make for warrant. The result is that it is particularly important for my defense of anti-reductionism to take up this matter.

In responding on behalf of AR + to the worry from rationality, my main conclusions will be two. First, considerations pertaining to communication-based knowledge and belief suggest that there is a notion of rationality on which rationality itself (like warrant) is 'socially diffuse'. Second, if the notion of justification is to be understood in terms of the notion of rationality, it is socially diffuse rationality that should provide that understanding. As a result, even if we grant that there are notions of rationality on which rationality is detached from considerations of warrant, *such notions are not the ones that are relevant to the notion of epistemic justification.*

The last point is worth underlining, given its dialectical importance. The aim here is not to deny that there are individualistic notions of rationality (of course there are), but rather to suggest that these notions do not provide the proper lens through which to understand the notion of epistemic justification.[1] My more general conclusion is that both anti-reductionism and AI–J are defensible, as embodying the sort of socially

---

[1] One might worry that my ecumenical spirit here weakens the interest of this chapter's conclusion. After all, if all that I am interested in showing is that there are anti-individualistic notions of justification and rationality, why couldn't an individualist – or, as they are more commonly known in epistemology, an internalist – simply concede this point without further ado? What then would be the interest of the present chapter?

In reaction, it must be borne in mind that individualism and internalism in epistemology, like their counterparts in the philosophy of mind and language, are strong claims. As I noted in chapter 5, internalism regarding an epistemic property e is the view that facts regarding whether a given cognitive state of S's has e supervene on conditions that are first-personally accessible to S. As I noted in footnote 5 of that chapter, such a thesis is not plausible with

diffuse rationality that, I will argue, is a core part of our assessment of the epistemological dimension of communication-based belief. From this perspective, the present worry about the rationality of testimonial belief, though identifying a real limitation on our ability to rationally police our beliefs, should not prompt us to a reactionary return to an unacceptable conception of epistemic justification.

7.2 THE SOCIAL DIFFUSION OF TESTIMONIAL WARRANT

As defended in chapter 5, AI–W tells us that the warrant (or total truth-conducive support) for a belief formed through accepting another's testimony depends on factors regarding interlocutors upstream in the chain of communication. It is for this reason that AI–W is an *anti-individualistic* thesis: the claim is that warranted testimonial belief implicates facts about (the cognitive processing of) the hearer's *interlocutor*(s). At the very least, such a claim implies an anti-supervenience claim to the following effect ('SDW' for the Social Diffusion of Warrant'):

SDW The total knowledge-relevant epistemic support enjoyed by a subject *S*'s testimonial belief is not exhausted by (i) the reasons *S* had for trusting her source, where *S* herself would cite these reasons upon (possibly searching) reflection, and (ii) the proper functioning of *S*'s cognitive system in the context in question.

SDW captures an important point: neither the reasons that the hearer has available to searching reflection, nor facts about the proper functioning of her cognitive system in the context in question, exhaust the total truth-conducive epistemic support enjoyed by her testimony-based belief. (Two subjects alike with respect to (i) and (ii) might nevertheless differ along the dimension of warrant.)

---

respect to the status of *knowledge*. But the internalist thesis is typically advanced, not regarding *knowledge*, but rather regarding *justification*, and, I would guess, regarding *rationality* as well. Such a view amounts to the strong claim that justification-facts and rationality-facts supervene on the first-personally accessible. Now it is simply not open to such a position to allow that there is a notion of rationality like the one I will be developing in this chapter, for in that case it would be false that justification and rationality *in that sense* supervene on the first-personally accessible. So at the very least the present chapter can be taken to show that, even as restricted to justification and rationality, epistemic internalism, as construed here, is unacceptable. This strikes me as an interesting result; and I submit that it remains an interesting result even after it is conceded that there are notions of rationality conforming to the internalist accessibility requirements.

In keeping with my use of 'warrant' whereby it designates the total knowledge-relevant (truth-conducive) epistemic support enjoyed by a belief, SDW is a thesis about warrant: it asserts that warrant in cases of testimonial belief does not supervene on (i) and (ii). What else do we need to add to (i) and (ii), such that we will have arrived at a supervenience base for testimonial warrant? AI–W itself provides the answer: we need to add the warrant enjoyed by the testimony itself. To return to the doppelgän-ger cases of Fred/Wilma and Fred*/Wilma* from chapter 5: Wilma knows that Swinegarten was at the stonecutter's conference, whereas Wilma* has a merely true belief to that effect, because Fred, but not Fred*, offered testimony that was based on a knowledge-sufficient war-rant. I will describe this situation by saying that testimonial warrant is *socially diffuse*: the warrant enjoyed by the hearer's testimony-based belief is a function of (among other things) the warrant enjoyed by the testi-monies upstream in the chain of communication. So much would appear patent.

7.3 RATIONALITY

But trouble looms. In her 2006 paper, Fricker herself gestures at the trouble. In a passage I cited in chapter 5, she notes the social diffusion of testimonial warrant:

Knowledgeable belief based on trusted testimony implicitly refers back to the existence of a non-testimonial ground or warrant for what is testified to: the ground or warrant in virtue of whose possession the original teller spoke from knowledge ... *When I know that P solely from trust in testimony, I do not possess the evidence for P.* Instead, my knowledge is premised on the existential supposition that there is non-testimonial evidence for P, although I myself do not possess it. I suppose that *a person or persons upstream in the chain of informants between them possess that evidence* – the grounds for believing P true. (Fricker 2006: 241; italics added)

However, Fricker immediately follows this acknowledgment with an editorial comment: "Epistemic dependence on others, while it extends one's knowledge base so enormously, also *lessens one's ability rationally to police one's belief system for falsity*" (2006: 242; italics added). The trouble at which she appears to be gesturing is this. Rational policing of one's beliefs is, at least in substantial part, a matter of tailoring one's beliefs (or one's degree of confidence in them) to the support enjoyed by those beliefs. This in turn requires surrendering a belief when one has evidence bearing against that belief, or against what one took to support that belief. Suppose I have the sensory experience as of a red surface over yonder, on the basis of which I form the belief that the surface is red. If I find out that a uniform red light is illuminating the surface, then so long as I have no reasons to distrust or discount the information I just acquired, I ought to withdraw my judgment (surrender my belief) that the surface is red. If I don't, I am ignoring the evidence: the persistence of my belief in the face of this evidence is epistemically remiss, warranting a charge of irrationality.

Consider now how this requirement of rationality, according to which we ought not to ignore relevant evidence, bears on beliefs acquired through testimony. You tell me that Mike Mussina (one of the Yankees' best pitchers) has seriously injured his pitching arm. Your evidence for this (which you do not share with me) is based on an observation you made while in the Yankees' dugout earlier today in New York: you saw a man whom you took to be Mussina clutching his right arm, wincing in pain. Some time later that same evening you and I are taking part in a conversation, when it comes out that Mussina has been in Chicago all week. You immediately draw the inference that the man you saw wincing in pain in the Yankees' dugout was not Mussina, and so you immediately (but privately) surrender your belief that Mussina has seriously injured his pitching arm. But I continue to believe that Mussina has been injured. Although I am aware that the Yankees' dugout is in New York and not Chicago, I do not realize that your testimony (on which I based my belief regarding Mussina's injury) was itself based on your having taken yourself – incorrectly, it now turns out – to have seen Mussina in the Yankees' dugout wincing in pain earlier in the day. This is a case in which I myself believe something that functions as a (doxastic) defeater of the warrant enjoyed by my testimony-based belief, yet I don't realize this, and so do not revise my confidence in my testimony-based belief accordingly.

This example can be described as a limitation in my ability to police my own beliefs for falsehood. It is clear that these limitations flow directly from the socially diffuse nature of the warrant my belief enjoys. In particular, the limitation in question arises because of the very feature that makes testimonial belief distinctive: in accepting testimony one is epistemically relying on the speaker to have testified appropriately, and one relies on another speaker in this way only when one oneself does not have access to the details regarding what considerations support the testimony one has accepted.[2] In any case in which this is so, one will not know when the support enjoyed by the testimony one has consumed – what in chapter 5 I called 'distinctly testimonial support' – is undermined by a defeater. The result is that one can acquire evidence that itself counts as a defeater of the warrant of the testimony she herself consumed, in which case the warrant for her belief based on that testimony is undermined as well – all without the hearer's awareness of what is going on.

It should be clear, then, that the social diffuseness of testimonial warrant makes trouble for a subject's efforts to police her beliefs for falsehood. But Fricker's description of such cases goes further: she alleges that they amount to a diminution in "our ability *rationally* to police our beliefs for falsehood." This characterization initially appears a bit odd. After all, as Fricker characterizes matters, the hearer doesn't even "possess the evidence" for her testimony-based belief (her interlocutor, or the original source, does). But in that case the subject's failure to see how the new evidence bears on the old evidence is a failure to appreciate something about evidence she does not possess. It can seem strange to describe this as a failure of *rationality*.

At the same time, I think that Fricker's basic idea here is not hard to appreciate. We want to think that we are sensitive to matters pertaining to the (likely) truth of our beliefs. That is, we want to think that if there are conditions that bear on the (likely) truth of our beliefs, then, insofar as we are in a position to discern that such conditions have obtained, we will *ipso facto* revise our belief (or perhaps merely our degree of confidence) accordingly.[3] Given our limited epistemic perspectives, we hope at least to be able to make the most with what limited information we do have. In this

---

[2] Compare Jonathan Adler: "Knowledge obtained purely by transmission or testimony is 'thin.' What the seeker knows via satisfying TK [a principle pertaining to testimonial knowledge] is simply the correctness of p. He does not, specifically, come thereby to understand at all why p is correct" (Adler 1996: 107).

[3] Admittedly, this principle breaks down in connection with conditions whose bearing on belief an ordinary human subject could not be reasonably expected to discern. Suppose that there is a worldly condition C, directly observable by humans, whose obtaining renders our beliefs about monkeys unreliable. Suppose that this fact is not yet known by medical science or psychology. One might be aware that C has obtained, without being aware of C's bearing on one's presently formed monkey beliefs. In this case, no one would think to describe such a subject as failing to rationally police her beliefs. But this is because the bearing of C on her monkey beliefs is not something any ordinary subject can be expected to know. Testimony cases are not like this since the way undercutting works there involves conditions whose bearing on belief an ordinary subject could be expected to know – at least if she is aware of the basis of the testimony she has consumed.

respect, the acquisition of beliefs through accepting another's say-so introduces something like a *cognitive access barrier* between our beliefs, on the one hand, and the materials that make for the total truth-relevant support they enjoy, on the other, such that we could have information accessible to us whose epistemic relevance in this respect we cannot discern through even searching reflection.

We can make clear the relevance of rationality in this connection as follows. Imagine a person who acquires all of her beliefs regarding a particular subject-matter through testimony, where the subject-matter in question is such that she does not have the competence to evaluate the relevant evidence. *Qua* epistemic subject, she is totally dependent on her sources, not only for what she believes about this subject-matter, but also for becoming apprized of the epistemic relevance (if any) of newly encountered evidence. While it may be too much to say that (taken by herself) she herself is *irrational* in the face of relevant new evidence, it would not be too much to say that she herself does not know her way about the terrain, and hence is limited in her ability to *employ* her rationality in policing her beliefs for falsity. I think this is the sort of thing Fricker has in mind.[4]

We are now in a position to characterize the problem for rationality posed by the socially diffuse nature of testimonial warrant. Given the socially diffuse nature of testimonial warrant, the recipient of testimony places herself at risk of losing her way about the relevant evidential terrain, in such a way that there will be a corresponding diminution in her ability to employ her rationality in policing her testimony-based beliefs for falsity. The problem ramifies, of course, insofar as beliefs acquired through testimony stand in rational (evidential; probabilistic; logical) relations to other beliefs we have. The result is that our present problem is not an isolated one, but rather will adversely affect our ability to employ our rationality in policing our entire belief corpus. It would be too dramatic to describe this situation as one in which we have lost our epistemic way in our own epistemic house; but it would not be an exaggeration to describe it as one in which we suffer from a diminution in our capacity to discern the relations of epistemic relevance between the various beliefs we hold. If

---

[4] Fricker's own description suggests as much. She writes that testimonial beliefs "will lack the characteristic sensitivity to defeating evidence, should it come along, which is usually taken to be a hallmark of belief which amounts to knowledge" (Fricker 2006: 242).

this is not a tragic condition, it is not a pleasant one either. It would be good to see how we might resist the conclusion that this *is* our situation; or, failing that, to see how we might modify our epistemic expectations accordingly.

7.4 POSSIBLE REACTIONS

The foregoing problem is generated by AI–W, without appeal to any doctrine regarding the conditions on the justified acceptance of testimony. Accordingly, it must be faced by everyone, independent of one's position on the reductionism/anti-reductionism dispute. Even so, it might be thought that the problem gives one a reason to prefer reductionism over anti-reductionism. Such a verdict could be reached, for example, if it could be shown that the reductionist but not the anti-reductionist has a plausible response to the difficulty above.

First appearances might suggest that this is the case. In chapter 5, I criticized the reductionist for detaching issues of justification from issues of warrant: my claim was that, as a result of this detachment, reductionist positions will be unable to accept JES, whose preservation (I argued) is a *desideratum* on accounts of the epistemic dimension of communication. But it might now seem that the reductionist can defend the detachment, and the ensuing repudiation of JES, as the price that needs to be paid in order to have a plausible reply to the problem from rationality. For once issues of justification are detached from issues of warrant, one need only identify rationality with justification to be in a position to conclude that AI–W – a thesis about warrant – has no untoward effects on rationality at all. Thus it would seem that, while the problem of rationality is generated by a doctrine (accepted by all parties) regarding the social diffuseness of warrant, nevertheless the problem promises more trouble for anti-reductionist positions than for their reductionist rivals.

Or so it might seem. Against the appearances, however, I will be arguing that rationality considerations do not give us a reason to prefer RD over AR + . While the anti-reductionist is limited in what she can say in response to the difficulty, she is not the worse off for that: one of the responses available to the reductionist is implausible on its face; the best reductionist response faces difficulties in its turn; and the anti-reductionist response employed here, though having far-reaching (and initially counter-intuitive) implications, is supported by independent considerations.

7.4.1

I begin with the most radical response to the problem posed by rationality, which is to deny AI–W itself. The motivation for doing so is clear enough: AI–W is needed to generate the problem in the first place, so denying it blocks the problem from arising right at the outset. What is more, such a response is open to the reductionist, but not to the anti-reductionist – at least not as I have been presenting the position. The move to deny AI–W is open to the reductionist: having detached the notion of justification from that of warrant, the move to reject AI–W (a thesis about warrant) will not prevent her from saying everything she wants to say about justification. But the move is not open to the anti-reductionist, at least not if she hopes to motivate anti-reductionism in the manner of chapter 5: that motivation depends essentially on the construal of justification in terms of the materials that make for warrant. So if it can be shown that the best response to the problem above is to deny AI–W, we could conclude that the rationality problem gives us a reason to prefer reductionism to anti-reductionism (at least as motivated here).

But the move to deny AI–W is unacceptable. (Since I have already had my say about this in chapter 5, here I will be brief.) First, AI–W is supported by AI–K, together with the imminently plausible doctrine that knowledge differs from merely true belief in enjoying a greater amount of truth-conducive support.[5] Second, as noted in chapter 5 section 5.2, AI–W can be supported even if independent of AI–K. Third, as we have already seen, core reductionists (Fricker (2006); Faulkner (2000)) already accept AI–W, and epistemic internalists more generally (Conee (in conversation); Feldman (2004); Foley (2004)) accept the distinction between warrant and justification, and so would appear to be in a position to accept AI–W without any need to modify their theories of justification. Thus it would appear that such theorists themselves recognize the plausibility of AI–W.

In short, if reductionism is to be preferred to anti-reductionism on grounds pertaining to the rationality problem under discussion, it cannot be through its rejection of AI–W itself.

---

[5] The plausibility of this doctrine, in turn, flows from the two further widely held assumptions: first, that knowledge is belief whose truth is non-accidental; and second, that it is the truth-conducive or truth-indicative support of a true belief which renders its truth non-accidental. In any case the doctrine itself maintains that knowledge differs from merely true belief in *at least* that much; not that this is the *only* difference.

7.4.2

But reductionists need not deny AI–W to suppose that they have a comparative advantage on the score of rationality. For suppose that the reductionist accepts AI–W. Even so, on the basis of an identification of rational belief with justified belief, the reductionist can maintain that AI–W has no more implications regarding the *rationality* of testimonial belief, than it has implications regarding the *justification* of testimonial belief. And since, for the reductionist, changes in (degrees of) warrant do not by themselves make for changes in (degrees of) justification, it can be maintained that the former do not by themselves make for changes in (degrees of) rationality either.

This position appears to put the reductionist at a competitive advantage over the anti-reductionist on the score of rationality. In chapter 5 (especially sections 5.6 and 5.7) it was brought out that, on the anti-reductionist view, AI–W has substantive implications regarding the justification of testimonial belief. The result is that if the anti-reductionist accepts the identification of rational belief with justified belief, then she will have to allow that AI–W has substantive implications regarding the rationality of testimonial belief as well. Alternatively, the anti-reductionist who wishes to deny that AI–W has any substantive implications for the rationality of testimonial belief must reject the identification of rational belief with justified belief. Such a move would greatly weaken the case I presented for anti-reductionism, as it would force a corresponding complication in our overall bookkeeping regarding the epistemological dimension of communication. It would seem, then, that if the reductionist's move to link rational belief to justified belief is otherwise acceptable, the rationality problem may well favor reductionism over anti-reductionism.

The proposal, then, is to combine RD with the thesis that rational belief is justified belief, and in this way to show that an endorsement of AI–W has no untoward implications for the rationality of testimonial belief. The core idea in this position is to deny that rationality is a matter of our sensitivity to those conditions that *as a matter of fact* bear on the (likely) truth of our beliefs, and to replace such a view with one that restricts the purview of rationality to matters entirely within our subjective ken. Indeed, such a position can be motivated by reflecting on the Fred–Wilma and Fred*–Wilma* cases from chapter 5. The proposed position will hold that, while the two cases are asymmetrical at the level of *knowledge* and *warrant*, they are perfectly alike at the level of *justification* and *rationality*.

183

On such a view, what justifies both Wilma and Wilma* in their respective testimony-based beliefs, and what enters into assessments of rationality with respect to each's formation and sustainment of this belief, are the reasons each subject has (and would cite on searching reflection) for regarding her interlocutor as trustworthy on this occasion. These reasons of theirs remain the same, even if it turns out that the actual warrant enjoyed by their interlocutors' testimonies differs in the two cases.

An explicit expression of this sort of position is found in the 'hybrid' view of Faulkner 2000. His commitment to reductionism itself comes out in his commitment to what he calls the "internalist" idea that "the formation of a warranted testimonial belief requires a justifying argument that articulates the audience's reasons for believing" (2000: 292). As noted in chapter 5, Faulkner accepts AI–W as well, as is clear when he writes that "in accepting testimony an audience frequently believes propositions whose warrant could not possibly be equated with whatever justification the audience has for its acceptance ..." (2000: 291–2). But it is also clear that he regards the rationality of testimonial belief as restricted to the reasons that are available to the subject's reflection:

> If the *process* of acceptance is essentially the *rational* process of assessing credibility ..., then it seems better to characterize the posited testimonial faculty in internalist terms [e.g. in terms of introspectively accessible justifying reasons]. (Faulkner 2000: 593; italics in original)

(I should add that context makes it patent that he accepts the antecedent of this conditional.)

Although such a position has much to say for it, it does have some untoward implications. These can be best appreciated once we recognize that the present problem of rationality itself, although raised above in connection with testimony, is not unique to testimony-based belief. It can also be generated for beliefs based on memory.[6] Take the following case. At time t_1 I take myself to have a visual experience as of p, and so

---

[6] Indeed, Fricker herself appears to acknowledge this. She writes, "... Once the original source of a testimonially spread belief is no longer available, the original warrant for the belief is no longer retrievable. However, this feature characterizes most of our beliefs. Cognitively limited beings that we are, we generally form a belief from the evidence then store the fact in memory and jettison the evidence" (Fricker 2006: pp. 249–50, fn 33). However she immediately goes on to note that "[t]he lack of sensitivity to potentially refuting new evidence is, *in contrast, a risk of testimonial belief only*" (italics mine). As against this last point, I am about to go on and describe a memory case that appears to have precisely this feature.

(on that basis) form the belief that p. At time t_2 I acquire the information that q, where q is the following proposition: *visual information regarding whether p is unreliable*. So my belief in q (acquired at t_2) provides an undercutting defeater for my belief that p (acquired at t_1). However, although I know the bearing of q on beliefs acquired through vision, I do not revise my belief that p at t_2, since at t_2 I no longer remember that my belief that p was acquired through vision. (By t_2 I do not remember which, of the various sources that might have provided the information that p, did so.) Although this case does not involve testimony, it is structurally parallel to the case involving testimony-based belief, from 7.3. So the sort of situation we are discussing, in connection with a diminution in our ability to rationally police our beliefs for falsity, is not unique to testimony.

Let us say that an individual is *individualistically insensitive* to possible (undercutting) defeaters when she is such that if she were to encounter what in fact is an undercutting defeater for her belief she would fail to realize this (remaining rational all the while).[7] The present point is that, in the first instance, what renders a subject individualistically insensitive has nothing to do with testimony: an individual is individualistically insensitive whenever she fails to have access to details about the epistemic support (warrant) enjoyed by a given belief of hers – support whose truth-indicativeness *vis-à-vis* her belief might come into question in the face of future evidence. What is unique about testimony cases is simply that, given the social diffusion of testimonial warrant, what provides the most direct truth-conducive support to our testimony-based belief (namely, whatever it is that supports the testimony we've consumed) is not something to which the hearer *ever* had access in the first place.[8] While this means that subjects will typically (always?) be individualistically insensitive *vis-à-vis* their testimony-based beliefs, in principle the same effects could be brought about (via memory failures, for example) in connection with non-testimonial beliefs (contra Fricker (2006: 250, fn 33)). So to the extent that one shares Fricker's worry about the diminution of our ability rationally to police our testimony-based beliefs, one's worry will expand into a worry regarding our ability to keep track

---

[7] Construing the problem posed by rationality as a matter of insensitivity to defeaters is in keeping with Fricker's own presentation of the problem. See her 2006: 242.

[8] See Goldberg 2006 for a defense of this point about the *directness* of the truth-conducive support provided by the testifier's warrant.

of the truth-conducive support of our beliefs more generally – no matter *how* they were initially acquired.

This fact spells trouble for the sort of position, like Faulkner's, that links rationality with justification while simultaneously detaching justification from the materials that make for warrant. The following case illustrates. A cognitively normal human in all other respects, Daphna suffers from a condition that I will call *source-forgetfulness*: it regularly happens that she fails to keep track of the source of her beliefs – i.e. whether it was through testimony, or through a sensory modality (and if so which one), or through reasoning from other beliefs, etc. – where what is lost through such source-forgetfulness is irrecoverable by her via methods of reflection. As a result, it often happens that she acquires doxastic defeaters to which she is individualistically insensitive, where her individualistic insensitivity is generated by her poor memory (her 'source-forgetfulness'), and where this condition cannot be rectified by her most searching reflection on the matter. She continues to have reasons for her beliefs, even as she forgets their sources; only her reasons are culled from that part of her belief corpus to which she continues to have memorial access.

Daphna once acquired the belief that there are albino penguins from having seen an albino-looking penguin in the zoo. Several weeks later she recalls that there are albino penguins, but has forgotten how she came to acquire this belief. She continues to believe that there are albino penguins; but if asked what reasons she has for believing this she would say such things as that she distinctly remembers having learned this somewhere, although she can't say where or when. The result is that when she reads in the paper that for the past several months the zookeeper has been playing tricks on visitors, painting some of the animals white, she accepts this but fails to see its epistemic relevance to her belief regarding the existence of albino penguins. (For all she knows, she acquired her belief about albino penguins through reliance on trustworthy testimony.) Nor is this an isolated example: it often happens that she is individualistically insensitive to doxastic defeaters she acquires.

Now Daphna's twin sister Dalia is very much like Daphna except that Dalia does not suffer from source-forgetfulness. On the contrary, Dalia's memory functions normally. As a result she is much better at 'policing her beliefs for falsity.' So, for example, whereas she, too, saw an albino-looking penguin in the zoo several weeks ago, and so on that basis acquired the belief that there are albino penguins, she gives this belief up as soon as she read the report about the zookeeper in the paper.

Now it is uncontroversial that Dalia is better than Daphna at 'policing her beliefs for falsity.' More controversial will be several other claims one might make about the *comparative rationality* of the two twins: for example, that Dalia's beliefs enjoy a better rational standing than do Daphna's; or that, given its dynamics, Dalia's belief-corpus exhibits a higher degree of rationality than that exhibited by Daphna's belief-corpus; or that Dalia's belief-revisions are more rational than those of her sister. And yet there would appear to be good grounds for endorsing these claims about the sisters' comparative rationality. It can hardly be denied, for example, that there is a clear epistemic difference between the two women: Dalia is in a happier epistemic situation than is her twin sister. Moreover, the more Daphna forgets the sources of her beliefs, the more removed she is from the original reasons she had for acquiring (and subsequently sustaining) these beliefs. Although she continues to regard herself as having reasons in support of her beliefs, these reasons are ever more abstract, and depend ever more on generic memory considerations, rather than on the specific details of the original reasons for acquisition. It remains true, of course, that, within what is available to her via searching reflection, Daphna behaves in an epistemically excellent way. Even so, she is extremely epistemically impoverished *vis-à-vis* her sister.

Consider how the sisters' comparative situations will be described according to the present position, on which issues of rationality and justification are detached from issues of warrant. Such a position will have to hold that whatever it is that differentiates Daphna's and Dalia's epistemic perspectives, Daphna's source-forgetfulness by itself has no negative implications along either the dimension of rationality or the dimension of justification. It can allow that Daphna is more susceptible than is Dalia to retaining false beliefs (in the face of doxastic defeaters); but even so, on the view presently under discussion, this is not a matter to be understood in terms of Daphna's ability to rationally police her beliefs for falsity, or of the justification enjoyed by her beliefs in the face of acquiring such doxastic defeaters. On the contrary, the present view holds that Daphna's epistemic perspective is not blemished along these dimensions, given that the flaws in her perspective are beyond her subjective ken.

But how plausible is such a view? Two reasons suggest that it is not very plausible. First, it should be readily conceded that, when it comes to the employment of rationality in policing one's beliefs for falsity, Daphna is in a poorer position than is Dalia: even though Daphna and Dalia are equally adept at the various skills needed for belief-updating (logic, probability theory, statistics, or what-have-you), Dalia is better able to put these skills to use in her efforts to acquire and retain interesting truths and to avoid and weed out falsity. Second, it seems curious indeed to suppose that Daphna's extreme cognitive impoverishment has no affect on assessments of how justified she is (how justified her beliefs are; I will return to the issue of rationality below). If both she and her sister recall (and so form the memorial belief) that *p*, do we really want to say that they are equally justified in doing so – that their respective memorial beliefs are justified to the same degree – as long as neither retains her belief in *p* in the face of what *she herself recognizes to be* doxastic defeaters? If so, then we reach the paradoxical conclusion that Daphna's cognitive deficit makes it easier for her to retain justified memorial beliefs than it is for Dalia, since Daphna's cognitive deficit shields her from recognizing doxastic defeaters. On the contrary, it seems better to say that Daphna's cognitive deficit renders her memorial belief that *p less justified* than is her sister's memorial belief that *p*. In defense of this description we can make a point here, in connection with the justification of memorial belief, that is an analogue of the point that Fricker herself made regarding the justification of testimonial belief: in both cases, justification appears to require some sort of "counterfactual sensitivity" to the kinds of factors that would undermine the trustworthiness of a content presented-as-true (Fricker 1994: 154). This is no less true when speaking of memorial belief, where it is *one's own memory system* that is presenting the content as true, than it is when speaking of testimonial beliefs, where it is *another speaker* who is presenting the content as true. It would thus seem that, to the extent that ascriptions of rationality go hand-in-hand with ascriptions of justification, Daphna's memory-sustained belief in *p* does not have the same rational standing as does Dalia's. Of course, what goes in the case of *memory*-induced individualistic insensitivity goes in the case of *testimony*-induced insensitivity as well: to the extent that a subject is individualistically insensitive, she suffers from a diminishment in her capacity to police her beliefs for falsity.

Now for those antecedently committed to internalist conceptions of justification and rationality, I do not imagine that the foregoing will convince them to abandon such conceptions; they will continue to retain those conceptions in the face of the problem of rationality, and will let the chips fall where they may. But I do think that the foregoing considerations make it reasonable to consider whether there are other ways for dealing with the problem of rationality – ways that would not have us detach the notions of rationality and justification from the notion of warrant (or total truth-conducive support). For, given the untoward implications of the foregoing position, we should be satisfied with such a position only if there are no other, more plausible ways to deal with the problem of rationality. By extension, it is only if there are no other such ways of dealing with that problem, that we can regard considerations of rationality as favoring reductionism over anti-reductionism. So our examination must consider other responses.

7.4.3

Before moving on to a response – and I think the only response – open to anti-reductionists, I want to consider one other response available to reductionists but not to anti-reductionists. This response detaches the link between justification and rationality, allowing that the social diffusion of warrant has implications for our capacity to rationally police our belief for falsity, while denying that it has any untoward implications for justification.

I am not certain how to motivate such a position. In fact, I would otherwise be inclined to skip over this position, for thinking that it is bound to degenerate into one or another of two positions (the one from 7.4.2 just discussed, or the one to be examined in 7.4.4). My reason for including it is simply that Fricker herself, an important theorist in the epistemology of testimony, appears to occupy something like this position. ('Appears': I am not certain of this attribution.)[9] I have already cited Fricker's own recent remarks in her (2006) about the nature of evidence in testimony cases – a remark which indicates her endorsement of the social diffusion of testimonial warrant. What is more, it is clear from her work on testimony that she comes at this with a solid commitment to employing an epistemically internalist notion of justification (see Fricker 1987 and 1994). And yet she also holds the view (cited earlier) that "Epistemic dependence on others, while it extends one's knowledge base so enormously, *also lessens one's ability rationally to police one's belief system for falsity*" (2006: 242). Since a belief sustained by a subject who suffers from a diminished ability rationally to police her belief system for

---

[9] For example, Fricker comments (2006: 240) that "My trust in another's word is rational when I have good grounds to believe her competent about her topic and sincere . . ." This would suggest that Fricker's view is like Faulkner's, described above. However, as I will go on to note, she says other things about the *sustainment* of one's testimonial belief, suggesting that her view is not like Faulkner's.

falsity is a belief whose rational credentials are themselves somewhat diminished, it would seem that Fricker's view recognizes that the social diffusion of warrant affects the rationality of a subject's beliefs, even as she denies that the social diffusion of warrant affects the justification of the subject's beliefs. Her difference with Faulkner, it would appear, can be traced to their respective conceptions of the scope of rationality. Fricker's is the more expansive conception: for her but not for Faulkner, full rationality requires a sensitivity not just to considerations that bear against one's internalistically accessible reasons, but also to considerations that bear against one's warrant. (If this isn't her view then I cannot see why she did not endorse the line of 7.4.2, according to which the social diffuseness of testimonial warrant has no implications for assessments of rationality.)

If this reconstruction of Fricker's view is correct, then she has implicitly endorsed the relevance to rationality of considerations bearing on testimonial warrant. But for precisely this reason, I suspect that the position she is (appears to be) trying to occupy is unstable. For I want to go on to suggest that, once one acknowledges the relevance to rationality of considerations bearing on testimonial warrant, then one would do better to endorse the next response to the rationality problem, according to which rationality itself, like warrant, should be seen as socially diffuse. If I am correct in this, then Fricker is best advised, either to side with Faulkner and reject the relevance to rationality of considerations bearing on testimonial warrant, or else accept this relevance but at the cost of having to endorse the anti-individualistic response presented below (and with it reject her own favored internalist approach to rationality and her reductionistic approach to epistemic justification).

7.4.4

So far we have considered three responses to the problem of rationality. The first rejected AI–W, and the next two involved accepting AI–W while denying any untoward implications regarding rationality and/or justification. The move to reject AI–W was seen to be implausible on its face; and the two attempts to deflate AI–W's implications regarding rationality and/or justification each raise questions regarding the epistemic import of the notions of justification and rationality so conceived. I now want to consider a position which endorses AI–W, but which conceives of justification, with the anti-reductionist, in terms of (reliability-generated) warrant. If such a view also endorses the link between justification and rationality, then the result will be a doctrine that I will call *the social diffusion of rationality*. Here I describe the view; in the section following I offer reasons to think that it is plausible – or at least no *less* plausible than the position described in 7.4.2.

The present reaction to the dialectic concerning rationality agrees with Fricker, that the sort of insensitivity to relations of epistemic relevance exhibited in testimony cases *is* correctly described as having a non-negligible effect on the subject's rational belief-policing. But the present reaction disagrees with her over the proper conclusion to draw. Whereas Fricker concludes, conservatively, merely by noting a diminution in our ability rationally to police our beliefs, the present reaction uses the subject's testimony-generated insensitivity to relations of epistemic relevance as the occasion to *re-think what is involved in rational belief-policing itself*. In particular, the present reaction proposes that we ought to move from a more individualistic conception, to a more social conception, of what is involved in the rational policing of one's beliefs. I examine this proposal in greater detail in the next section.

7.5 TOWARDS A CONCEPTION OF RATIONALITY AS SOCIALLY DIFFUSE

The proposal of 7.4.4 is to reconceive (the nature of) the resources available to an individual for the purpose of managing her own individualistic insensitivity. The key idea is that the hearer utilizes other speakers in her attempt to manage the very insensitivity which her reliance on her co-linguals helped to bring about in the first place. This will involve utilizing other speakers, not merely as testifiers, but also as critics of testimony.

Suppose hearer H believes that p on the basis of S's testimony to that effect, where S's testimony is itself supported by e. Some time later H acquires information i, which as a matter of fact undermines the truth-conducive support e provides to H's belief that p. Since H does not appreciate the bearing of i on the support enjoyed by her belief that p, H is unaware that her belief that p has been epistemically imperiled. As a result, she is not sensitive to the need to do anything to rectify this situation. But in the course of everyday life, she often does something that addresses this situation: she subjects her beliefs to social scrutiny. Sometimes she does so deliberately: realizing that she has a roomful of experts on some topic relating to her belief that p, she raises the issue of the truth-value of p, and in this way works to minimize whatever individualistic insensitivity she might have *vis-à-vis* her belief that p. (Her hope here is that, while she herself may be individualistically insensitive to relevant evidence, those in her audience will bring such evidence – if there is any – to her attention.) But far more frequently her beliefs are subjected to social scrutiny in a way that is not the effect of some deliberate act on her part: sometimes she asserts p, taking herself to know (and so to be letting her audience know) that p, and yet she finds herself with someone who disagrees over whether p – thereby occasioning the sort of disagreement that typically requires each party to offer support for its contention. Such disagreements enable her beliefs to be socially 'groomed' (as it were) even as it was not her intention to do so.

Now the appeal to social scrutiny, by itself, will not serve to differentiate the proposal of 7.4.4 from the previous proposals. This is because even those who conceive of justification in internalist terms, and those who favor reductionist accounts of testimonial justification, can ascribe a rationality-enhancing role to social scrutiny. On such a view, social scrutiny regarding S's belief that p enhances the rational standing of that belief insofar as such scrutiny is explicitly represented in S's own belief-system – that is, insofar as S herself forms reasonable beliefs about (for example) the epistemic utility of such scrutiny, the relevant knowledge-ableness of her peers, the (explicit or implicit) confirmation she receives when they agree with her (or at least don't object to her statements), and so forth. These beliefs of S's (about the utility of social scrutiny etc.) in turn become further reasons S has in support of her belief that p, rationalizing its continued sustainment. The upshot is that, on a reductionist (or internalist) view, it is not others' scrutiny *per se*, but rather what S believes about that scrutiny, that enhances the rational standing of S's belief that p.

As against this, the distinctive nature of the proposal of 7.4.4 lies in its repudiation of the intermediary role played by S's own beliefs regarding the epistemic utility of social scrutiny. On the present proposal, it is not S's own beliefs about the role played by such scrutiny, but instead *the actual reliability-enhancing (or -undermining) effects of that scrutiny*, that matters to the rational standing of S's belief that p. As we might put it: in subjecting one's beliefs to social scrutiny (whether deliberately or not), the task of rationally policing one's beliefs is *distributed*, as it includes aspects of one's larger epistemic community.

It will be helpful to formulate more clearly the proposal in question, which I will designate as the Social Diffusion of Rationality. To a first approximation, it can be formulated as a claim about the supervenience base of ascriptions of rationality (as these pertain to beliefs formed and sustained through would-be rational belief-policing). The following formulation is meant to recall the corresponding anti-supervenience thesis regarding warrant from section 7.1 above:

SDR The rational standing of S's belief that p is not exhausted by (i) considerations pertaining to the coherence of S's belief that p within S's own belief corpus, and (ii) the proper functioning of S's cognitive system in the context in question.

SDR entails that there could be two subjects, alike with respect to how well each's belief that p coheres with the rest of her belief corpus, and alike as well with respect to the proper functioning of their respective cognitive system in the contexts, yet where they differ in the rational standing enjoyed by their respective beliefs that p.

Consider the following illustration. Let A and B be two believers who are as individualistically alike as any two believers can be. Both believe that p, and both would cite the same reasons in support of their belief that p. What is more, each believes with respect to her current peer group that some of its members are better-positioned than she is *vis-à-vis* the truth-pertinent support bearing on p; so both A and B subject their respective p-beliefs to social scrutiny. Now imagine that in both cases, their current peer groups are silent in the face of the statement that p, and that both A and B interpret this silence as indicating an absence of relevant defeaters within the respective peer communities. But now imagine that there is this difference: only A's peers really are, as believed, well-positioned regarding the truth-relevant support for p. (B's belief that his peers are well-positioned, though based on very good reasons, is mistaken: the silence of his peers actually reflects the fact that they don't so much as understand what B said.)

Next, let us consider how this case will be treated by the two competing proposals. The proposal of 7.4.2 regards rational standing as exclusively a matter of one's sensitivity to factors bearing on one's introspectively accessible reasons. Proponents of this view will hold that A's and B's respective p-beliefs enjoy the same rational standing. After all, the reasons A and B would cite in support of their respective p-beliefs are the same, both A and B would cite the same reasons for presuming their peers to be relevantly knowledgeable, and they would cite the same reasons for interpreting the silence of their peers as providing an indication of no relevant defeaters. The proponents of the view of 7.4.4, by contrast, will hold that, despite the type-identity in the introspectively accessible reasons each subject brings to bear on the question whether p, A's belief enjoys a better rational standing – alternatively, a higher degree of justification – than does B's belief. This is in virtue of the fact that only A's peers really are well-positioned regarding the truth-relevant support for p.

Below I will argue in support of such a view over its rivals in 7.4.2 and 7.4.3. First, however, it is worth pointing out one implication of the present position. In particular, the truth of SDR would entail the truth of the corresponding anti-individualistic doctrine regarding rationality:

AI–R   A complete account of the rational standing of S's (testimonial) belief that p depends on facts regarding one (or more) of S's social peers.

The social diffusion of rationality, SDR, stands to the anti-individualistic AI–R precisely as the social diffusion of warrant, SDW, stands to the corresponding anti-individualist thesis AI–W.

7.6 IN DEFENSE OF SDR AND AI–R

I have been suggesting that, in reaction to the problem of rationality under consideration, the proponent of an anti-reductionist view of testimonial justification ought to endorse the position of 7.4.4 (and with it, AI–R). I now want to offer independent reasons in support of such a position. The main source of support comes from a parallel between the rationality- and justification-enhancing role played by social scrutiny, on the one hand, and that played by individualistic coherence considerations, on the other. Here I want to develop this parallel. The conclusions I will draw are two: first, that (without calling into question the existence or the utility of more 'individualistic' notions of rationality) there is an importantly anti-individualistic kind of rationality at play in beliefs acquired through testimony; and second, that it is this kind of rationality that is most directly linked to the notion of justification. Arguing for these conclusions will complete my case for the position of 7.4.4, and with it AI–R.

I begin first with a truism concerning the degree to which considerations of individualistic coherence – that is, coherence within *one's own* belief corpus – enhance the rational standing of one's belief. The truism is this: individualistic coherence considerations enhance the rational standing of one's belief that p to the degree that the background corpus in question is *robust* and *systematic*, involving such things as probabilistic consistency and explanatory relations (see Bonjour 1985; Thagard 2000, chapter 3; Bonjour and Sosa 2003: 46–8; Sosa 2004). This truism reflects the following idea: passing the test of coherence is more rigorous to the degree that one's background belief corpus is robust and systematic. Now there are various connections we might see between the rigorousness of passing the test of coherence, on the one hand, and the rational standing of belief, on the other. For one thing, more rigorous tests are harder to pass, and it it arguable that the greater the difficulty of passing coherence tests, the more likely it is that beliefs that pass are true. Alternatively, perhaps passing a more difficult coherence test indicates that the corpus has resources for answering a range of objections. Whatever explanation we prefer, the point remains that the degree of difficulty in passing the coherence test correlates with degree of the coherence-generated contribution to a belief's rational standing. A corresponding point holds regarding justification as well: in a case where a new piece of information does succeed at fitting into the subject's belief corpus, the (coherence-generated) epistemic justification enjoyed by the newly acquired belief is enhanced in proportion to the antecedent difficulty of fitting. Now if this is so – and I do not intend the foregoing remarks to be controversial – then we can say that coherence contributes to rational standing, and so to justification, in direct proportion to how severe the test of coherence is.

Now the proposal of 7.4.4 is supported by the idea that the very same thing can be said of subjecting one's beliefs to social scrutiny. Subjecting one's beliefs to the scrutiny of the appropriate epistemic community – one that is both relevantly knowledgeable and outspoken – typically amounts to a *more rigorous testing* of one's belief, than that which is provided by considerations of internal coherence alone. On such an account, the rational standing of one's belief is enhanced to the degree that one's epistemic community *is* relevantly knowledgeable and outspoken. If *S* happens to be in the unhappy situation of *believing falsely* that she is interacting with an epistemic community that is both outspoken and knowledgeable whether *p*, then, *no matter how good her reasons for this false belief seem to her*, her interaction with that community (and her interpretation of their silences in the face of her assertion that *p*) will not greatly enhance the rational standing of her belief that *p*. Compare: if a person falsely (but coherently) believes that her belief corpus is robust and systematic, then, no matter how good her reasons are (or at least seem to her to be) for this meta-belief, the rational standing of her belief that *p* will not be greatly enhanced by the fact that it coheres within her (actually anemic) belief corpus. If this holds with respect to the relevance of individualistic coherence to rationality, it should also hold, *mutatis mutandis*, with respect to the relevance of social scrutiny to rationality. In this way we see that the hypothesis of the social diffusion of rationality itself follows from (what I claim is) a parallel between the way considerations of internal coherence enhance a belief's rational standing, and the way considerations of social scrutiny enhance do.

Of course, a given subject can usually tell something about how knowledgeable and outspoken her audience is. But unless subjects always know when their peers are relevantly knowledgeable and outspoken, there will be occasions on which what a subject *believes* regarding her peers (which will constitute her reasons for thinking her belief in question has passed through a rigorous process of social scrutiny) will not match the *actual knowledgeableness* of her peers (and so will not match the actual rigorousness of the process of social scrutiny). On those occasions, the subject's reasons for thinking that a given belief of hers successfully passed the test of social scrutiny – reasons which include other beliefs of hers (some of which are false) regarding the knowledgeableness of her peers – will not reflect the actual rational standing of the belief in question. That is, her reasons will not reflect the actual rational standing of the belief in question, *assuming* that the rational standing of the belief is determined in part by the actual difficulty (as opposed to what she takes to be the difficulty) of having passed the test of social scrutiny.

7.6.1

So far we have examined four distinct reactions to a problem regarding the rational policing of beliefs one acquires through the acceptance of testimony. Of these reactions the first three were open only to the reductionist, and the last is open only to the anti-reductionist (as it is open only to those willing to link rationality and justification to the materials that make for warrant). At this point is should be clear that each of the positions comes at a cost. The question is which of the four positions, with its combination of virtues and drawbacks, is the most attractive overall position. I submit that the position of 7.4.4 would appear to be the best of the options, and in any case is no worse off than the position of 7.4.2 (which, I argued, is the best of the positions open to the reductionist).

The position of 7.4.2 held that the only considerations relevant to issues of rationality and justification were those pertaining to the thinker's reasons for believing as she does – reasons she herself could cite on searching reflection. It is a virtue that, on such a position, SDW (the Social Diffusion of Warrant), which everyone should want to embrace, has no untoward implications for justification or rationality. But this same position also had seriously revisionary (even 'paradoxical') implications, brought out in connection with the case of Daphna and her source-forgetfulness. Consider then the position of 7.4.4. The virtues of such a position are several: it preserves the link between rationality and justification; it avoids the 'paradoxical' implication of the position of 7.4.2; and its analysis is independently supported by a parallel between the rationality- and justification-enhancing role played by considerations of individual coherence, and that played by considerations of social scrutiny. Admittedly, the position of 7.4.4 has revisionary implications regarding our conception of rationality; but these implications stop short of paradoxicality, and in any case are directly supported by the parallel just noted. All things considered, then, it would seem best to endorse the position of 7.4.4; or, at the very least, it is no less reasonable to do so, than to accept one of the other positions on offer. And so it would seem that considerations of rationality do not favor reductionism over anti-reductionism.

7.7 SIGNIFICANCE OF THE SOCIAL DIFFUSENESS OF RATIONALITY

In the foregoing section I spelled out some of the virtues of a position that would have us infer, from the social diffuseness of (testimonial) warrant (SDW), to the social diffuseness of rationality (SDR), and from there to anti-individualism regarding rationality (AI–R). Before bringing this chapter to a close I want to make two remarks about the significance of the latter hypothesis. These comments are offered in the spirit of suggesting further work.

A first point has to do with the overall ideological context of the hypothesis. In broad outline, this hypothesis concerns what we might call (broadly speaking) the 'marketplace of ideas.' The idea that there is such a marketplace, or that it might play an important role in our inquiries, is not new. My aim, rather, was to indicate that this marketplace may have an epistemic significance that has been largely overlooked. Traditionally, those who see an epistemic significance in the 'marketplace of ideas' articulate that significance in terms of its effects on the (likely) truth of our inquiries: the claim is often made that an unfettered marketplace aids our search for truth. (But see Goldman 1999 for a dissenting opinion.) Here I am making a slightly different point. My present claim is that participating in the marketplace of ideas – at least insofar as one's participation is in the appropriate marketplace – can affect the *rational standing* of the beliefs one brings to market. That is, subjecting one's beliefs to potential criticism is epistemically valuable not only in connection with one's attempt to acquire *true* beliefs, but also in connection with one's attempts to *enhance the rationality* of one's beliefs.[10]

A second point is this. If we are to put much stock in others' say-so for the purpose of managing our individualistic insensitivities, then we must be willing to see others as sometimes better-positioned, epistemically, on the subject-matter of our own beliefs. But it is clear that we should not always favor the opinion of others over our own, when the two conflict. This raises interesting questions regarding the epistemic significance of disagreement – a topic that has only recently begun to attract the attention that it deserves.[11] Here I note only that the proposal of the present chapter presupposes an adequate account in that domain.

7.8 CONCLUSION

In this chapter I have argued that, given the socially diffuse nature of testimonial warrant, we ought to endorse the claim that a belief's rational

---

[10] Compare van Gulick (2005: 281). I quote him at length (italics mine): "Many of the critical and corrective processes that keep our beliefs consistent, coherent, and in correspondence with the available evidence operate within the realm of social interchange and mutual discussion. The need to articulate and defend our beliefs in conversation with others often forces us to recognize inferential connections we might otherwise ignore. Contradictions and unsupported beliefs that might persist in the isolation of a single mind will more readily be detected and removed if exposed to the rational pressures of social dialogue. Like mutually interacting metering systems, cognitive agents can keep each other's belief more accurately anchored to the evidence. *Nor are social processes limited to the removal of error and the reduction of cognitive dissonance. They have a positive rational aspect as well. Through communication and cooperative intellectual activity we often extend the inferential reach of our beliefs and more fully draw out their positive implications and overall coherence.*" (Of course, van Gulick's point here can be accommodated within an epistmecially individualistic account as well as by the reliabilist account I favor.)

[11] Recent work includes Feldman (forthcoming) and Kelly (2005); and for a topic that bears on this, see also Goldman (2001b).

standing, insofar as it is relevant to its epistemic justification, is a socially diffuse affair as well. Admittedly, endorsing such a claim does not silence the worry, first noted in Fricker (2006), that arises out of an acknowledgment of the socially diffuse nature of testimonial warrant. This worry involved what I called the generation of individualistic insensitivity to the epistemic relations holding between some of one's own beliefs. However, we can now see that this worry ought to be acknowledged as part of the human epistemic condition. For one thing, the phenomenon in question obtains not just in cases of testimonial belief, but more generally in any case in which one fails to keep track of the sources or grounds of one's belief – with the result that, given well-documented limitations on human memory,[12] all epistemological theories are going to have to face this worry. For another, though the worry regarding individualistic insensitivity is not silenced by the socially diffuse nature of rationality, the former is mitigated by the latter. So while humans have to live with the fact that we often (whether through testimonial acquisition or memory limitations) fail to know or otherwise keep track of the details regarding what it is that most directly supports our beliefs, we have evolved what would appear to be a useful technique for addressing this situation, in the form of social scrutiny. My claim has been that a proper epistemic account of such scrutiny ought to regard the actual (relevant) knowledgeableness and outspokenness of one's peers as affecting the rational standing, and hence the epistemic justification, of beliefs subjected to such scrutiny. Such a view is recommended by a parallel with how internal coherence contributes to epistemic justification; and the result of endorsing the proposed view is to acknowledge the need for an anti-individualistic account of the sort of rationality relevant to epistemic justification.

---

[12] The empirical literature has documented that adults often have difficulties retaining information in long-term memory about the source of a given piece of information. See Loftus and Ketchum 1991; Zaragoza and Lane 1994; Zaragoza and Mitchell 1996.

8

Towards an 'active' epistemic anti-individualism

From the results we have so far in Part II, considerations pertaining to knowledge communication support a rather substantive rethinking of the central epistemic statuses mentioned above. In particular, given the role of condition (a), the reliable testimony condition, on testimonial knowledge, we arrived at anti-individualistic results regarding the nature of knowledge, warrant, justification, and rationality. The arguments for these results suggest that, when it comes to the epistemic status of a hearer's (testimonial) belief, the relevance of her linguistic peers is seen in the epistemic properties of the peers' testimonies – in particular, in the epistemically relevant properties of the cognitive processes that underwrite the formation and sustainment of the beliefs expressed in those testimonies. But for all these arguments have to say, this *exhausts* the epistemic relevance of the hearer's linguistic peers: once we specify the (epistemically relevant) properties of the testimonies upstream in the chain of communication, and those (epistemically relevant) properties related to the process of social scrutiny, we have exhausted the anti-individualistic considerations relevant to the epistemic status of the hearer's (testimonial) belief. The overarching aim of this chapter is to show that the anti-individualistic character of the epistemic dimension of communication involves even more than this. In particular, my thesis will be that there are cases in which a hearer S satisfies condition (c), the reliable discrimination condition, only if we assume that the relevant credibility monitoring is performed *for* her *by others*. If this is correct, then the relevance of S's linguistic peers to the epistemic status enjoyed by S's own testimonial beliefs is not exhausted by the epistemic properties *of their testimonies*, but extends to include properties regarding how well her peers themselves monitor testimony for credibility.

I aim to show this by appeal to considerations pertaining to young children's consumption of testimony. My claim will be that a proper account of testimonial knowledge in early childhood will require us to reconceive the process that eventuates in the child's consumption of testimony: this process will need to be seen as involving features of the child's social environment. In particular, if, for the purposes of epistemic appraisal, we do *not* hold these features to be part of the process that eventuates in the child's acquisition of a testimonial belief, then we will not be able to account for our battery of intuitions regarding the scope, and arguably even the existence, of testimonial knowledge in early childhood. The result will be what I will call an 'active' anti-individualism regarding (testimonial) knowledge.

8.2 THE CONSUMPTION OF TESTIMONY IN EARLY CHILDHOOD: PSYCHOLOGY AND EPISTEMOLOGY

Since my argument from this chapter will involve a close look at the epistemic features of testimonial beliefs acquired by very young children, I want to begin by having a look at the psychology of testimonial belief-fixation in very young children. More specifically, I will be looking at this consumption in what I will call 'cognitively immature' children, those who, out of their negligible or undeveloped capacity for monitoring testimony for credibility, exhibit simple (uncritical) trust in the say-so of others. The precise extent to which children are cognitively immature is still unknown. However, some aspects of this immaturity are well documented in the literature on child development. Here I briefly review this literature and suggest how it bears on an account of the epistemology of testimony in early childhood.

It should be noted straight away that children are not uniformly uncritical of the speech of others. Children as young as sixteen months react differently to true and false testimony in cases involving the labelling of simple objects (Koenig and Echols 2003). Children as young as three are sensitive to some source credibility cues, especially when their attention is drawn to such cues (Lampinen and Smith 1995). Preschool children can distinguish, more or less reliably, those speakers who are engaging in obvious story-telling (Dias and Harris 1990; Richards and Sanderson 1999; Harris 2002). And children aged six and older discriminate between various types of testimonies and testifiers (Bar-Tal *et al.* 1990; Baldwin and Moses 1996; Lutz and Keil 2002; Mills and Keil 2004; and Heyman and Legare forthcoming). The result is that even young children can keep their credulity within certain limits (Pea 1982; Lampinen and Smith 1995;

201

Mitchell and Nye 1995; Robinson *et al.* 1999; Robinson and Whitcombe 2003; Clément *et al.* 2004; Koenig *et al.* 2004).

At the same time, various additional studies suggest that credulity in early childhood, though limited in the ways discussed, is nevertheless substantial. In particular, the distinction between true and false statements, though registered in behavior in children as young as sixteen months, is not exploited in any systematic way in a child's consumption of testimony until some time between the ages of three and four, before which the children exhibit a high degree of 'indiscriminate trust' (Koenig *et al.* 2004).[1] For example, children younger than three typically have a hard time making judgments regarding the reliability of reporters on the basis of the reporters' past track record, and so typically respond to adult testimony with indiscriminate trust in any situation in which the child lacks explicit knowledge incompatible with what they are being told (Clément *et al.* 2004). Moreover, the widely cited 'false belief test' indicates that pre-schoolers (three- to four-year-olds) are insensitive to an interlocutor's access to the truth of what she is reporting (Wimmer and Perner 1983). This result was extended by Taylor and colleagues (Taylor *et al.* 1994), who concluded that the young child's insensitivity to an interlocutor's access to the truth extends beyond features of locally observed objects, to include more general information about the world. More recently, Wellman and colleagues (2001) have drawn the general lesson implicit in the foregoing studies: that, until the age of four, children do not appear to appreciate that beliefs (whether their own or others') can be false.

Nor do gullibility-making characteristics disappear after preschool. On the contrary, there is a good deal of evidence regarding the persistence of such features in older children. For example, it is not until late elementary school that children regard discrepancies between a speaker's verbal and nonverbal communication as indicating dishonesty (Rotenberg *et al.* 1989). Children younger than six are likely to endorse self-report as a means to learn about such highly esteemed qualities as the intelligence of the self-reporting person (Heyman and Legare, forthcoming), thereby rendering themselves potentially gullible in matters in which others have a strong motive to lie. Even older children (six to ten) are susceptible to suggestibility by sources they regard as powerful (Wheeless *et al.* 1983) or

---

[1] Various developmental psychologists have speculated about what might account for this surprising result. See Lampinen and Smith 1995; Giles *et al.* 2002; Koenig and Echols 2003; Koenig *et al.* 2004; and Clément *et al.* 2004.

whom they perceive as in a position to reward or punish them (Loftus and Ketchum 1991; Ceci and Bruck 1993).

This brief review of the empirical literature suggests that the move to more 'skeptical trust' develops gradually, and in any case is significantly less well-developed in three-year-olds than it is in four-year-olds (Koenig *et al.* 2004). In this connection, one final point is worth making. Even among children who have initiated the move to a more skeptical trust, the effects of this move are limited by the fact that children typically do not have a great deal of relevant worldly knowledge on which to draw when assessing the likely truth of testimony in real-life cases. The result is that, while the young child may reject false testimony when she has observational knowledge contradicting the testimony (Mitchell *et al.* 1997, Harris 2002), in everyday life children often confront testimony regarding whose likely truth they have no relevant first-hand information (Koenig *et al.* 2004).

What to say, then, of the epistemological dimension of young children's consumption of testimony? A first suggestion might be that the child acquires knowledge through testimony only *after* her consumption of testimony is regularly informed by her knowledge of source credibility cues, types of testimony, other relevant background information, and so on. The thought here might be that, prior to this, the child is too gullible to count as having acquired knowledge, even on those occasions when her acceptance of testimony yields true belief. The basis for such a contention would be that the credulity of the cognitively immature child renders her unable to satisfy condition (c), the reliable discrimination condition, on testimonial knowledge – with the result that the cognitively immature child cannot acquire *knowledge* (as against merely true belief) through testimony.

But do we really want to say that little two-year-old Johnny cannot come to know through his mother's (reliable) testimony that there is ice cream in the freezer?, that little Sally cannot come to know through her father's (reliable) testimony that the object over yonder is a book?, or that little Ramona cannot come to know through her parent's (reliable) testimony that there will be a babysitter tonight? On the contrary, even if little Johnny, Sally, and Ramona are cognitively immature, it seems perverse to deny them knowledge in these cases.

This contention is supported by more than intuition. Suppose that little Ramona tells her visiting uncle that there will be a babysitter tonight, and that, when he asks her how she knows this, she replies by saying that her parents told her so.² If her uncle has no reason to think she failed to understand her parents, or that (having understood what she was told) she failed to remember what her parents told her, it seems reasonable for him to describe her as *knowing* that there will be a babysitter tonight. I submit that the reasonableness of this knowledge ascription persists, even after we add that Ramona is indiscriminately trusting. What is more, in a good number of the cases in which very young children acquire beliefs through accepting another's testimony, their belief can be described as *locally reliable* in the sense introduced in chapter 5. Little Johnny wouldn't have formed the belief that there is ice cream in the freezer, in the manner he did, unless it were true. For consider: had he believed that there is ice cream in the fridge in a similar situation, this belief would have been true, since none of the informants in his house would have lied or spoken unreliably about such a matter; and, alternatively, had there been no ice cream in the freezer, no one would have testified that there was, and so he would not have believed through testimony that there was. Admittedly, not everyone is moved to ascribe knowledge on such (local reliability) grounds; but these considerations, together with the battery of intuitions about particular cases, make a strong *prima facie* case for the idea that even cognitively immature children can acquire knowledge through testimony.

Indeed, it would appear that a good many epistemologists working on testimony acknowledge the intuitiveness of the claim ('TKC' for Testimonial Knowledge in early Childhood) that

TKC Cognitively immature children acquire knowledge through testimony.

A telling indication of TKC's plausibility is the fact that it is accepted not only by those whose epistemological views enable an easy accommodation of TKC, but also by many whose views provide them with an ideological motive for repudiating TKC.

Consider those who endorse anti-reductionist views about testimonial justification, which as it is standardly formulated amounts (not to AR + but rather) to the claim that

---

² It is true that young children's ability to keep track of the sources of their knowledge is seriously impoverished. However, there are circumstances in which they can do so. For discussion, see Flavell 1979; O'Neill and Gopnik 1991; O'Neill *et al.* 1992; Taylor *et al.* 1994; and especially Gopnik and Graf 1988. The relevant literature is also discussed in Harris 2002.

AR A hearer is epistemically justified in accepting (has the epistemic right to accept; is epistemically entitled to accept) another's testimony so long as there are no undefeated good reasons *not* to accept the testimony.

AR entails that it is not necessary for a hearer to *have positive reasons to trust* (on a particular occasion), in order for the hearer to be justified in accepting a piece of testimony (on that occasion).[3] For this reason it is unsurprising that those committed to AR accept TKC:[4] TKC itself, together with the thesis that knowledge requires justification, would appear to offer some support for AR, as against any 'reductionist' view of testimonial justification. The reason for this is easily appreciated once we have the reductionist thesis before us. I repeat it here:

RD A hearer does not have the epistemic right to – is not justified in – accepting another's testimony unless she has (inductive or *a priori*) reasons, ultimately not themselves based on still further testimony, for regarding the testimony she confronts as credible.

The trouble posed for RD by TKC is this. The cognitive immaturity of very young children – especially those younger than four – precludes them from having positive reasons for believing that a given piece of testimony is credible. So if testimonial knowledge requires testimonial justification, then the proponent of RD appears forced to deny TKC.[5]

In light of this, it is surprising to find that a number of prominent proponents of RD, who can resist the pressure on RD by rejecting TKC outright, do not do so. Rather, these proponents of RD endorse TKC, and opt instead to respond to the preceding argument in one of two alternative ways. The first sort of response, typified by Elizabeth Fricker, is to argue that, while TKC is true, RD does not apply to subjects during the 'immature phase' of early childhood (Fricker 1995: 401–3). The second sort of response, exemplified in the work of Robert Audi, is to

---

[3] Matters are more complicated when it comes to AR +; I will be returning to this below.

[4] For examples of proponents of AR who endorse something in the neighborhood of TKC, see Reid 1872/1993: 281–2; Coady 1992: 115; Millgram 1997: 143; Insole 2000: 51; and Davis 2002: 521.

[5] This sort of argument, as an argument for preferring AR to RD, is criticized in Lackey (2005). I discuss her criticism below.

square RD with TKC by rejecting instead the thesis that knowledge requires justification (Audi 1997: 414–16).[6] (A third sort of response, which might be motivated by Goldman's recent reflections on children's consumption of testimony in the process of education (1999; 2001) and by Paul Harris' interests in cognitive development (see Harris 2002), would be to argue that children *do* have adequate evidence to accept what people tell them. But as the cognitive impoverishment of preschool children has been amply documented in the literature cited above, I do not regard this as a live option with respect to TKC.)[7]

I think that it is telling that proponents of RD endorse TKC, even though they have some clear motivation for rejecting it. I take it to indicate that TKC itself has some strong intuitive plausibility no matter one's background ideology regarding the nature of testimonial justification.

Above I noted that TKC appears to give us a *prima facie* reason to prefer anti-reductionist to reductionist accounts of the conditions on the justified acceptance of testimony. It is worth noting, though, that the line of argument leading to this conclusion is threatened, both by the way I have argued for anti-reductionism, and by my formulation of anti-reductionism as AR +. I have argued (chapters 5 and 6) that anti-reductionist views should be seen as built on an empirical presupposition regarding the existence and reliability of subcognitive processing going on in the background – subcognitive processing aimed at 'filtering out' testimonies that are not reliable. In light of this I suggested that the anti-reductionist view might be explicitly formulated (albeit perhaps at the cost of some redundancy) as

AR + A hearer *H* is epistemically justified in accepting (has the epistemic right to accept; is epistemically entitled to accept) another's testimony on occasion *O* so long as (i) there are no undefeated good (doxastic, factual, or normative) reasons *not* to accept the testimony, and (ii) on *O H*'s acceptance was the outcome of a process that exhibited a

---

[6] Arguably, this is a move that Fricker, too, has to endorse. For, on the assumption that RD states a necessary condition on the only sort of justification relevant to testimonial belief, the combination of RD and TKC entails that cognitively immature children have testimonial knowledge but that they are not justified in accepting the testimony.

[7] This is not meant as a criticism of either Goldman (1999; 2001c) or Harris (2002), since neither of them address themselves to the issue of TKC: Goldman does not, as he does not address his epistemological theorizing to the issue of *cognitively immature* children; and Harris does not, because, while he does address himself to the issue of cognitively immature children, his interests are primarily developmental rather than epistemological.

'counterfactual sensitivity' to the presence of defeaters (which, given (i), turns up no such defeaters on *O*).

Note, though, that AR + does not appear to be at a comparative advantage over RD on the score of TKC. We run into trouble on the score of (ii): given the cognitively immaturity of very young children, it would seem that, when they accept testimony, they do so in a way that fails to satisfy condition (ii). So if justification is a necessary condition on knowledge, then it would appear that AR + is no better off than RD in accounting for the truth of TKC. And if AR + merely makes explicit the empirical presuppositions of AR itself, the same could be said of AR, too. Thus it would seem that proponents of anti-reductionist views, far from seeing TKC as helping their cause, may have their own difficulties accounting for TKC.

In sum, I have argued that TKC is true, but that its truth raises challenges – or at least appears to raise challenges – for both reductionists and anti-reductionists. In what follows I will assume that an adequate account of the epistemology of testimony ought to preserve TKC; my main aim will be to identify and then respond to two challenges that arise on this assumption. If unmet, these challenges would show that, no matter one's views on the issues that separate reductionism and anti-reductionism, there is no adequate account of testimonial knowledge in early childhood.

8.3 THE *DEFEATER* CHALLENGE

As noted, the claim that very young children acquire knowledge through testimony has been traditionally cited by proponents of AR as a *prima facie* reason to favor traditional anti-reductionist approaches in the epistemology of testimony over their reductionist opponents. In a recent provocative paper, Jennifer Lackey (2005) argues that the appeal to testimonial knowledge in early childhood does not provide even a *prima facie* reason to favor anti-reductionism as against RD. What is of interest to me, however, is not Lackey's conclusion, so much as her argument for that conclusion. Though Lackey herself does not treat it in this way, her argument extends quite naturally into a case against TKC itself. In particular, the main premise of her argument is that there is no non-trivial sense in which very young children can be said to satisfy a no-relevant-defeater condition. If we supplement this with the premise that knowledge presupposes that

207

the would-be knower satisfies a no-relevant-defeater condition, then TKC itself appears to be in trouble.

As Lackey herself notes (and as we saw in chapter 6 in any case), the No-Defeater condition is an important part of any AR approach to the epistemology of testimonial justification. Within that framework, the point of the condition is to avoid the absurd conclusion that "hearers could be epistemically justified in accepting *any report* that was as a matter of fact reliable, no matter how irrational or epistemically irresponsible such acceptance was" (Lackey 2005: 165; italics in original). Generalizing, we might say that a No-Defeater condition ought to be part of any account, not only of testimonial justification, but also of testimonial *knowledge*, on pain of ascribing the epistemic status in question in cases in which intuitively such a status ought not to apply.[8]

Lackey points out, however, that to play this role in particular cases, the No-Relevant-Defeater condition must be *substantively* satisfied. As she presents matters, the No-Defeater condition is substantively satisfied in a particular case if "it is possible for it to fail to be satisfied" in that case (Lackey, 2005). She explains:

[O]ne of the reasons it doesn't make sense to impose a 'no-lying condition' on a chair is because chairs cannot lie. To say that a chair has satisfied such a condition merely because it hasn't lied, without taking into account the chair's capacity to lie, trivializes what satisfaction of such a condition means (166).

The intended parallel is this. If cognitively immature children are to be credited with satisfying the No-Defeater condition, it is not sufficient to cite the fact that there are a good many cases in which such children believe that *p* in the absence of any relevant defeaters. For this no more shows that they satisfy the No-Defeater condition, than the fact that chairs haven't lied establishes that chairs satisfy the 'no-lying condition.' So on the assumption that the cognitive immaturity of young children precludes them from having *positive* reasons for their testimonial beliefs (for example, in the form of reasons to think that a piece of testimony is credible), their cognitive immaturity also precludes them from having defeaters for their testimonial beliefs – as defeaters are really nothing more than a kind of

---

[8] We are confirmed in this by the reductionist Fricker, who writes that "sensitivity to defeating evidence, should it come along, ... is usually taken to be a hallmark of belief which amounts to knowledge" (Fricker 2006: 242). It is clear from context that Fricker is sympathetic to this idea.

An 'active' epistemic anti-individualism

negative reason. On the further assumption that testimonial knowledge requires *substantive* satisfaction of the No-Defeater condition, Lackey's argument can be used to argue against TKC itself. The *defeater challenge* is to rebut such an argument.[9]

8.4 THE *EXTENSION* CHALLENGE

It is uncontroversial that knowledge requires the satisfaction of some non-accidentality condition: the belief purportedly amounting to knowledge must be reliable (sensitive; safe; or what-have-you). In chapter 1 I argued that the non-accidentality condition of knowledge, as applied to the acquisition of knowledge through testimony, requires (a) that the testimony consumed be reliable,[10] (b) that the hearer have a reliable method for recovering the proposition attested to, and also that (c) the hearer herself be a *reliable consumer* of reliable testimony. A failure along any of these dimensions, I argued, will result in a testimonial belief that does not satisfy the non-accidentality condition of knowledge, and so will fail to amount to knowledge even if it is true.

The extension challenge focuses on the *consumer reliability* condition, condition (c). That such a condition will be part of any adequate account of testimonial knowledge was argued in connection with Polyanna in chapter 6, but it will be helpful to have a new case in front of us. Consider the following case. Sid is gullible in the extreme: he accepts anything anyone says merely in virtue of the fact that someone said so. Sid is in a room full of inveterate liars. He immediately and uncritically believes everything each of them says. At one point he happens to bump into Nancy, the only reliable person around. Nancy reliably tells Sid that *p*, and (as a matter of course) he believes her. Even so, it seems patent that Sid

---

[9] Two distinct but related arguments from the cognitively immature child's relation to defeaters can be found in Weiner 2003 and Pritchard 2004. Of these, Pritchard's own view is most relevant here. He remarks that agents in the developmental stage – that is, in the stage of cognitive immaturity – "lack the competency in evaluating testimony (*and, relatedly, defeaters*) that comes with repeated exposure to instances of testimony within a social milieu, and this is bound to undermine their reliability in forming TBBs [testimonially based beliefs]" (p. 341; my italics). An adequate response to the defeater challenge should address Pritchard's point regarding reliability as well. I do so below, in section 5.

[10] But see chapter 1 section 1.4, as well as Goldberg 2005b and (forthcoming b), for some special circumstances in which this condition might fail to be satisfied, and yet the subject still counts as knowing through testimony.

does not know that *p* through her testimony. The obvious diagnosis is that, though her testimony is perfectly reliable, he is not a reliable consumer of reliable testimony. Condition (c) is the generalization of this. I take it that the underlying point, which has been made by others in a variety of different contexts,[11] is more or less patent.

Consider now that cognitively immature children are like Sid in at least one important respect: they are credulous to the point of gullibility. An initial question, then, is whether naive credulity is compatible with the satisfaction of condition (c), and hence with the acquisition of a reliable testimonial belief on a given occasion (see Pritchard 2004: 341). But even if we accept an affirmative answer to this question – as I did above in connection with little Johnny's ice cream belief, and as I will defend in greater detail below – the further question arises as to whether we can give an account of the conditions under which a belief formed through cred-ulously accepted testimony satisfies the externalist (or non-accidentality) condition on knowledge. The challenge here is to offer an account that accommodates our intuitions in particular cases. I call this the *extension* challenge, since a failure to meet it will result in a need to modify our views about *the extent* of the phenomenon of testimonial knowledge in early childhood.

I just said that the young child's credulity need not preclude her from counting (at least on particular occasions) as a reliable consumer of reliable testimony. Given such credulity, the young child's testimonial belief-forming *process* will be unreliable in any world, like ours, in which there is a decent amount of false testimony. However, unless one is a *process-reliabilist*, it does not follow that each and every one of her testimonial *beliefs* is unreliable.[12] Nor is it clear that the case of Sid and Nancy can be generalized to cover *all* cases involving the credulous consumption of testimony. For example, suppose the situation were inverted: it is a regular feature of Sid's epistemic situation that the environments he occupies are

---

[11] See Burge 1993: 485–6; Plantinga 1993a: 86; Faulkner 2000: 591–2; the 'newspaper case' in Graham 2000a: 134; and Lackey 2003 and 2006.

[12] In this and the following section I will be restricting my focus to the epistemic properties of particular beliefs, not of belief-forming processes. In doing so I am following various theorists who have argued that testimonial knowledge in general (and so TKC in parti-cular) turns on the epistemic properties of particular *beliefs*. See Fricker 1987; Fricker 1994: 147; Graham 2000a: 141–2; and Graham 2000b for arguments to this effect. I return to the question of processes, briefly, in section 8.6.

full of only reliable reporters. If in such an environment he credulously accepts the word of a reliable reporter, do we still want to say that he does not count as acquiring knowledge through testimony? This is far from obvious (see chapter 6). Suppose that very young children were regularly exposed only to reliable testifiers. (Below I will suggest that a weakened version of this supposition is actually true.) The result would be that (contra Pritchard 2004: 341) they would be reliable consumers of reliable testimony, at least insofar as their caretakers were both generally knowledgeable and also vigilant in policing those who were given access to the children. But then childish credulity is compatible with the reliable consumption of reliable testimony, and so would appear to be compatible with TKC as well (at least insofar as reliability considerations go).

Of course, compatibility claims are weak claims. The real question is whether the credulity of immature children can be squared with our intuitions regarding whether they have acquired knowledge in particular cases. This is the question that is raised by the extension challenge. This challenge remains no matter one's views about the nature of testimonial justification. For while the assumption of RD would make this challenge acute – here we are in the ballpark of the contention, questioned by Lackey (2005), that TKC gives us a reason to prefer AR over RD – the extension challenge remains even on the assumption of AR. This is because even after it is granted that childhood credulity is compatible with testimonial knowledge acquisition, the question remains whether cognitively immature children satisfy the externalist (non-accidentality) conditions on knowledge in *all and only* those cases in which we want to ascribe testimonial knowledge to the child.

A failure to meet the extension challenge would have broad ramifications for our understanding of the epistemology of testimony more generally. For consider that young children's testimonial knowledge is a special instance of the case in which testimonial knowledge is ascribed under conditions in which the subject of the knowledge *can provide no positive reasons to trust the testimony she has consumed*. We might then say that the case of young children articulates the minimum epistemic burden on the hearer, compatible with the ascription of testimonial knowledge to her. So if our intuitions about when knowledge is had in these cases must themselves be revised, it may well be that we will also have to revise our views about the distinct epistemic demands made on the hearer even in cases in which the hearer is *not* a simple truster (but rather is a mature adult consumer of testimony).

211

8.5 SIMPLE TRUST AND THE EXTERNALIST CONDITION ON (TESTIMONIAL) KNOWLEDGE

I begin by taking up the extension challenge. Under what conditions can one exhibit *simple trust in another's word*, and yet proceed to acquire a testimonial belief that satisfies the externalist condition on knowledge (including condition (c), the reliable discrimination condition)? In exploring this matter, I will continue to employ the reliability account of the externalist (non-accidentality) condition on knowledge; the same points could be made no matter how one understands reliability, that is, whether in terms of sensitivity, safety, etc.

Let S be a hearer who has reliably comprehended another speaker's testimony that p, and who has no other basis for believing that p other than the testimonial basis.[13] Where S forms the belief that p through having accepted the speaker's say-so on occasion O, S knows through testimony that p only if the following condition holds on O:

REL If S were to form the testimonial belief that p, it would be true that p.

Given standard semantics for the subjunctive conditional, this can be reformulated as:

RL* In most or all of the nearby worlds in which S forms the testimonial belief that p, p.

I will evaluate S's belief in two different types of case. In the first type of case, the proposition believed – the proposition that p – is true in all nearby worlds, such that we must go quite some distance from the actual world to find a world in which $\sim p$. (Propositions satisfying this condition will be called 'safe' propositions.) In the second kind of case the proposition believed is not a safe proposition, i.e., there are nearby worlds in which $\sim p$. (I distinguish these cases since there are occasions on which the question of the reliability condition's satisfaction turns on whether $\sim p$-worlds are close.)

Now let us turn to a case. Babe is a cognitively immature child; his attitude towards observed testimony is one of simple trust. We will

---

[13] The testimonial basis for S's belief that p includes the epistemic support (if any) that the testimony itself provides for S's belief, together with whatever epistemic support (if any) S has for thinking that the testimony was credible. (This characterization of 'testimonial basis' is meant to be neutral as between RD and AR.)

suppose that *the testimony* he consumes satisfies the relevant externalist condition regarding proferred testimony: it is reliable, sensitive, and/or safe (as you please). And we assume as well that the process of comprehension was reliable, in the sense explored in Part I of this book. Our question is whether Babe's *uncritical and credulous acceptance* of this reliable testimony satisfies the reliable discrimination condition, and so whether his testimonial belief (in reliable testimony) is itself reliable. The case we will consider is one in which he observes his mother tell him that there is milk in the fridge, and where on the basis of accepting her testimony he goes on to form the belief that there is milk in the fridge. I will call this case the Milk case.

Does Babe's belief in the Milk case satisfy RL$\star$? Where *m* is the proposition *there is milk in the fridge*, we can start by noting that Babe forms the testimonial belief in *m* in *any* situation in which he happens to observe an attestation of *m* (whether the testimony issues from his mother or from someone else). So we need to go to the nearest worlds in which he confronts an attestation of *m*. Suppose *m* is a safe proposition. Then such worlds are worlds in which *m* is true, and so (by extension) Babe's testimonial belief in *m* is true.[14] In that case, Babe's testimonial belief in *m* satisfies RL$\star$. Suppose then that *m* is not safe: there are nearby worlds in which $\sim m$. Our question then is whether there are, among the nearby $\sim m$-worlds, worlds in which Babe observes an attestation of *m*: if there are, then given his credulity he would believe that testimony, in which case his belief in that possible world is false, and so his actual-world belief fails to satisfy RL$\star$;[15] but if there are no (or very few) such worlds – if in none (or very few) of the worlds in which $\sim m$ does Babe confront an attestation of *m* – then Babe's actual-world belief can be seen as satisfying RL$\star$, since in that case the nearest worlds in which he observes an attestation of *m* (and so forms a testimonial belief in *m*) will all (or mostly) be worlds in which *m* is true.

The foregoing analysis of the reliability of Babe's testimonial beliefs makes clear that, in cases involving an unsafe proposition, Babe is at the

---

[14] *m*'s safety ensures that Babe's testimonial belief that *m* is true in the nearest worlds in which Babe confronts testimony that *m*, even if such testimony is from a source other than his mother. (Unless otherwise noted, we are assuming that the testimony Babe consumes is reliable.)

[15] Here I am assuming that if there are $\sim p$-worlds in which Babe encounters the testimony that *p*, then such worlds are not uncommon (among the set of worlds in question).

mercy of his environment. If he is regularly in environments in which he would confront only or mostly reliable testimony regarding the matter at hand, he will be a reliable consumer of reliable testimony, and so his testimonial beliefs (even in unsafe propositions) will satisfy RL*; but if he is in an environment in which he would be exposed to a good deal of unreliable as well as reliable testimony regarding the matter at hand, then he is not a reliable consumer of reliable testimony, in which case at least some of his testimonial beliefs (in unsafe propositions) will fail to satisfy RL*.[16]

So far, this result would appear to be perfectly acceptable. However, our analysis leads to some unacceptable results in particular cases. Consider the following expansion of the Milk case. As before, Babe is told by his mother that there is milk in the fridge, and this testimony is reliable. But the refrigerator in Babe's house rarely contains milk. And, what is more, Babe's notorious Uncle Marfman, who gulls little children every chance he has, is in the next room. Then it would seem that the following counterfactual scenario occupies a nearby possible world: although there is no milk in the fridge, Uncle Marfman, knowledgeable of the milk-less condition of the fridge but aiming to pull his nephew's leg, tells Babe that there *is* milk in the fridge. In that case, Babe's actual belief, formed through his mother's reliable testimony, does not satisfy RL*, since there are nearby possible worlds in which he forms the testimonial belief that there is milk in the fridge, under conditions in which there is no milk in the fridge. Since in that case Babe's testimonial belief does not satisfy RL*, it is not reliable, and hence Babe does not count as knowing (through his mother's testimony) that there is milk in the fridge.

This result might not strike one as particularly unhappy. After all, it might be contended that the case of Babe and his Mother (with Marfman nearby) is structurally parallel to the case of Sid and Nancy (with the liars nearby). Since there was no knowledge transmission in the latter case, we should expect no knowledge transmission in the former case either. Or so one might contend. However, in response I note that there is one important relevant difference between the two cases: as Babe's parent and

---

[16] If we could but restrict our attention to the worlds in which the only testimony regarding *m* Babe observes is his mother's testimony, then his testimonial belief in *m* would be reliable even given unsafe *m*; but since Babe forms a testimonial belief in *m* *whenever* he confronts an attestation of *m* (no matter its source), we cannot so restrict ourselves. See below.

caretaker, Mother takes a distinct interest in helping Babe to consume only true testimony, whereas Nancy takes no such interest in Sid's consumption of testimony. This difference, I submit, underlies an *epistemic* difference between the two cases: in the final analysis, Mother's interest in Babe's consumption of testimony has an effect on the reliability of Babe's testimonial belief, whereas Sid's belief in Nancy's testimony is unreliable (even in the final analysis), as there is no external check on his credulity. Precisely how to model this epistemic difference is a matter I discuss in section 8.6, below. Here I merely note that, because of this difference, there are clear grounds for regarding it as an unhappy result if Marfman's proximity forces us to treat Babe as failing to know through his acceptance of Mother's reliable testimony.

Even if it is granted that this result is unhappy, it might be wondered how devastating this result is. Might we simply bite the bullet? Such a reaction is less attractive once we recognize that the type of case in question – in which we will have to deny knowledge in situations in which the intuition to the contrary is tugging at us – is actually widespread. Call cases of this type 'unhappy' cases. A case will be unhappy in any situation in which the child receives reliable testimony from a caretaker, under conditions in which one or more nearby testifiers would have testified falsely regarding the matter at hand. Given such a situation, even if the child consumes what in fact is reliable testimony, the fact that she would have formed a false testimonial belief (had one of those other testifiers testified) prevents her actual belief from being counted reliable. Now, let it be granted that few children have in their midst people who actively aim to deceive them: the Marfmans of the world are few and far between. Even so, it is quite common for cognitively immature children to be in contexts that are *rife* with unreliable reporters, since they are often in contexts in which *other* cognitively immature children are present. (Cognitively immature children are terribly unreliable reporters, often asserting things that are, to the adult's more knowledgeable mind, obviously false or unreasonable.) Admittedly, children have a tendency to regard the testimony of other children with some skepticism (Lampinen and Smith 1995), and in any case they exhibit greater trust in the testimony of those they regard as teachers than in the testimony of those they do not regard as authorities (Bar-Tal *et al.* 1990). But again we are interested in *cognitively immature* children, in whom such discriminations do not play as significant a role, if any, in guiding subsequent patterns of testimonial consumption (Ceci *et al.* 1987; Clément *et al.* 2004). It appears, then, that the Marfman case is just a drop in the bucket: on a good many occasions the bite-the-bullet reaction would have us deny that (say) Babe acquires knowledge from his preschool teacher, since Babe's preschool classroom contains a good deal of unreliable children; and on a good many occasions it would have us deny as well that Babe acquires knowledge from his parents when they are in the mall (or on the street), since the mall (street) contains a good deal of unreliable reporters; etc. In both cases, the presence of unreliable reporters renders Babe unreliable in his consumption of reliable testimony, with the result that his testimonial belief in what in fact is reliable testimony is not itself reliable. (Once again, these examples might be thought of as actual testimonial versions of Fake Barn Country.)

It might be thought that the foregoing still overstates the extent of unhappy cases. Even if Babe is amidst reporters who are unreliable in the sense that they would testify to a barrage of false propositions, even so, so long as $\sim p$ is not among those propositions to which they would attest, then Babe's testimonial belief that p, formed through his acceptance of reliable testimony that p, is itself reliable, and so can count as knowledge.[17]

But this stop-gap reply to the allegedly wide extent of unhappy cases is unsatisfactory. For one thing, it makes the issue of whether Babe has acquired testimonial knowledge turn on the contingencies of others' speech dispositions. So, for example, what Babe can come to know through his preschool teacher's testimony will depend on the subjects regarding which his classmates are disposed to make false reports. If Babe's pal Ruthie is disposed to assert all sorts of falsehoods about gender roles (her sexist family fills her with all sorts of falsehoods about what girls have and have not accomplished), then, although Babe's teacher gives reliable lessons regarding the history of girls' accomplishments, Babe cannot learn (in the sense of *come to know*) very much through these lessons, since for many of the things his teacher says Ruthie would have testified otherwise (and given his gullibility Babe would have believed her). Surely one cannot respond to this unhappy result by pointing out that, still, Babe can come to know his shape and color facts through his teacher's reliable

---

[17] Of course, if one is a process-reliabilist, one remains in trouble, since in that case the unreliability of the process by which cognitively immature children form testimonial beliefs is likely to swamp the reliability of the result of that process on the particular occasion of the child's acquiring the testimonial belief that p.

testimony (as, happily, no child in the classroom would have testified otherwise).

But there is a second reason to be suspicious of what I am calling the stop-gap reaction to the charge of extensive unhappy results. Whether or not the speakers surrounding Babe are *actually* disposed to assert the negation (or something implying the negation) of a proposition reliably attested to by (say) Babe's mother or preschool teacher, surely we want to say that, even if Babe's compatriots *had* been so disposed, *still* he would count as having acquired knowledge through his acceptance of his mother's (or his teacher's) reliable testimony. Let a 'relevantly unreliable testifier' be one who is such that he or she would testify that ~p in a situation in which Babe confronts the reliable testimony that p. Then the following diagnosis seems pertinent. We want to be able to say that the mere background presence of relevantly unreliable testifiers *need not affect* (although it *can* affect; see below) the epistemic status of Babe's testimonial beliefs in those cases in which Babe acquires his belief from a reliable parent or other adult caretaker. The trouble is that, given Babe's credulity and the proximity of a relevantly unreliable testifier, we appear to be prevented from saying this on reliabilist grounds. This is because, had the relevantly unreliable testifier falsely testified to Babe, Babe would have believed her – in which case condition (c), the reliable discrimination condition, is not satisfied, and so Babe's testimonial belief fails to be reliable even though it is true.

It seems, then, that if we are to honor our intuitions in particular cases – that Babe *does* know (through his mother's reliable attestation) that there is milk in the fridge, or that Babe *does* learn (through his teacher's reliable lesson) that there have been great female scientists and great female athletes – then we need a way to discount the epistemic effects of Marfman's and Ruthie's proximity. Now in cases involving *adult* consumers of testimony, the mere presence of a relevantly unreliable testifier need not have the reliability-undermining (and hence knowledge-undermining) effect it has in the case of Babe: this is because the adult, being a critical consumer of testimony, would not be as quick to extend trust to testimony from such a source, as she would to testimony from a reliable source. But, since Babe is undiscriminating in his consumption of testimony, the proximity of a relevantly unreliable testifier cannot be discounted in this way, and hence the proximity of a relevantly unreliable testifier undermines the ascription of reliable belief (and hence knowledge) to Babe. If we are to avoid this result, we need a way to discount the epistemic effects of the proximity of a relevantly unreliable testifier *even in the case in which the testimony is being consumed uncritically.* This is the face of the extension challenge, when presented in the guise of reliability considerations.

Before moving on to address this, I should note that there are other cases in which we do *not* want to discount the epistemic significance of a nearby relevantly unreliable testifier. These are cases where, though the testimony Babe accepted was reliable, the background proximity of a relevantly unreliable speaker *would* militate against treating Babe's testimonial belief as a case of knowledge (and hence as a case of reliable belief). Consider the following 'used car' case. Babe is taken by his parents to a used car lot. As his parents are engaged by a salesperson, he wanders off by himself and overhears someone saying of a particular car that it was owned by a grandmother. Credulous as ever, Babe accepts this testimony, and so comes to believe of that car that it was owned by a grandmother. It just so happens that the testimony was reliable (the speaker was the grandson of the car's owner). Even so, we want to say that Babe's resulting testimonial belief does not amount to knowledge. In this case, the fact that there is an unscrupulous salesperson (or two) on the lot seems perfectly relevant to whether Babe counts as having acquired testimonial knowledge. Ideally, an account of testimonial knowledge in early childhood should be able, both to accommodate this description of the used car case, but also to *explain* it, articulating the conditions under which the presence of a relevantly unreliable testifier does/does not undermine an ascription of testimonial knowledge to a child.

Let us take stock. Our question concerned the conditions under which a subject accepts the say-so of another out of simple trust, yet nevertheless satisfies the externalist condition on (testimonial) knowledge – and in particular whether we could formulate such conditions so as to yield the right verdicts in particular cases. Our results so far are mixed: while a standard reliabilist analysis appears to capture our intuitions in a good deal of particular cases, it yields unintuitive verdicts in cases in which the simple truster is in a situation involving relevantly unreliable sources nearby. The difficulty is that, in a good many of these cases, our intuitions support the ascription of testimonial knowledge to the simple truster. (In 'a good many' of these cases, but not in all of them: there remains the used car case and other cases like it.) Can we bring any order to this mess? Or should we concede that there is no way to vindicate the intuitions tugging at us in the battery of situations in which the child acquires a testimonial belief through accepting the reliable testimony of an adult guardian?

8.6 TOWARDS AN ACCOUNT OF TESTIMONIAL KNOWLEDGE IN EARLY CHILDHOOD

Leaving intact the standard reliabilist account of the external condition on knowledge, in what follows I propose to reconceive the process eventuating in the child's testimonial belief. Doing so will enable me to throw out the unhappy results of 8.4, as the effect of an unacceptable (because *overly individualistic*) conception of the process that eventuates in the young child's testimonial belief.[18]

I begin with a guiding analogy. Samantha is a teenager who has just received her drivers' permit, which allows her to drive a car only under certain very restrictive conditions: she can only drive during the day, in good weather, and when in the company of an experienced driver. If we consider Samantha herself, independent of these restrictions on her driving, she is not a particularly safe driver (yet): she has difficulties making a left-turn into oncoming traffic, does not allow herself sufficient braking distance, has a tendency to drive too close to the cars ahead of her, rarely uses her turn signals, tends not to obey the speed limit, and cannot parallel park. At the same time, when she drives under the restricted conditions set forth by her permit – and these are the only conditions under which she drives – she drives very safely: she only drives during the day and in good weather; she is gradually desensitized to making a left into oncoming traffic; she is reminded to use her turn signals; she is urged to slow down when she starts to go too fast, and to speed up when she goes too slowly; and so forth. Under these conditions, it would be correct to say that her driving is safe to the extent that her experienced cohort is vigilant in policing her. This is so for two reasons: first, the occasions on which she confronts the sort of conditions that would elicit her driving flaws are minimized, as her experienced cohort does not let her travel on the more dangerous roads, or in bad weather/at night, or in great traffic, etc.; and second, her experienced cohort serves as an external reminder,

---

[18] It might be wondered why I am focusing on *the process* eventuating in the young child's testimonial belief. After all, I have already argued (in 8.1 and 8.2) that the question of knowledge in such cases turns on the epistemic properties, not of *the process* by which the child acquires testimonial beliefs, but rather of *the beliefs* themselves. My claim here will be that, such is the process in question (as reconceived here), that the child's testimonial beliefs themselves will have the desired epistemic properties. It is a further question, but one that I do not consider here, whether this reconception can be used by the proponent of process-reliabilism as a way to reconcile process-reliabilism with TKC.

guiding Samantha through difficulties and correcting Samantha's driving errors as soon as they arise (before they have a chance to become dangerous).

Is Samantha a good (safe, reliable) driver? In one sense, she is not: if she were to drive alone, she would likely exhibit many serious driving flaws. In another sense, she is: as a matter of fact, she only drives in the restrictive conditions set forth by her permit, with the result that her environment is structured in such a way as to reduce the occasions on which she exhibits those flaws, and to minimize her flaws' effects on those occasions when she does begin to exhibit them. We might then describe this state of affairs by saying that, although Samantha herself is not yet a safe driver, she drives safely in the very restrictive conditions under which she drives (i.e. those set forth by her permit).

I want to suggest that something parallel occurs in the case of young children's consumption of testimony. My claim is that, just as we do not adequately characterize Samantha's driving without taking into account the social context of her driving (in particular, the laws restricting when she can drive, and with whom), so too we do not adequately characterize the process involved in young children's consumption of testimony without taking into account the child's *social environment*.[19] Rather, we should consider the role that the child's adult guardians play in the process that eventuates in the young child's consumption of testimony. I submit that adult guardians play three epistemically relevant roles in this process. First, adult guardians make social arrangements in such a way that children are typically shielded early in life from those who might abuse their trust; second, adult guardians serve as an explicit check on the trustworthiness of interlocutors whom children encounter in the presence of their parents or adult guardians (as in: "Rachel, do you really believe Uncle Myron's story about being the richest man in the world?"; or "Sam, don't believe your brother, he's just saying silly things again"); and third, adult guardians continue to vet the child's subsequent assertions for signs of his having consumed unreliable testimony. I will describe these three roles as the roles

---

[19] It is interesting to note that both this explanation, and the recognition of the explanation's potential philosophical significance, were offered by Reid in his remarks on testimony. See Reid 1872/1993: 281–2. In addition, the case of Samantha might also be thought to be accommodated within Goldman's (1986) notion of local reliability: Samantha's driving is (as it were) locally but not globally reliable.

of (i) *access-restriction*, (ii) *pro-active monitoring* for credibility, and (iii) *reactive monitoring* for credibility.[20]

The present proposal can be developed in relation to the idea that, if the cognitively immature child is really to count as coming to know something through her (more-or-less credulous) acceptance of testimony, the process eventuating in this acceptance must be such that her belief is reliable. My claim is that the roles adult guardians play in connection with (i)–(iii) are such as to enhance the reliability of a good many of the beliefs that are elicited by the child's encounters with testimony.

Consider first the epistemic significance of (i). During her waking hours, a young child is typically either at home, or else (if outside the home) in the company of an adult guardian. Access to the child is restricted while she is at home, since the walls of the house enable the adults to monitor (literally) who is permitted to enter the home (and so who has access to the child). When not at home the child will encounter strangers, but will do so typically only in the presence of her adult caretaker, where the caretaker's interest in protecting the child will render the caretaker more attentive to the child's environment. Part of this attentiveness, I submit, is a greater attentiveness on the adult's part to the testimony proferred in their mutual presence. The result is that, given the role adults play in achieving (i), the child is typically either in a pre-screened environment, or if she is not, her guardians are more vigilant; but either way, the risk of the child's accepting false testimony is significantly decreased, whether because the risk of *encountering* it is decreased, or because (though the child encounters it) the risk of *consuming* it is decreased.

Next consider (ii), pro-active monitoring. For one thing, the looming presence of the child's adult caretaker will already serve to ward off many of those who might otherwise try to exploit the child's gullibility. But it is noteworthy as well that children are much less suggestible when the question of the credibility of a source is *merely raised* by an adult

---

[20] Where proactive monitoring can be seen as a filter on *incoming* testimony (aiming to prevent unreliable testimony from entering into Babe's belief corpus in the first place), reactive monitoring can be conceived as a kind of filter which acts on Babe's belief corpus *as it actually is*, aiming to detect and eliminate any unreliable belief (no matter its source) that has managed to make its way into that corpus. As such, reactive monitoring does not figure among the features that determine the epistemic properties of a testimonial belief that the young child *forms* (at least not at the time of formation); rather, it serves to groom those beliefs, and so factors among the features that determine the epistemic properties of testimonial beliefs that the young child *sustains*. For this reason I will not be speaking much of reactive monitoring in what follows.

(Lampinen and Smith 1995; Giles *et al.* 2002). So to protect the child against consuming false testimony, it is typically sufficient that the adult merely make manifest her own doubts regarding a given speaker (or a given piece of testimony).

In order to realize the reliability-enhancing role I am describing in connection with (i) and (ii), it is not necessary that the child's adult guardian(s) be hyper-vigilant, listening to every sentence and remaining disposed to jump in whenever she regards the source as having said something false. Here a comparison with credibility monitoring *in adults* is helpful. As Fricker notes (and as discussed at length in chapter 6), the point of monitoring among adults is to provide the hearer with a "counterfactual sensitivity", such that it is "true throughout of the hearer that if there were signs of untrustworthiness, she would register them and respond appropriately" (Fricker 1994: 154). Now adult hearers can be more or less counterfactually sensitive in this way, and so can be more or less reliable in their consumption of reliable testimony. I submit that the role that adults play in connection with (i) is to provide a pre-filter that does not give access to the child to those speakers whom the adult deems to be unreliable; and the role that the adult plays in connection with (ii) is simply that of enabling the cognitively immature child to consume the testimony that does reach her ears with a greater degree of 'counterfactual sensitivity' than the child would enjoy on the basis of her cognitive resources alone. If adults are less vigilant in connection with either (i) or (ii), then the cognitively immature children in their presence will enjoy a correspondingly lower degree of this 'counterfactual sensitivity.' The limiting case here is complete non-vigilance, on which the very young child is left to fend for herself, and so attains knowledge only in those cases (if any) in which she is suitably supported by her surrounding environment.

The foregoing account makes two predictions.

First, the account predicts that, given the roles adults play in connection with (i) and (ii), false (or otherwise unreliable) testimony from mature speakers reaches children's ears much less than one might have initially expected.[21] Initially, one might have expected that false testimony from mature speakers reaches children's ears roughly as frequently as such

---

[21] The need for the modification involving false testimony *from mature speakers* is generated by the fact, noted above, that young children are often in the presence of (other) young children.

testimony reaches the ears of mature hearers. But the foregoing predicts that this is not so. Merely in virtue of the role adults play in connection with (i), children are less often in places where the chances of false or unreliable testimony are greatest. Since adult commerce in the world beyond the home forces adults into such places, the result is that adults will encounter such testimony far more frequently. The result, I submit, is that the epistemic situation of the credulous child can seem worse than it actually is. In particular, we distort matters if we think of the credulous child as a hearer, like any other, who will encounter the ordinary range of speakers (some reliable, others not) that we as adults encounter in our daily commerce with the world. If this is the standard we use in evaluating the reliability of the child's testimony-based beliefs, then a good many of those beliefs will be evaluated to be unreliable. But imposing this standard on the child distorts the epistemology of credulous belief in early childhood, since young children do not encounter the same range of speakers that adults do.

But the present account makes a second prediction, which is that our inclination to ascribe testimonial knowledge to a cognitively immature child in contexts involving relevantly unreliable testifiers will vary in strength in direct proportion to the degree of vigilance exhibited by the adult guardian(s) present. Take a case in which the child consumes what in fact is a reliable piece of testimony, but does so in a context involving one or more relevantly unreliable testifier(s) lurking about. If the context is what I will call a *poorly monitored context* – one in which unreliable testifiers are not pre-screened, and/or no caretaker in that context would take steps to prevent the child from consuming false testimony had she been pre-sented with it – then the present account predicts that the child will not be regarded as coming to know through her consumption of what in fact was reliable testimony. But if the context is what I will call a *well-monitored context* – one in which there is some pre-screening of testifiers, and one or more of the child's caretakers in that context would take steps to prevent the child's consumption of unreliable testimony on those occasions if such reached their ears – then the present account predicts that the child will be regarded as coming to know through her consumption of the testimony.

I submit that these predictions accord with intuition. The case involving the *poorly monitored context* is structurally identical to the case of Sid and Nancy from section 8.4 above: in each, the recipient could easily have come to form the belief he did, in the (testimonial) manner he did, even if the proposition believed were false. Thus, just as it is intuitive to think that gullible Sid fails to count as having acquired knowledge from reliable

Nancy given the prevalence of the talented liars, so too it is intuitive to think that a cognitively immature child fails to count as having acquired knowledge through her acceptance of a reliable piece of testimony when the belief is acquired in a poorly monitored context involving other relevantly unreliable testifiers. Indeed, this analysis gives us a plausible way to explain the intuitive verdict in the used car case: given that Babe's parents left him alone on the used car lot, this case can be seen as one taking place in a poorly monitored context. So the present account both accommodates and explains the independently plausible verdict that Babe does not count as acquiring knowledge in the used car case, despite the fact that he consumed reliable testimony. By contrast, cases involving a *well-monitored context* are such that the child would not easily have come to form the belief he did, in the (testimonial) manner he did, even if the proposition believed were false. On the contrary, to the extent that the context is well-monitored, it is that much more likely that the child would have been prevented from accepting any false testimony by the monitoring adult.

With this in mind we can now return to an objection which received only superficial treatment in section 8.4. This was the objection that it is unprincipled to ascribe knowledge to Babe in the Milk case in which Uncle Marfman is lurking nearby, while at the same time withholding an ascription of knowledge from credulous Sid in the case where liars lurk nearby. In 8.4 I responded by remarking that the interest Mother takes in Babe's consumption of testimony enhances the reliability of his (credulously formed) testimonial belief, in a way that has no parallel in the case of Sid's credulous belief in Nancy's testimony. We now have a label for this phenomenon: Babe's case, but not Sid's, takes place in a *well-monitored context*. But a key question remains unanswered: by what right do we hold fixed (in counterfactual scenarios) the active monitoring role Mother is disposed to play in the actual scenario? (Note too that if we don't hold Mother's monitoring fixed across the range of those nearby possible worlds in which we evaluate Babe's belief, this will affect the reliability, and hence the epistemic status, of Babe's belief in the actual world.) My answer is simply this, that the active monitoring role Mother is disposed to play on this occasion is itself part of the process that eventuates in Babe's forming the testimonial belief he did, and so cannot be separated out from that process on pain of distorting the relevant scenario.

In defense of this answer, consider that it is natural for parents to take an active interest in protecting their children. (Presumably there is an evolutionary explanation for this.) The role Mother plays in connection with Babe's consumption of testimony is an instance of the protective role she plays toward him more generally. Only here the protection concerns, not bodily harms, but rather *epistemic* harms that might befall Babe. Such protection is not only natural, it is also a systematic feature of Mother's relationship with Babe: it is not as if she monitors only when the mood strikes her, rather she always exhibits some degree of vigilance towards Babe (in accordance with the general risks she anticipates, i.e., less at home, more outside the home). We might say that she is *reliable* in the protection she affords Babe, both in general, and with respect to Babe's consumption of testimony in particular. But then Babe, whose consumption of testimony would otherwise be globally unreliable, is reliably monitored by an agent (in this case, Mother) who herself is a reliable consumer of testimony. Since in her pro-active monitoring Mother brings to bear the very same cognitive resources that make her a reliable consumer of testimony in her own right, the result is that Babe is *reliably rendered a reliable consumer* of reliable testimony. It is this, I submit, that warrants regarding Mother's role as part of the process that eventuates in Babe's testimonial belief, at least on those occasions when she is present (and is disposed to monitor for Babe). And it is because no similar story can be told in connection with Sid, that his case is to be treated differently.[22]

I should add (what is clear in any case) that not all guardians perform equally well when it comes to playing the roles of (i)–(iii), and not all children have the same amount of protection from guardians playing the roles of (i)–(iii). But it is a fact of life that such roles do get performed with some regularity. From this perspective, we can consider the process involved in the young child's consumption of testimony as one of blind trust *in a largely sheltered and closely monitored environment*, where both access to the testimony of others is severely restricted and, when testimony is observed by the young child, it is often closely monitored (pro-actively and/or reactively) by those parents and guardians who themselves take an interest in ensuring that only credible testimony be consumed by their

---

[22] Of course, if Nancy had been disposed to take the same interest in Sid's consumption of testimony that Mother took in connection with Babe's consumption of testimony, the cases would have been parallel. This suggests that even in a case not involving a cognitively immature child, a recipient of testimony can acquire knowledge even under conditions in which (a) she herself is uncritical in her consumption of testimony and (b) there are relevantly unreliable testifiers nearby. I discuss the case of a cognitively mature recipient relying on the monitoring of another adult in Goldberg 2005b.

wards. Just as we can say that Samantha drives safely under the restrictive conditions set forth by her permit even though, left to her own devices, she does not yet count as a safe driver, so too we can say that testimony consumed by the young child is being consumed reliably even in situations in which, left to his own devices, the child himself would not count as having acquired a reliable testimonial belief.

The aspects of the child's protected epistemic environment described in (i)–(iii) above are contingent aspects of the child's world. But as they reflect the deep human instinct to protect our young, they are deep features of a child's world; and any community that is like ours will be characterized by epistemic environments of this sort. And it is these aspects, I submit, that enable us to diminish the epistemic effects of the background presence of relevantly unreliable testifiers in those cases in which Babe consumes reliable testimony from an adult guardian. For, given any piece of false testimony that p proffered to Babe in Mother's presence, so long as Mother *herself* is aware that $\sim p$, she will do what she can to prevent Babe from consuming testimony that p – in which case RL* holds of Babe. Of course, if Mother is not aware that $\sim p$, then Babe's belief would be unreliable – since in that case Mother would not protect Babe against consuming the testimony (or against sustaining the testimonial belief, once formed). But in that case Mother herself would not be a reliable consumer of reliable testimony bearing on whether p – so the fact that, under such conditions, Babe's testimonial belief would be unreliable, is itself a welcome result: Babe's belief should not enjoy a *higher* degree of reliability than that of his adult guardian.[23]

In sum, I submit that the proposed account of the process eventuating in the young child's consumption of testimony, conceived to include the role adults play in restricting access to the child and monitoring the testimony that does reach the child's ears, provides a principled and systematic response to the extension challenge.

8.7 OBJECTIONS FROM EPISTEMIC AGENCY

The present proposal is to regard the process that eventuates in a young child's consumption of testimony as including the monitoring of his adult caretakers. It is this monitoring that enables such children to consume testimony in a way that satisfies the reliable discrimination condition.

---

[23] See Weiner 2003 for an expression of a similar intuition.

But there are at least two objections to this proposal that are worth considering.[24] The first charges that the proposal surrenders the idea of knowledge as a cognitive achievement *of the knowing subject*, and in so doing fails to square with the idea – motivating much externalist epistemology – that knowledge is (in John Greco's words) "credit for true belief." The second objection aims to raise an unflattering parallel in other domains, where the proper description of sheltered immature children appears to tell against describing them in the same terms as those with which we describe adults. These two objections are not unrelated: at heart, they both derive from the assumption that knowledge is correctly ascribed only to those individuals who meet certain threshold requirements for cognitive/epistemic agency.

I begin with the objection from cognitive achievement. The idea that knowledge involves a cognitive achievement does seem to underlie much epistemology, especially externalist epistemology. The point is nicely made by John Greco, himself a virtue-theoretic reliabilist, in a recent paper entitled "Knowledge as Credit for True Belief." He writes,

> when we attribute knowledge to someone we mean to give the person credit for getting things right. Put another way, we imply that *the person is responsible for getting things right*. The key idea here is ... that knowledge requires responsibility for true belief ... To say that someone knows is to say that his believing the truth can be credited to him. It is to say that the person got things right *due to his own abilities, efforts, and actions*, rather than due to dumb luck, or blind chance, or something else. (Greco 2004: 111; italics mine)

Although Greco is speaking of knowledge in terms of desert of credit rather than in terms of the attainment of a cognitive achievement, it is clear that his credit view is of a piece with the cognitive achievement view. For surely a case in which one "is responsible for getting things right" is a case in which one has achieved something through cognition. The achievement is in getting things right; and the achievement is a cognitive one since 'getting things right' is a matter of mentally representing things to be as they are. Assuming that Greco is correct to regard knowledge as credit for true belief, we can ask: does my proposal regarding young children's consumption of testimony square with Greco's doctrine, or with the associated idea of knowledge as a cognitive achievement (by the knowing subject)?

---

[24] I owe these objections to two anonymous referees.

Initially, it might seem not. Given that knowledge is ascribed to a cognitively immature child in virtue of cognitive work being done by her adult guardian(s), it is by no means clear that the child can be given credit for her true testimonial belief, or that her attainment of such knowledge can be counted a cognitive achievement *on her part*. But before we address this, we need to be clear about the sort of credit and/or achievement that is in play. Consider the case of perceptual knowledge. Joe knows by looking that there is a book in front of him. In what sense does Joe deserve credit for having attained this happy status? Two considerations suggest that the sort of credit at play, and the sort of achievement attained, are not very substantial. For one thing, Joe is relying on the proper functioning of his visual system, where this functioning is – at least to a very large extent – something that is not in his control. For another, Joe, like most others, doesn't know very much about the workings of the visual system, and so he wouldn't know quite what to say if asked to defend his entitlement to rely on his visual system. To be sure, if queried in this way he might appeal to past experience to cite the reliability of that system. But such a response faces the well-known difficulty of assuming what it is trying to show: how else does Joe know that past experience has shown vision to be reliable, other than by further reliance on vision? I do not bring these points up in order to undermine the thesis that knowledge is a cognitive achievement, or that knowledge is credit for true belief. I do so, rather, to support the conclusion that, if knowledge is or implies credit for true belief (or is a cognitive achievement), then the sort of credit (or cognitive achievement) in question must be one whose ascription to a subject is compatible with her relying on her native cognitive endowments – endowments for whose functioning she is not responsible, regarding whose workings she is (typically) ignorant, and the entitlement to rely on which she could not adequately defend. This point is readily granted by Greco and should not be controversial in any case.

Consider next the credit deserved (or cognitive achievement attained) in cases where the knowledge is acquired through testimony. In what sense are you to be given credit for your knowledge that *p*, when you know it through having taking someone else's word for it? It is tempting to regard testimonial knowledge as a counterexample to the thesis about knowledge as credit for true belief, and indeed others have done so.[25] However, let us waive this possible move; let us assume for the sake of

---

[25] See Lackey (forthcoming b).

argument that some (minimal) credit is due to the subject who knows through testimony. We can then ask: what is the knowing subject (whose knowledge is through testimony) being given credit for? What sort of cognitive achievement does the acquisition of testimonial knowledge amount to? My characterization of such knowledge, from chapter 1, suggests that the knower can be credited for a cognitive achievement along two distinct dimensions. First, she can be credited for having reliably comprehended the testimony; and second, she can be credited for having been reliable in her discrimination of reliable from unreliable testimony. This may not be much to credit her for, but it is something.

With these two points in mind – that credit to (or cognitive achievement by) a knowing subject is consistent with the subject's reliance on native cognitive endowments, and that credit in testimony cases in particular is minimal – we can now defend the thesis that the cognitively immature child deserves some credit, minimal though it may be, for the testimonial knowledge she acquires. For one thing, the young child deserves credit for having reliably comprehended the testimony. For the task of comprehension does call on her to use her cognitive faculties, and as such it can be seen as a minimal cognitive achievement. For another, while it is true that she alone cannot be given credit for having been reliable in her discrimination of reliable from unreliable testimony – after all, according the proposal above she relies on the credibility-monitoring of her adult guardians – nevertheless the young child can be given at least a minimal sort of credit for having allowed herself to be properly guided by the adult caretakers in her life. After all, the cognitively immature child could have reacted to an adult's guidance by ignoring the adult caretaker (and continuing to believe the discredited testimony), or by jumping up and down, or by yodeling, or by what-have-you. Admittedly, this too is a minor sort of credit, and it is also credit for something that (as it were) comes naturally to the child. But our first point above noted that credit can be given – a cognitive achievement can be ascribed – even when the subject is relying on her native cognitive endowment, under conditions in which she knows little about the workings of that endowment, and where she can do little in the way of offering an independent vindication of her reliance on it.

The foregoing suggests that the cognitively immature child is nevertheless to be given a minimal sort of credit for the cognitive achievement(s) involved in her consumption of reliable testimony. However, one might argue in response that the cognitive achievement(s) for which she is being 'credited' is/are not robust enough for this to preserve the thesis that

229

knowledge is credit for true belief. But this move threatens to falsify the credit thesis itself. The problem is that it is dubious whether there is a reading of the credit thesis that is strong enough to rule out crediting cognitively immature children for their true testimonial beliefs, but weak enough to allow that the acquisition of perceptual and testimonial knowledge by mature subjects is creditable. The burden is surely on the other side to establish that there is such a reading.

Still, one might try to press the objection from cognitive achievement as follows: if we allow children to have knowledge in virtue of the monitoring activities performed by their adult caretaker(s), won't we be forced to allow children to have knowledge in virtue of other sorts of activities performed by their adult caretaker(s)? For example, imagine a case in which a parent plays the role of a 'friendly demon', making sure to so arrange the world that the child's beliefs come out true. Won't we have to allow, implausibly, that this too can count as a case of the adult's enabling the child to acquire knowledge?[26] But this objection can be met by noting a crucial difference between the two cases. In the case of testimonial knowledge but not in the adult 'friendly demon' case, the child is employing (the underdeveloped versions of) processes that everyone should acknowledge as providing a route to knowledge. Nor is it *ad hoc* to regard the adult's credibility monitoring to be part of a legitimate way she can help the child to acquire knowledge, while still maintaining that the help provided by the adult 'friendly demon' is not a legitimate way to help the child to acquire knowledge. For not only does the former case but not the latter involve the employment of a type of process that is acknowledged by all parties to be knowledge-yielding; what is more, in the former case this process is supplemented by the adults' use of *the very same process*. This supports the idea that the case in which the adult monitors testimony for the child can be seen as an 'extended' version of a case involving a familiar knowledge-producing process. The same cannot be said for the case of the adult 'friendly demon': this introduces an knowledge-undermining element of luck, as much in the case of the child, as it would in the case where a 'friendly demon' helped an adult.

However, it remains to be seen whether knowledge presupposes a certain development in one's epistemic agency, and if so, whether the required degree of development obtains in those cases in which the above proposal would ascribe knowledge to cognitively immature children. To

---

[26] I thank an anonymous referee for raising this objection.

get a handle on this question, consider the proper description of children in other domains in which they are sheltered from the outside world. For example, consider a child who is sheltered from having to confront moral dilemmas.[27] Such a child would not thereby be counted a good moral agent. Presumably, this verdict is grounded in the idea that the child has not yet attained the minimum development of moral sensibility and/or self-control to count as a moral agent in the first place. This suggests an unflattering parallel: a child who is sheltered from the epistemic harms of unreliable testimony has not yet attained the minimum cognitive development and/or cognitive self-control to count as an epistemic agent in the first place.

But the psychological literature above suggests that this "parallel" is not a good one. Take the moral case. Assuming (with the objection) that young children who are sheltered from moral dilemmas have not yet developed to the point where they can be counted as moral agents, this will be in part because they do not yet have the capacity to see the world in the proper moral terms. But as noted in section 8.2, cognitively immature children are able to react to the world in terms appropriate to the epistemology of testimony: they react differently to true and false testimony in simple situations (Koenig and Echols 2003), are sensitive to some source credibility cues (Lampinen and Smith 1995), and are able to distinguish reporting from obvious story-telling (Dias and Harris 1990; Richards and Sanderson 1999; Harris 2002). The trouble, we noted above, was that children often have trouble *using* this knowledge to guide their consumption of testimony, in addition to having little background knowledge on which to draw in their credibility-assessments. So on this particular point, the parallel between the moral case, where we want to say that the child has not yet attained the status of a moral agent, and the epistemic case, where we want to credit the child with knowledge (and hence regard her as an epistemic agent), breaks down. Now it might be that, contrary to the suggestion above, the child development literature suggests a similar phenomenon with respect to the young child's moral competencies: she does see the world in moral terms, but simply lacks the capacity to put this knowledge into action. But if this is the correct way to describe the moral development of young children, then it is no longer clear whether the morally sheltered child fails to count as a moral agent (in which case the parallel holds but the case no longer presents an objection to my proposal).

---

[27] This potential parallel was suggested to me by an anonymous referee.

The foregoing suggests the following picture. The cognitively immature child does have the rudimentary cognitive tools of an epistemic agent,
but cognitive immaturity prevents their deployment in appropriate set-
tings. The role – I would speculate, the *evolutionarily given role* – of the adult
here is to structure the child's environment, and the child's relations to her
adult caretaker(s), so as to foster the development and appropriate use of
the cognitive tools she does have. In 'relying' on the adults' interventions,
the child is 'relying' on regularities which, though not part of her own
(individualistically conceived) cognitive resources, are nevertheless environmental regularities that are exploited by those resources.[28] Here the fact
that the exploited regularities are regularities *in the environment*, rather than
regularities within her own (individualistically conceived) cognitive
resources, should not be used to establish the epistemic irrelevance of
these broadly environmental regularities. After all, research into perceptual
representation has long noted that human perceptual systems systematically exploit regularities and invariances in our perceptual environment;[29]
and no one should want to say that, since these regularities are broadly
environmental, they are irrelevant to the epistemology of perception. (At
the very least, they contribute to the reliability of our perceptual beliefs and
belief-producing processes.) Thus it would appear that we have a solid
basis for saying, and no good reasons not to say, that, whatever the minimal
cognitive threshold is for counting as an epistemic agent, very young
children meet this threshold.

I conclude that my proposal above, to regard the child's reliance on an
adult's monitoring as part of what enables the child to satisfy the reliable

---

[28] The child, of course, is unaware that she is so 'relying', which is the reason for the scare-
quotes.

[29] It is widely recognized that our perceptual representations of the world are formed on the
basis of sensory evidence that underdetermines the set of possible physical arrangements
that could have given rise to the relevant sensory evidence. The trick employed – what
renders our perceptual representations reliable, despite this underdetermination – is that
perceptual systems make certain environmental/perceptual *invariance* assumptions, which
in effect helps the system narrow down the set of perceptual 'hypotheses' it will find
acceptable in a given situation. In most cases this narrowing, together with other information available to the environmentally situated cognitive system, enables the selection of
single 'hypothesis'. (I use the scare-quotes as this process takes places below the level of
consciousness and so should not be modeled on the case of conscious hypothesis-selection.)
See Gibson 1966 pp. 3, 52–4, 81–4, 156–63, 186–223, 250–65, 284–6; Shepard 1987 and
1992; Hubel 1995 Chapter 8; Zeki 1993, chapters 23 and 25; and see Pinker 1997, chapter 4
for a nice overview of the literature.

discrimination condition on testimonial knowledge, can be defended against the objections from epistemic agency.

8.8 THE DEFEATER CHALLENGE REVISITED

On the present proposal, the process eventuating in the child's consumption of testimony is seen as incorporating the role played by credibility-monitoring by the young child's adult caretaker. In 8.6 I argued that this proposal meets the extension challenge; and in 8.7 I defended this proposal against various objections from epistemic agency. In this section I want to argue that this very same proposal also provides a natural reply to the defeater challenge.

We recall that the defeater challenge was to square TKC – the thesis that cognitively immature children acquire testimonial knowledge – with the claim that

LAK Children cannot properly be described as satisfying the No-Defeater condition.

Suppose that LAK is true. Even so, it would not follow that young childrens' testimonial beliefs cannot be said to satisfy a No-Defeater condition. On the contrary, I submit that Lackey's argument for LAK,[30] together with two plausible auxiliary assumptions, can be seen as offering support to the proposal of section 8.6.

To see this, let us grant LAK (see footnote 30). I submit that LAK, together with TKC and the thesis that

NT Knowledge presupposes a non-trivial satisfaction of the No-Relevant-Defeater condition.

supports the following anti-individualistic conclusion regarding the nature of the process involved:

---

[30] Lackey herself doesn't advance LAK itself. Rather, she argues that if cognitively immature children lack positive reasons for accepting testimony, as the infant/child objection to RD maintains (for which see section 8.2 above), then LAK holds. In what follows I am assuming (what Lackey does not take sides on) that cognitively immature children lack positive reasons for accepting testimony. This assumption is concessive: making it jeopardizes TKC, a thesis I am trying to preserve. My claim here is that even if we make this assumption, and so put in jeopardy a thesis I am trying to preserve, that thesis (TKC) can still be preserved by endorsing an anti-individualistic account of the process by which children consume testimony.

AI–P The process that eventuates in young children's consumption of
testimony (and hence in the child's testimonial belief) extends to include
aspects of the child's social environment – in particular, the coherence-
monitoring that is performed for her by her adult guardian(s).

The argument here is one of inference to the best explanation. Given
NT, knowledge involves the non-trivial satisfaction of the No-
Relevant-Defeater condition; but LAK asserts that immature children
do not meet this condition; so if immature children do have testimonial knowledge, as TKC asserts, then the No-Relevant-Defeater
condition must be satisfied by something other than the children.
Whatever it is that satisfies this condition must itself be part of the
process that eventuates in the child's testimonial belief – otherwise it
will not be relevant to the epistemic assessment of that belief. And
the only thing that appears to be distinct from the child's cognitive
system, yet relevant to the process that eventuates in the child's
acquisition of a testimonial belief, is the role adults play in monitoring the child's consumption of testimony. AI–P is simply a generalization of this idea.

We can develop this line of reasoning by seeing how the truth of AI–P
might account for the truth of TKC given NT and LAK. The basic idea
here is straightforward. There can be no doubt that adults' beliefs can
satisfy (or fail to satisfy) the No-Relevant-Defeater condition: their cognitive maturity is such that they can have negative reasons bearing against
particular beliefs they have (or against the support enjoyed by those
beliefs). But above I argued that adult guardians bring their cognitive
resources to bear in the process that eventuates in the child's consumption
of testimony. The cognitive resources in question are those with which
adults anticipate and identify cases of unreliable testimony. Since it is these
very same cognitive resources that render the adults' beliefs susceptible to
evaluation in terms of the No-Relevant-Defeater condition, the result is
that the child's testimonial beliefs, when formed as the outcome of a
process involving these cognitive resources of the adult, are themselves
evaluable in terms of the No-Relevant-Defeater condition.

To illustrate, we can use a variant on the simple Milk case. When
Mother opened the refrigerator this morning, she saw a little milk left
over from the day before. However, she soon sees Father take the milk out
of the fridge. What is more, she knows that Father has a selfish tendency to
finish off the milk, and has been known on occasion to put empty milk

cartons back in the fridge. Now suppose that Liz (an adult whom Babe does not know) shows up on the scene. And suppose further that Mother suspects (incorrectly, it turns out) that Liz did not see Father take the milk out of the fridge. In this situation, if Liz tells Babe (in Mother's presence) that there is milk in the fridge, Mother should regard the testimony as unreliable: after all, Mother thinks that it is more likely that Father drank the milk and returned the empty carton to the fridge (thereby misleading Liz into thinking that there was milk in the fridge), than that Father returned the milk carton with milk left in it to the fridge. In that case, Mother should try to prevent Babe from consuming Liz's testimony. I submit that if, instead of doing so, she lets Babe consume Liz's testimony, then this would be a case in which Babe's belief fails to satisfy the No-Relevant-Defeaters condition.[31] This is so even if Liz's testimony was in fact reliable (unbeknownst to Mother, Liz saw what Mother herself did not: Father put the milk back without having consumed any). This illustrates that, just as the successful proactive monitoring of an adult guardian can put a cognitively immature child in a position to acquire testimonial knowledge which, left to her own devices, the child would not be in a position to acquire, so too this monitoring (when not performed in a manner that is up to epistemic standards) can undermine the child's claim to know under conditions in which, left to her own devices, the child might have been in a position to know. But the present point is simply that the child's belief is appropriately evaluated in terms of the No-Relevant-Defeaters condition.

I just argued that if AI–P holds, then even if LAK is true, the young child's belief can satisfy (or fail to satisfy) the No-Relevant-Defeaters condition. Of course, if AI–P does *not* hold, then, on the assumption of LAK, the process that eventuates in the young child's consumption of testimony does not yield testimonial beliefs that can

---

[31] It might be objected: if Babe cannot acquire knowledge through Liz's reliable testimony under these circumstances, why should we regard Babe as acquiring knowledge through Mother's reliable testimony in the original Milk case? A correct but unhelpful answer is that the one case but not the other involves a relevant defeater. This is unhelpful, since the objector will want to know why we should we regard Mother's defeater as relevant to Babe's belief. A more helpful answer is this: insofar as Mother is the one whose regular monitoring of Babe renders Babe reliable in his consumption of reliable testimony, it is Mother whose background beliefs are relevant to the assessment of the epistemic status of Babe's belief. If these background beliefs contain a relevant defeater regarding Babe's consumption of testimony regarding the presence of milk in the fridge, then his testimonial belief is defeated.

be said to satisfy (or fail to satisfy) the No-Defeater requirement. In that case, the options facing those who still want to preserve TKC would appear to be three.[32] One would be to hold that the No-Defeater requirement pertains to justification, not knowledge, and that one can have knowledge without justification. (In effect, this is the view of Audi 1997.) A second (related) option would be to distinguish various kinds of knowledge, such that not all kinds of knowledge require the truth of NT. Such a view might hold, for example, that there are (at least) two kinds of knowledge (say, animal and reflective), and that it is only with respect to one of these kinds (reflective knowledge) that NT holds.[33] If so, then TKC, construed as a thesis about animal knowledge, can be true even though NT is false. But it is worthwhile noting that, for those who want to preserve TKC, LAK, and NT, and who hold both that knowledge requires justification and that the kind of knowledge implicated in TKC just is the kind of knowledge ascribed to cognitively mature hearers, there remains the option of endorsing AI–P. On such a view, although cognitively immature children (taken in isolation from their surrounding social environment) fail to satisfy the No-Defeater requirement, nevertheless such children (taken in the context of their surrounding social environment) can be said to acquire beliefs in such a way as to satisfy this requirement. In that case, even assuming that knowledge requires justification and that justification requires NT, TKC is true.

In sum, given LAK, one who denies AI–P does so at the cost of having *either* to deny TKC, *or else* to deny that knowledge requires justification, *or else* to maintain that there are types of knowledge not requiring the truth of NT. For those for whom the latter three options are not palatable, I offer the possibility of retaining TKC by endorsing AI–P. Given the pretheoretic intuitiveness of TKC, discussed in 8.2, I conclude that the considerations in Lackey's argument are better seen as an argument for AI–P, than for ~TKC – even for those for whom the various alternative options are not palatable. In short, our conclusion from 8.6 is supported in ways that go beyond the ability of the proposal to meet the extension challenge. Our confidence in AI–P should be reinforced by the fact of such convergence.

[32] I thank Peter Graham for indicating the dialectical situation here.
[33] The distinction between animal and reflective knowledge is owed to Ernest Sosa. See Sosa (1991: 240), as well as Sosa 2001.

8.9 TOWARDS AN 'ACTIVE ANTI-INDIVIDUALISM' ABOUT KNOWLEDGE

In this concluding section I want to make a few remarks about the radicalness of this chapter's main contention, that the process that eventuates in young children's consumption of testimony extends to include aspects of the child's social environment. AI–P goes beyond the other epistemically anti-indvidualistic results of Part II (AI–K, AI–W, AI–J, and AI–R). More specifically, AI–P amounts to a particularly radical form of externalism about knowledge. If the foregoing account is sound, when cognitively immature children count as knowing through testimony, this knowledge reflects more than (the young hearer's sensitivity to) the epistemic properties of the testimonies upstream in the chain of communication; it also reflects the epistemic properties of the credibility-monitoring performed by the child's adult guardians. For it is this credibility-monitoring that renders the child's consumption of testimony both *reliably discriminating* and *appropriately evaluated in terms of relevant defeaters*. We might then say that the processing relevant to an epistemic evaluation of a very young child's testimonial beliefs *is 'extended' into the social world itself*.[34]

One gets a sense of the radicalness of AI–P by comparing it to the other epistemically anti-individualist positions argued for in this book. AI–P goes beyond the various anti-individualism argued for in Part II – AI–K, AI–W, AI–J, and AI–R – in the role that AI–P assigns to social (anti-individualistic) factors. Whereas each of the previous anti-individualistic doctrines are motivated in connection with the satisfaction of condition (a), the reliable testimony condition on testimonial knowledge, AI–P is motivated in connection with the satisfaction of condition (c), the reliable discrimination condition, on testimonial knowledge.

This difference is significant. It is no part of my arguments from earlier chapters that the social environment plays an *active role* in the process through which the hearer consumes the testimony. Rather, the epistemic relevance of previous speakers in a chain of communication was restricted

---

[34] I borrow the idea of 'extended' cognitive processing from Clark and Chalmers 1998. The foregoing proposal can be seen to illustrate the *epistemic* dimension of extended processing. This said, the forgoing does not imply the thesis of extended cognition. Granted that the adult's cognitive processing is relevant to the epistemic assessment of the child's testimonial belief, this processing need not be counted as part of the *cognitive* process that eventuates in the child's testimonial belief – any more than the broadly environmental regularities exploited by the perceptual process are part of the cognitive process that eventuates in perceptual belief.

to their serving as repositories of what I called 'distinctly testimonial support'; but beyond contributing such support to the recipient's testimony-based belief, previous speakers play no role in the process that eventuates in the recipient's acquisition of that belief. In the case I have presented for AI–P, in contrast, adult caretakers play an *active* role in the process eventuating in the child's acquisition of a testimonial belief, for example, by monitoring testimony proffered in their joint presence. Thus we might contrast AI–P with the other epistemically anti-individualistic theses by distinguishing between active and passive anti-individualism.[35] The conclusion of this chapter, then, is that then the epistemic dimension of knowledge communication is even more social than traditional epistemic categories ('knowledge,' 'warrant,' 'justification,' 'rationality') would lead us to expect.

---

[35] Once again, in speaking of 'active' and 'passive' epistemic anti-individualism, I am mirroring the language of Clark and Chalmers 1998, who speak of 'active' and 'passive' externalism in the philosophy of mind.

References

Adler, J. 1994. "Testimony, Trust, Knowing." *Journal of Philosophy* 91, 264–75

  1996. "Transmitting Knowledge." *Noûs* 30: 1, 99–111

  1997. "Lying, Deceiving, or Falsely Implicating." *Journal of Philosophy* 94: 9, 435–52

Alston, W. 1986. "Internalism and Externalism in Epistemology." *Philosophical Topics* 14, 179–221

Armstrong, D. 1973. *Belief, Truth, and Knowledge* (Cambridge: Cambridge University Press)

Audi, R. 1988. "Justification, Truth, and Reliability." *Philosophy and Phenomenological Research* 49: 1, 1–29

  1993. *The Structure of Justification* (Cambridge: Cambridge University Press)

  1997. "The Place of Testimony in the Fabric of Knowledge and Justification." *American Philosophical Quarterly* 34: 4, 405–22

Bach, K. 1988. "Burge's New Thought Experiment: Back to the Drawing Room." *The Journal of Philosophy* 85, 88–97

  1994. "Conversational Implicitures." *Mind and Language* 9, 24–62

  1997a. "Do Belief Reports Report Beliefs?" *Pacific Philosophical Quarterly* 78: 3, 215–41

  1997b. "The Semantics-Pragmatics Distinction: What It Is and Why It Matters." *Linguistiche Berichte* 8, 33–50

Bach, K. and Elugardo, R. 2003. "Conceptual Minimalism and Anti-Individualism: A Reply to Goldberg," *Noûs* 37: 1, 151–60

Baldwin, D. and Moses, L. 1996. "The Ontogeny of Social Information Gathering." *Child Development* 67, 1915–39

Bar-Tal, D., Raviv, A., Raviv, A., and Brosh, M. 1990. "Perception of Epistemic Authority and Attribution for its Choice as a Function of Knowledge Area and Age." *European Journal of Social Psychology* 21, 477–92

Bezuidenhout, A. 1997. "Pragmatics, Semantic Underdetermination and the Referential- Attributive Distinction." *Mind* 106, 375–409

  1998. "Is Verbal Communication a Purely Preservative Process?" *Philosophical Review* 107, 261–88

Bilgrami, A. 1992. *Belief and Meaning* (Oxford: Basil Blackwell)

Boghossian, P. 1989. "Content and Self-Knowledge." *Philosophical Topics* 17: 1, 5–26

Bonjour, L. 1985. *The Structure of Empirical Knowledge* (Cambridge: Harvard University Press)

  1999. *In Defense of Pure Reason* (Cambridge: Cambridge University Press)

Bonjour, L. and Sosa, E. 2003. *Epistemic Justification* (London: Blackwell)

Brandom, R. 1983. "Asserting." *Noûs* 17, 637–50

    1994. *Making It Explicit* (Cambridge: Harvard University Press)

Brown, J. 2004. *Anti-Individualism and Knowledge* (Cambridge: MIT Press)

Burge, T. 1979. "Individualism and the Mental." Reprinted in D. Rosenthal (ed.) *The Nature of Mind* (Oxford: Oxford University Press, 1991), 536–67

    1982a. "Other Bodies." In A.Woodfield (ed.) *Thought and Object* (Oxford: Oxford University Press), 97–120

    1982b. "Two Thought Experiments Reviewed." *Notre Dame Journal of Formal Logic* 23: 3, 284–93

    1986. "Intellectual Norms and the Foundations of Mind." *Journal of Philosophy* 83, 697–720

    1986b. "Individualism and Psychology." *Philosophical Review* 95, 3–45

    1987. "Individualism and Self-Knowledge." *Journal of Philosophy* 85: 11, 649–63

    1988. "Cartesian Error and the Objectivity of Perception." In R. Grimm and D. Merrill, *Contents of Thought* (Tucson: University of Arizona Press)

    1989. "Wherein is Language Social?" In A. George (ed.) *Reflections on Chomsky* Oxford: Basil Blackwell

    1993. "Content Preservation." *Philosophical Review* 102: 4, 457–88

    1996. "Our Entitlement to Self-Knowledge." *Proceedings of the Aristotelian Society* 96, 91–116

    1997. "Interlocution, Perception, and Memory." *Philosophical Studies* 86, 21–47

    1998. "Memory and Self-Knowledge." In P. Ludlow and N. Martin, eds, *Externalism and Self-Knowledge* (Palo Alto: CSLI Publications), 351–70

    1999. "Comprehension and Interpretation." In Lewis Hahn (ed.), *The Philosophy of Donald Davidson* (Chicago: Open Court Press), 229–50

    2003. "Perceptual Entitlement." *Philosophy and Phenomenological Research* 67: 3, 503–48

Brueckner, A. 1997. "Externalism and Memory." *Pacific Philosophical Quarterly* 78: 1, 1–12

Byrne, A. and Thau, M. 1995. "In Defense of the Hybrid View." *Mind* 105, 139–49

Cappelen, H. and Lepore, E. 1997. "On an Alleged Connection between Indirect Speech and the Theory of Meaning." *Mind and Language* 12, 278–96

Carston, R. 1988. "Implicature, Explicature, and Truth-Theoretic Semantics." In S. Davis (ed.) *Pragmatics: A Reader* (New York: Oxford University Press, 1991), 33–51

    2002. "Linguistic Meaning, Communicated Meaning, and Cognitive Pragmatics." *Mind and Language* 17, 127–48

Ceci, S., Ross, D., and Toglia, M. 1987. "Age Differences in Suggestibility: Psycholegal Implications." *Journal of Experimental Psychology* 117, 38–49

Ceci, S. and Bruck, M. 1993. "Suggestibility of the Child Witness: a Historical Review and Synthesis." *Psychological Bulletin* 113, 403–39

Chisholm, R. 1977. *Theory of Knowledge*, 2nd edn (Englewood Cliffs, NJ: PrenticeHall)

Chomsky, N. 1980. *Rules and Representations* (New York: Columbia University Press)

1986. *Knowledge of Language: Its Nature, Origin, and Use* (New York: Praeger)

Clark, A. and Chalmers, D. 1998. "The Extended Mind." *Analysis* 58, 7–19

Clément, F., Koenig, M., and Harris, 2004. "The Ontogenesis of Trust." *Mind and Language* 19: 4, 360–79

Clifford, W. K. 1999. "The Ethics of Belief." In *Ethics of Belief and Other Essays* (NY: Prometheus Books, 1999)

Coady, C. 1992. *Testimony: A Philosophical Study.* (Oxford: Oxford University Press)

2002. "Testimony and Intellectual Autonomy." *Studies in History and Philosophy of Science* 33, 355–72

Cohen, S. 1984. "Justification and Truth." *Philosophical Studies* 46, 279–95

Coady, C. A. J. 1992. *Testimony: A Philosophical Study* (Oxford: Clarendon Press)

1994. "Testimony, Observation and 'Autonomous Knowledge.'" in *Knowing From Words*, Matilal, B., and Chakrabarti, A., eds. (Dordrech: Kluwer, 1994), 225–50

2002. "Testimony and Intellectual Autonomy," *Studies in the History and Philosophy of Science* 33: 2, 355–72

Conee, E. 2007. "Externally Enhanced Internalism." In S. Goldberg (ed.) *Internalism and Externalism in Semantics and Epistemology* (Oxford: Oxford University Press)

Conee, E. and Feldman, R. 2004. *Evidentialism* (Oxford: Oxford University Press)

Danto, A. 1969. "Semantical Vehicles, Understanding, and Innate Ideas." In S. Hook (ed.), *Language and Philosophy* (New York: New York University Press)

Davidson, D. 1984. *Inquiries into Truth and Interpretation* (Oxford: Oxford University Press)

1986. "A Nice Derangement of Epitaphs." In E. Lepore (ed.) *Truth and Interpretation.* Oxford: Basil Blackwell, 433–46

1999. "Reply to Tyler Burge." In Lewis Hahn (ed.) *The Philosophy of Donald Davidson* (Chicago: Open Court Press), 251–4

2001. *Subject, Intersubjective, Objective* (Oxford: Oxford University Press)

Davis, S. 2002. "Conversation, Epistemology, and Norms." *Mind and Language* 17: 5, 513–37

DeRose, K. 1991. "Epistemic Possibilities." *Philosophical Review* 91, 581–605

Dias, M. and Harris, 1990. "The Influence of the Imagination on Reasoning by Young Children." *British Journal of Developmental Psychology* 8, 305–18

Dretske, F. 1982. "A Cognitive Cul-de-Sac." *Mind* 91, 109–11

Dummett, M. 1978. "Frege's Distinction between Sense and Reference." In M. Dummett, *Truth and Other Enigmas* (Cambridge: Harvard University Press), 116–44

1994. "Testimony and Memory." In B. K. Matilal and A. Chakrabarti, eds. *Knowing from Words* (Amsterdam: Kluwer Academic Publishers), 251–72

Ebbs, G. 1997. "Can We Take Our Words at Face Value?" *Philosophy and Phenomenological Research* 56: 3, 499–530

Egan, F. 1991. "Must Psychology be Individualistic?" *Philosophical Review* 100, 179–203

1992. "Individualism, Computation, and Perceptual Content." *Mind* 101, 443–59

1995. "Computation and Content." *Philosophical Review* 104: 2, 181–203

1999. "In Defense of Narrow Mindedness." *Mind and Language* 14, 177–94

Elgin, C. 2002. "Take It from Me: The Epistemological Status of Testimony." *Philosophy and Phenomenological Research* 65: 2, 291–308

Elugardo, R. 1993. "Burge on Content." *Philosophy and Phenomenological Research* 53: 2, 367–84

Evans, G. 1982. *The Varieties of Reference* (Oxford: Oxford University Press)

Falvey, K. and Owens, J. 1994. "Externalism, Self-Knowledge, and Skepticism." *Philosophical Review* 103: 1, 107–37

Faulkner, 2000. "The Social Character of Testimonial Knowledge." *Journal of Philosophy* 97: 11, 581–601

Feldman, R. 2004. "In Search of Internalism and Externalism." In R. Schantz (ed.) *The Externalist Challenge* (Berlin: Walter de Gruyter), 143–56

Forthcoming: "Epistemological Puzzles about Disagreement." In S. Hetherington (ed.) *Epistemology Futures* (Oxford: Oxford University Press)

Flavell, J. 1979. "Metacognition and Cognitive Monitoring: A New Area of Cognitive-Developmental Inquiry." *American Psychologist* 34: 906–11

Fodor, J. 1983. *The Modularity of Mind*. Cambridge: MIT Press

2002. *The Mind Doesn't Work That Way: The Scopes and Limits of Computational Psychology*. Cambridge: MIT Press

Foley, R. 1994. "Egoism in Epistemology." In F. Schmitt (ed.) *Socializing Epistemology: The Social Dimensions of Knowledge* (Lanham, MD: Rowman and Littlefield), 53–73

2004. "A Trial Separation between the Theory of Knowledge and the Theory of Justified Belief." In J. Greco (ed.) *Ernest Sosa and his Critics* (Oxford: Blackwell Publishers), 59–71

Fricker, E. 1987. "The Epistemology of Testimony." *Proceedings of the Aristotelian Society*, Supplemental Vol. 61, 57–83

1994. "Against Gullibility." In B. K. Matilal and A. Chakrabarti, eds. *Knowing from Words* (Amsterdam: Kluwer Academic Publishers), 125–61

1995. "Telling and Trusting: Reductionism and Anti-Reductionism in the Epistemology of Testimony." *Mind* 104, 393–411

2003. "Understanding and Knowledge of What is Said." In A. Barber (ed.) *The Epistemology of Language* (Oxford: Oxford University Press), 325–66

2006. "Testimony and Epistemic Autonomy." In J. Lackey and E. Sosa, eds. *The Epistemology of Testimony* (Oxford: Oxford University Press), 225–52

Gauker, C. 1991. "Mental Content and the Division of Epistemic Labor." *Australasian Journal of Philosophy* 69: 302–18

1994. *Thinking Out Loud* (Princeton: Princeton University Press)

2001. "Situated Inference versus Conversational Implicature." *Noûs* 35, 163–89

Gibbons, J. 1996. "Externalism and Knowledge of Content." *Philosophical Review* 105: 3, 287310

Gibson, R. 1966. *The Senses Considered as Perceptual Systems* (Boston: Houghton Mifflin)

Gilbert, D. T. 1991. "How Mental Systems Believe." *American Psychologist* 46: 107–19

    1992. "Assent of Man: Mental Representation and the Control of Belief." In D. M. Wegner and J. Pennebaker, eds. *The Handbook of Mental Control* (New York: Prentice-Hall)

Gilbert, D. T., Krull, D. S., and Malone, S. 1990. "Understanding the Unbelievable: Some Problems in the Rejection of False Information." *Journal of Personality and Social Psychology* 59: 601–13

Gilbert, D. T., Tafarodi, R. W., and Malone, S. 1993. "You Can't Not Believe Everything you Read." *Journal of Personality and Social Psychology* 65, 221–33

Giles, J., Gopnik, A., and Heyman, G. 2002. "Source Monitoring Reduces the Suggestibility of Preschool Children." *Psychological Science* 13: 3, 288–91

Goldberg, S. 1997. "Self-Ascription, Self-Knowledge, and the Memory Argument." *Analysis* 57: 3, 211–19

    1999. "The Relevance of Discriminatory Knowledge of Content," *Pacific Philosophical Quarterly* 80: 2, 136–56

    2000. "The Semantics of Interlocution." *Communication and Cognition* 33: 3, 243–80

    2000b. "World-Switching, Word-Ambiguity, and Semantic Intentions," *Analysis* 60: 3, 260–4

    2001. "Testimonially Based Knowledge from False Testimony." *Philosophical Quarterly* 51: 205, 512–26

    2002a. "Do Anti-Individualistic Construals of the Attitudes Capture the Agent's Conceptions?" *Noûs* 36: 4, 597–621

    2002b. "Reported Speech and the Epistemology of Testimony." *Protosociology* 17, 57–75

    2003a. "Anti-Individualism, Conceptual Omniscience, and Skepticism."*Philosophical Studies* 116: 1, 53–78

    2003b. "What do you Know When you Know your Own Thoughts?" In S. Nuccetelli (ed.), *New Essays on Semantic Externalism and Self-Knowledge* (Cambridge, MA: MIT Press, 2003), 241–56

    2004a. "Radical Interpretation, Understanding, and Testimonial Transmission."*Synthese* 138: 3, 387–416

    2004b. "Descriptions, Context-Sensitivity, and the Epistemology of Testimony." In João Sàágua (ed.) *The Explanation of Human Interpretation.* (Lisbon: Colibri Editions, 2004), 473–85

    2005a. "The Dialectical Context of Boghossian's Memory Argument." *Canadian Journal of Philosophy* 35: 1, 135–48

    2005b. "Testimonial Knowledge from Unsafe Testimony." *Analysis* 65: 4, 302–11

    2005c. "(Non-standard) Lessons from World-Switching Cases," *Philosophia* 32: 1, 95–131

    2006. "Reductionism and the Distinctiveness of Testimonial Knowledge." In J. Lackey, and E. Sosa, eds. *The Epistemology of Testimony* (Oxford University Press), 127–44

References

Forthcoming a. "The Epistemic Utility of *What is Said*." In R. Stainton and C. Viger, eds. *Compositionality, Context, and Semantic Values: Essays in Honor of Ernie Lepore*. (Springer Verlag)

2007a. "Anti-Individualism, Content Preservation, and Discursive Justification." *Noûs*

Forthcoming b. "How Lucky Can you Get?" *Synthese*

Forthcoming c. "The Knowledge Account of Assertion and the Conditions on Testimonial Knowledge." In D. Pritchard and Greenough. eds. *Williamson on Knowledge* (Oxford: Oxford University Press, in preparation)

2007b. "Brown on Discriminability and Self-Knowledge." *Pacific Philosophical Quarterly*

2007c. "Semantic Externalism and Illusions of Epistemic Relevance." In S. Goldberg (ed.) *Internalism and Externalism in Semantics and Epistemology* (Oxford: Oxford University Press, in preparation)

Unpublished Manuscript. "Justification as the Entitlement to Regard one's Belief as Warranted"

Goldberg, S. and Henderson, D. 2007. "Monitoring and Anti-Reductionism in the Epistemology of Testimony." *Philosophy and Phenomenological Research*

Goldman, A. 1976. "Discrimination and Perceptual Knowledge." *Reprinted in Goldman* 1992

1980. "The Internalist Conception of Justification." *Midwest Studies in Philosophy* 5, 27–52.

1986. *Epistemology and Cognition* (Cambridge: Harvard University Press)

1992. *Liaisons: Philosophy Meets the Cognitive and Social Sciences* (Cambridge: MIT Press)

1999. *Knowledge in a Social World* (Oxford: Oxford University Press)

1999b. "Internalism Exposed." Reprinted in Goldman 2002

2001a. "The Unity of the Epistemic Virtues." In A. Fairweather and L. Zagzebski, *Virtue Epistemology* (Oxford: Oxford University Press). Reprinted in Goldman 2002

2001b. "Experts: Which Ones Should You Trust?" *Philosophy and Phenomenological Research* 63: 1, 85–110. Reprinted in Goldman 2002

2001c. "Social Routes to Belief and Knowledge." *Reprinted in Goldman* 2002

2002. *Pathways to Knowledge: Public and Private* (Oxford: Oxford University Press)

2004. "Group Knowledge vs. Group Rationality: Two Approaches to Social Epistemology." *Episteme* 1, 11–22

Gopnik, A., and Graf, P. 1988. "Knowing How you Know: Young Children's Ability to Identify and Remember the Sources of Their Beliefs." *Child Development* 59: 1366–71

Graham, P. 1997. "What is Testimony?" *The Philosophical Quarterly* 47: 187, 227–32

1999. "Transferring Knowledge." *Noûs* 34, 131–52

2000a. "Conveying Information." *Synthese* 123: 3, 365–92

2000b. "The Reliability of Testimony." *Philosophy and Phenomenological Research* 61: 3, 695–709

Greco, J. 2000. *Putting Skeptics in their Place* (Cambridge: Cambridge University Press)

2004. "Knowledge as Credit for True Belief." In Michael DePaul and Linda Zagzebski, eds. *Intellectual Virtue: Perspectives from Ethics and Epistemology*, (Oxford: Oxford University Press, 2004)

Grice, H. P. 1989. "Logic and Conversation." In *Studies in the Way of Words* (Cambridge: Harvard University Press)

Grundmann, A. 2004. "Counterexamples to Epistemic Externalism Revisited." In R. Schantz (ed.) *The Externalist Challenge* (Berlin/New York: Walter de Gruyter)

Haack, S. 1993. *Evidence and Inquiry* (Oxford: Basil Blackwell)

Hardwig, J. 1991. "The Role of Trust in Knowledge." *Journal of Philosophy* 88, 693–708

Harris, 2002. "Checking our sources: The Origins of Trust in Testimony." *Studies in History and Philosophy of Science* 33: 2, 315–33

Heal, J. 1998. "Externalism and Memory II." *Proceedings of the Aristotelian Society* 72 (Supplemental Volume), 95–109

Heck, R. 1995. "The Sense of Communication." *Mind* 104, 79–106

1996. "Communication and Knowledge: A Rejoinder to Byrne and Thau." *Mind* 105: 139–49

Henderson, D. and Horgan, T. 2000. "Iceberg Epistemology." *Philosophy and Phenomenological Research* 61: 3, 497–535

Forthcoming. "The Ins and Outs of Transglobal Reliability." In S. Goldberg (ed.) *Internalism and Externalism in Semantics and Epistemology* (Oxford: Oxford University Press)

Heyman, G. and Legare, C. forthcoming. "Children's Evaluation of Sources of Information about Traits." *Developmental Psychology*

Horgan, T., and Tienson, J. 1995. "Connectionism and the Commitments of Folk Psychology." In J. Tomberlin (ed.) *AI, Connectionism, and Philosophical Psychology*, (Ridgeview: Atascadero)

1996. *Connectionism and the Philosophy of Psychology*. Cambridge: MIT Press

Hubel, D. 1995. *Eye, Brain, Vision* (New York: W. H. Freeman)

Insole, C. 2000. "Seeing Off the Local Threat to Irreducible Knowledge by Testimony." *Philosophical Quarterly* 50: 198, 44–56

Jack, J. 1994. "The Role of Comprehension." In B. K. Matilal and A. Chakrabarti, eds. *Knowing from Words* (Amsterdam: Kluwer Academic Publishers), 163–93

Jackson, F. 2005. "On an Argument from Properties of Words to Broad Content." In Schantz, R. (ed.) *The Externalist Challenge* (Berlin: Walter de Gruyter), 319–27

Kelly, T. 2005. "The Epistemic Significance of Disagreement." In J. Hawthorne, and T. Gendler, eds. *Oxford Studies in Epistemology: Volume 1* (Oxford: Oxford University Press)

Koenig, M., Clément, F., and Harris, 2004. "Trust in Testimony: Children's Use of True and False Statements." *Psychological Science* 15: 10, 694–8

Koenig, M., and Echols, C. 2003. "Infants' Understanding of False Labeling Events: The Referential Roles of Words and the Speakers who Use Them." *Cognition* 87, 179–208

Kornblith, H. 1988. "How Internal Can You Get?" Reprinted in Kornblith 2001
    2001. *Epistemology: Internalism and Externalism*. H. Kornblith (ed.) (London:
    Blackwell)

Kutsch, M. 2002a. "Testimony in Communitarian Epistemology." *Studies in the*
    History and Philosophy of Science 33
    2002b. *Knowledge By Agreement: The Programme of Communitarian Epistemology*
    (Oxford: Oxford University Press)

Kvanvig, J. 1996. *Warrant in Contemporary Epistemology: Essays in Honor of*
    Plantinga's Theory of Knowledge. (Savage, MD: Rowman and Littlefield)
    2003. *The Value of Knowledge and the Pursuit of Understanding* (New York:
    Cambridge University Press)

Lackey, J. 1999. "Testimonial Knowledge and Transmission." *The Philosophical*
    Quarterly 49: 197, 471–90
    2003. "A Minimal Expression of Non-Reductionism in the Epistemology of
    Testimony." *Noûs* 37: 4, 706–23
    2005. "Testimony and the Infant/Child Objection." *Philosophical Studies* 126:
    163–90
    2006. "It Takes Two to Tango." In J. Lackey and E. Sosa, eds. *The Epistemology*
    of Testimony (Oxford: Oxford University Press), 160–89
    Forthcoming a. "Learning From Words." *Philosophy and Phenomenological*
    Research
    Forthcoming b. "Why We Don't Deserve Credit for Everything We Know."
    Synthese
    Unpublished Manuscript. "Assertion without Knowledge"

Lampinen, J. and Smith, V. 1995. "The Incredible (and Sometimes Incredulous)
    Child Witness: Child Eyewitnesses' Sensitivity to Source Credibility Cues."
    Journal of Applied Psychology 80: 5, 621–7

Lehrer, K. 1981. "A Self Profile." In R. Bogdan (ed.) *Keith Lehrer*. Dordrecht:
    D. Reidel, 3–104
    1989. "Knowledge Reconsidered." In M. Clay and K. Lehrer, eds. *Knowledge*
    and Skepticism (Boulder: Westview Press)

Lewis, D. 1975. "Language and Languages." In K. Gunderson (ed.) *Language,*
    Mind, and Knowledge (Minneapolis: University of Minnesota Press), 3–35

Loar, B. 1988. "Social Content and Psychological Content." In R. Grimm and
    D. Merrill, eds., *Contents of Thought* (Tucson: University of Arizona Press),
    99–110

Loftus, E., and Ketchum, K. 1991. *Witness for the Defense: The Accused, the Eyewitness*
    and the Expert who Puts Memory on Trial (New York: St. Martin's Press)

Ludlow, P. 1995. "Externalism, Self-Knowledge, and the Prevalence of Slow
    Switching." *Analysis* 55: 1, 45–9

Lutz, D. and Keil, F. 2002. "Early Understanding of the Division of Cognitive
    Labor." *Child Development* 73: 1073–84

Lyons, J. 1997. "Testimony, Induction, and Folk Psychology." *Australasian Journal*
    of Philosophy 75: 2, 163–77

McDowell, J. 1980. "Meaning, Communication, and Knowledge" Reprinted in
    McDowell 1998

References

1981. "Anti-Realism and the Epistemology of Understanding." Reprinted in McDowell 1998

1994. "Knowledge by Hearsay." Reprinted in McDowell 1998

1998. *Meaning, Knowledge, and Reality* (Cambridge: Harvard University Press)

McGinn, C. 1984. "The Concept of Knowledge." *Midwest Studies in Philosophy* 9, 529–54

McKinsey, M. 1994. "Individuating Beliefs." In J. Tomberlin (ed.) *Philosophical Perspectives 8: Logic and Language.* Ridgeview: Atascadero

1999. "The Semantics of Belief Ascriptions." *Noûs* 33: 4, 519–57

McLaughlin, B. and Tye, M. 1998. "Is Content-Externalism Compatible with Privileged Access?" *Philosophical Review* 107: 3, 349–80

Martinich, A. P. 2001 (ed.). *The Philosophy of Language*, 4th edn. (Oxford: Oxford University Press)

Millgram, E. 1997. *Practical Induction* (Cambridge: Harvard University Press)

Mills, C. and Keil, F. 2004. "Knowing the Limits of One's Understanding: The Development of an Awareness of an Illusion of Explanatory Depth." *Psychological Science* 87: 1–32

Millikan, R. 1995. *White Queen Psychology and Other Essays for Alice* (Cambridge: MIT Press)

2004. "Existence Proof for a Viable Externalism." In R. Schantz (ed.) *The Externalist Challenge* (Berlin: Walter de Gruyter), 227–38

Mitchell, Robinson, E., Nye, R., and Isaacs, J. 1997. "When Speech Conflicts with Seeing: Young Children's Understanding of Informational Priority." *Journal of Experimental Child Psychology* 64, 276–94

Morton, 1993. "Supervenience and Computational Explanation in Vision Theory." *Philosophy of Science* 60, 86–99

Nozick, R. 2001. *Invariances: The Structure of the Objective World* (Cambridge: Harvard University Press)

O'Neill, D., Astington, J., and Flavell, J. 1992. "Young Children's Understanding of the Role that Sensory Experiences Play in Knowledge Acquisition." *Child Development* 63, 474–90

O'Neill, D., and Gopnik, A. 1991. "Young Children's Ability to Identify the Sources of their Beliefs." *Developmental Psychology* 27, 390–7

Patterson, S. 1990. "The Explanatory Role of Belief Ascriptions." *Philosophical Studies* 59, 313–32

Pea, R. 1982. "Origins of Verbal Logic: Spontaneous Denials by Two- and Three-Year-Olds." *Journal of Child Language* 9, 597–626

Peacocke, C. 2004a. "Explaining Perceptual Entitlement." In R. Schantz (ed.) *The Externalist Challenge* (Berlin: Walter de Gruyter), 441–80

2004b. *The Realm of Reason* (Oxford: Oxford University Press)

Pettit, D. 2002. "Why Knowledge is Unnecessary for Understanding Language." *Mind* 111: 443, 519–50

Pinker, S. 1997. *How the Mind Works* (New York: Norton)

Plantinga, A. 1993a. *Warrant: The Current Debate* (Oxford: Oxford University Press)

1993b. *Warrant and Proper Function* (Oxford: Oxford University Press)

Pritchard, D. 2004. "The Epistemology of Testimony." *Philosophical Issues* 14, 326–48

    2005. *Epistemic Luck* (Oxford: Oxford University Press)

Putnam, H. 1975. "The Meaning of 'Meaning'." In *Mind, Language, and Knowledge: Philosophical Papers, Volume II* (Cambridge: Cambridge University Press)

    1996. "Introduction." In A. Pessin and S. Goldberg, eds. *The Twin Earth Chronicles* (Armonk, New York: M. E. Sharpe), xv–xxii

Recanati, F. 1989. "The Pragmatics of What is Said." *Mind and Language* 4: 4, 295–329

    2002. "Does Linguistic Communication Rest on Inference?" *Mind and Language* 17: 1/2, 105–26

Reid, T. 1872/1993. *The Complete Works of Thomas Reid*. Sir William Hamilton (ed.) (Edinburgh: Maclachlan and Stewart)

Richards, C. and Sanderson, J. 1999. "The Role of the Imagination in Facilitating Deductive Reasoning in 2-, 3-, and 4-year-olds." *Cognition* 72: B1–B9

Robinson, E., Champion, H., and Mitchell, 1999. "Children's Ability to Infer Utterance Veracity from Speaker Informedness." *Developmental Psychology* 35, 535–46

Robinson, E., Mitchell, and Nye, R. 1995. "Young Children's Treating of Utterances as Unreliable Sources of Knowledge." *Journal of Child Language* 22, 663–85

Robinson, E., and Whitcombe, E. 2003. "Children's Suggestibility in Relation to their Understanding of Sources of Knowledge." *Child Development* 74, 48–62

Ross, A. 1986. "Why Do We Believe what We Are Told?" *Ratio* 28: 1, 69–88

Ross, J. 1975. "Testimonial Evidence." In K. Lehrer, ed. *Analysis and Metaphysics: Essays in Honor of R. M. Chisholm* (Dordrecht: Reidel), 35–55

Rotenberg, K. Simourd, L., and Moore, D. 1989. "Children's Use of a Verbal-Nonverbal Consistency Principle to Infer Truth and Lying." *Child Development* 60, 309–22.

Russell, B. 1924/1993. *The Philosophy of Logical Atomism* (La Salle, IL: Open Court)

Sabbagh, M. and Baldwin, D. 2001. "Learning Words from Knowledgeable versus Ignorant Speakers: Links between Preschoolers' Theory of Mind and Semantic Development." *Child Development* 72, 1054–70

Sartwell, C. 1991. "Knowledge is Merely True Belief." *American Philosophical Quarterly* 28, 157–65

    1992. "Why Knowledge is Merely True Belief." *Journal of Philosophy* 89, 167–80

Saul, J. 2002. "Speaker Meaning, What is Said, and What is Implicated." *Noûs* 36: 2, 228–48

Schiffer, S. 2003. *The Things We Mean* (Oxford: Oxford University Press)

Schmitt, F. 1994. *Socializing Epistemology* (Maryland: Rowman and Littlefield)

    2002. "Testimonial Justification: The Parity Argument." *Studies in History and Philosophy of Science* 33, 385–406

    2006. "Testimonial Justification and Transindividual Reasons." In J. Lackey, and E. Sosa, eds. *The Epistemology of Testimony* (Oxford University Press), 193–224

References

Searle, J. 1965. "What is a Speech Act?" In M. Black (ed.) *Philosophy in America* (Ithaca: Cornell University Press), 221–39. Reprinted in A. Martinich (ed.) *The Philosophy of Language* 4th edn. (Oxford: Oxford University Press, 1995)

Segal, G. 1989. "Seeing What is Not There." *Philosophical Review* 98, 189–214.

Shagrir, O. 2001. "Content, Computation and Externalism." *Mind* 110, 369–400

Shepard, R. 1987. "Evolution of a Mesh between Principles of the Mind and Regularities of the World." In J. Dupre (ed.) *The Latest on the Best* (Cambridge: MIT Press), 251–76

    1992. "The Perceptual Organization of Colors: An Adaptation to Regularities of the Terrestrial World?" In J. Barlow, L. Cosmides, and J. Tooby, eds. *Adapted Mind* (New York: Oxford University Press, 1992)

Shogenji, T. 2006. "A Defense of Reductionism about Testimonial Justification of Beliefs." *Noûs* 40: 2, 331–46

Sosa, E. 1991. *Knowledge in Perspective: Selected Essays in Epistemology* (Cambridge: Cambridge University Press)

    1994. "Testimony and Coherence." In B. K. Matilal and A. Chakrabarti, eds. *Knowing from Words* (Amsterdam: Kluwer Academic Publishers), 59–67

    1999. "How to Defeat Opposition to Moore." In James Tomberlin (ed.) *Philosophical Perspectives*, 13: *Epistemology* (Atascadero, CA: Ridgeview Publishing, 1988)

    2001. "Human Knowledge, Animal and Reflective." *Philosophical Studies* 106: 3, 193–6

    2002. "Goldman's Reliabilism and Virtue Epistemology." *Philosophical Topics* 29: 1–2

    2004. "Replies." In Grecs, J. (ed.) *Ernest Sosa and his Critics* (Oxford: Blackwell), 275–326

Sosa, E. and Bonjour, L. 2003. *Epistemic Justification* (London: Blackwell)

Sperber, D. and Wilson, D. 1986. *Relevance: Communication and Cognition* (Oxford: Blackwell)

Stanley, J. 2000. "Context and Logical Form." *Linguistics and Philosophy* 23, 391–434

    2002. "Making it Articulated." *Mind and Language* 17, 149–68

Stevenson, L. 1993. "Why Believe What People Say?" *Synthese* 94, 429–51

Strawson, 1994. "Knowing from Words." In B. K. Matilal and A. Chakrabarti, eds. *Knowing from Words* (Amsterdam: Kluwer Academic Publishers, 1994)

Taylor, M., Estbensen, B., and Bennett, R. 1994. "Children's Understanding of Knowledge Acquisition: The Tendency for Children to Report That They Have Always Known What They Have Just Learned." *Child Development* 65: 1581–604

Tye, M. 1998. "Externalism and Memory I." *Proceedings of the Aristotelian Society* 72 (Supplemental Volume), 77–94

Unger, P. 1975. *Ignorance: A Case for Skepticism* (Oxford: Oxford University Press)

Van Cleeve, J. 2005. "Externalism and Disjunctivism." In R. Schantz (ed.) *The Externalist Challenge* (Berlin: Walter de Gruyter), 481–92

Van Gulick, R. 2005. "Outing the Mind: A Teleopragmatic Perspective." In R. Schantz (ed.) *The Externalist Challenge* (Berlin: Walter de Gruyter), 255–85

References

Warfield, T. 1995. "Externalism, Self-Knowledge, and the Irrelevance of Slow Switching". *Analysis* 57, 282–4

1998. "A Priori Knowledge of the World." *Philosophical Studies* 92: 127–47

Webb, M. O. 1993. "Why I Know About as Much as You: A reply to Hardwig." *Journal of Philosophy* 90, 260–70

Weiner, M. 2003. "Accepting Testimony." *Philosophical Quarterly* 53, 256–64

Welbourne, M. 1979. "The Transmission of Knowledge." *Philosophical Quarterly* 29: 114, 1–9

1981. "The Community of Knowledge." *Philosophical Quarterly* 31, 302–14

1986. *The Community of Knowledge* (Aberdeen: Aberdeen University Press)

1994. "Testimony, Knowledge, and Belief." In B. K. Matilal and A. Chakrabarti, eds., *Knowing From Words* (Dordrecht: Kluwer)

Wellman, H., Cross, D., and Watson, J. 2001. "Meta-Analysis of Theory of Mind Development. The Truth about False Belief." *Child Development* 72, 655–84

Wheeless, L., Barraclough, R., and Stewart, R. 1983. "Compliance-Gaining and Power in Persuasion." In R. N. Bostrom (ed.) *Communication Yearbook* 7 (Beverly Hills, CA: Sage Publishing), 105–45

Williamson, T. 1996. "Knowing and Asserting." *The Philosophical Review* 105: 4, 489–523

2000. *Knowledge and its Limits* (Oxford: Oxford University Press)

Wimmer, H. and Perner, J. 1983. "Beliefs about Beliefs: Representation and Constraining Function of Wrong Beliefs in Young Children's Understanding of Deception." *Cognition* 13, 103–28

Wilson, D. and Sperber, D. 2002. "Truthfulness and Relevance." *Mind* 111, 583–632

Zaragoza, M. and Lane, S. 1994. "Source Misattributions and the Suggestibility of Eyewitness Memory." *Journal of Experimental Psychology: Learning, Memory, and Cognition* 20, 934–45

Zaragoza, M. and Mitchell, K. 1996. "Repeated Exposure to Suggestion and the Creation of False Memories." *Psychological Science* 7, 294–300

Zeki, S. 1993. *A Vision of the Brain* (Oxford: Blackwell Scientific)

Index